"Early on the morning of April 25, 1961, I went up on deck and saw, not far off, a golden glow which was the city of Haifa being batted hard in the eyes by the Mediterranean sun. Without a moment's delay I fell in love with Israel. That first trip, I liked everything about the place: the children, the landscape, the ruins, the Jordan, the kibbutzim, the hazardous frontiers, the mosques, the poster hoardings, the poppies, the trains, the festivals, even the food. On later visits—of which there were many—the obvious shortcomings which had been veiled by my first rapture made me more critical, sometimes irritable, sometimes almost abusive. There were occasions when maddening encounters with the bureaucracy made me vow never to go back. But I always did. The more I knew the place, the more I learned what was wrong with it, the more I loved it."

—Gerald Kaufman

TO BUILD
THE PROMISED LAND
Gerald Kaufman

BANTAM BOOKS · TORONTO · NEW YORK · LONDON

*This low-priced Bantam Book
has been completely reset in a type face
designed for easy reading, and was printed
from new plates. It contains the complete
text of the original hard-cover edition.*
NOT ONE WORD HAS BEEN OMITTED.

TO BUILD THE PROMISED LAND
A Bantam Book

PRINTING HISTORY
Weidenfeld and Nicolson edition published February 1973
Bantam edition published July 1974

*Bantam Books are published by Bantam Books, Inc. Its trade-
mark, consisting of the words "Bantam Books" and the por-
trayal of a bantam, is registered in the United States Patent
Office and in other countries. Marca Registrada. Bantam
Books, Inc., 666 Fifth Avenue, New York, New York 10019.*

PRINTED IN THE UNITED STATES OF AMERICA

To Benny

*who taught me about Israel
from Metulla to Eilat*

Contents

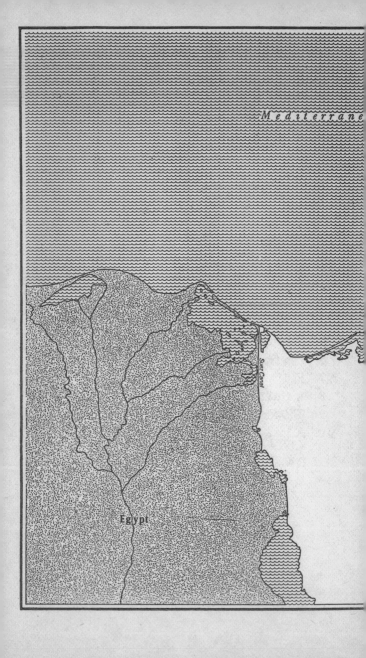

Syria

Sea

Acre

Safad

Sea of Galilee

Haifa

Tiberias

Nazareth

Beisan

Caesarea

Givat Chaim

Baka al Gharbieh

Kfar Vitkin

Netanya

West Bank

(occupied by Israel 1967)

Jordan

Petach Tikva

Tel Aviv

Kfar Kasim

Jaffa

Rishon Lezion

Lod

Ramleh

Jerusalem

Ashdod

Dead Sea

Ashkelon

Ein Gedi

Massada

Arad

Beersheba

I S R A E L

Sodoma

Dimona

Yerucham

Neot Hakikar

Sde Boker

Oron

Mitzpea Ramon

Sinai

(occupied by Israel 1967)

Jordan

Saudi Arabia

Yotvata

Timna

Eilat

80 km
50 miles

Introduction

The establishment of the State of Israel passed me by; it happened when I wasn't looking. I was brought up in a staunchly Zionist household, where there was for so long so much talk of the desirability of a Jewish national home in Palestine that its actual arrival, which occurred when I was in my teens, seemed to have slipped surreptitiously by in the general flow of conversation. I was an avid reader of the newspapers, yet cannot remember noting any item about the United Nations debate on the partition resolution. And I must have been the only Jewish boy in the Western world who did not hear the famous broadcast of the 1947 UN vote which is described so breathlessly in Leon Uris' *Exodus*.

It was indeed this novel which first sent me to Israel. Once the State had been safely founded, and the coins dropped into that tin box on the shelf had a homeland to be sent to, I paid little attention to what was going on there. True, the Suez war of 1956 was a time of political excitement for me; but it was to protest against this war—and, by associative guilt, against Israel—that I took part in my first march upon Downing Street. Then, in 1960, an American relative gave me a dog-eared paperback copy of *Exodus*. I found it to be one of those profoundly bad works of fiction which are, at the same time, transfixingly readable. After I had finished it I felt that I had to see Cyprus and Israel, the places in which it was set. So the following spring I headed east by night flight to Nicosia, visited Famagusta and Kyrenia for a couple of days, and then got on a ship sailing from Limassol.

Early on the morning of 25 April 1961 I went up on deck and saw, not far off, a golden glow which was the city of Haifa being batted hard in the eyes by the Mediterranean sun. Without a moment's delay I fell in love with Israel. That first trip, I liked everything about the place: the children, the landscape, the ruins, the Jordan, the kibbutzim, the hazardous frontiers, the mosques, the poster hoardings, the poppies, the trains, the festivals, even the food. On later visits—of which there were many—the obvious shortcomings which had been veiled by my first rapture made me more critical, sometimes irritable, sometimes almost abusive. There were occasions when maddening encounters with the bureaucracy made me vow never to go back. But I always did. The more I knew the place, the more I learned what was wrong with it, the more I loved it.

This book is therefore proffered in contrition for my having taken so long to notice the country which was eventually to become an inextricable part of my life. As an act of contrition, some Israeli readers may regard it as decidedly unsatisfactory. But only in 1961, when I knew hardly anything about the place, could I have supplied an entirely unflawed encomium. What I have sought to do in this volume is to provide an account of the State since its foundation not by means of a baldly chronological narrative, which would have been tedious to write, nor by an attempt to deal comprehensively with all developments during the life of the State, which would certainly have been indigestible to read and a little heavy for the reader to manhandle.

Instead, I have selected aspects of Israel which seem to me to convey a prismatic view of what has been taking place since independence, within the boundaries laid down by the armistice agreements of 1949. I have deliberately omitted all but the most passing mention of the wars which succeeded those armistices, since I feel that over-concentration on these martial events, crucial though they have been, has served to obscure what ex-

actly it is that the people of Israel have fought so single-mindedly to preserve. I have instead scrutinized the
political seeds from which everything else has grown;
and the efforts to build up the country by providing an
educational framework for its young, establishing industries which create the wealth to make that education
available, and settling the desert spaces where Israel's
future lies. I have looked at how Israeli independence
has affected the two unique creations of Jewish colonial
Palestine: the kibbutz, a socialist experiment which en-
raptures some and enrages others, and Tel Aviv, the
garden suburb which grew into modern Jewry's very
own metropolis.

Since Israel is not just a land of Jews, I have examined what life has been like in these decades for the
Arab minority there. And since Jews do not live just in
Israel, I have traced what impact the creation of the
State has had on the majority of Jews who live in minority communities outside it. I have tried to find out how
all these agglomerated events have been reflected by the
artistic creativeness of those who have experienced
them. And I have attempted to arrive at some estimate
of what all this has added up to within the context of an
only recently independent state anxious—sometimes
over-anxious—to be compared with the established democracies of the Western world.

In addition to referring to all appropriate printed
sources which were available, I made several visits to Israel in order to meet and question those best equipped
to provide me with first-hand information. I talked to
some dozens of people, ranging from the former Prime
Minister, David Ben Gurion (who cross-examined me
unrelentingly on why I did not come to settle in the
country), to the film director Uri Zohar (who almost
immediately afterwards was arrested on a drugs
charge). Politicians, civil servants, industrialists, farmers, artists, they were touchingly generous to me with
both time and material; some of them even pursued me
back to Britain either via the postal service or personally.

I am grateful to them all, and especially to Aloush
Hareven and Hannah Grinberg of the Israeli Foreign

Office; when in Jerusalem, I had only to mention to either of them my wish to meet some particular person or read some particular document, and they saw to it that my wish was granted. Eddie Ruppin, at the Embassy in London, was similarly generous both in providing information and in casting a dispassionate eye over the first draft of this book. I should like to thank also my colleague and friend, Eric Varley, who was kind enough to read that bedraggled first draft as it gradually emerged, and to offer helpful comments, as well as valued encouragement. None of these persons is in any way responsible for errors I have committed, and I am sure that the Israelis would wish to be absolved from all culpability for any opinions I have expressed—as well as for the inconsistency in transliteration of Israeli names, which began in helplessness and ended as a deliberate stylistic policy. My thanks are offered, too, to my secretary, Marian Craythorne, whose typing made sense of an original script which on occasion resembled one of the more recondite of the Dead Sea scrolls.

1

A Simple Little System

The State of Israel was born through politics, lives by politics, and, if it ever dies, will perish not on the battlefield but because of politics. It was created on 29 November 1947, under the provisions of a United Nations resolution. David Ben Gurion, nascent Israel's leader, presently its Prime Minister, and inevitable hero and ogre of any account of his country's vicissitudes, readily accepted the resolution but proceeded to ignore its provisions. Attacked on every side by Arab armies, the Israelis appropriated to themselves not only all the territory which the United Nations had allotted to them, but also sizeable chunks of Galilee in the north and the Negev in the south, as well as the western part of Jerusalem.

The Israelis surprised the world, and perhaps themselves, by turning out to be rather good at fighting. It was no surprise to anyone that they were extremely adept at politics. Under the British Mandate they had set up a trade union federation, the Histradrut, and begun to form characteristically quarrelsome political parties. On 6 April 1948, six weeks before the British were due to withdraw from Palestine, the World Zionist General Council met in Tel Aviv and set up a thirteen-member National Administration and a thirty-seven-member National Council. Ben Gurion, Chairman of the Jewish Agency's Executive, became government head. The declaration of independence in the Dizengoff Museum, Tel Aviv, at 4.00 p.m. on Friday, 14 May, automatically transmuted these bodies into a Provisional Government and a Provisional Legislature. From there on they made it up as they went along.

Even with a war going on, Israel was obviously not going to be a self-respecting independent state until it had had an election. There had, after all, been four elections to the representative Vaad Leumi under a British colonial administration which had not even made any provision for elected institutions. Organizing this indispensable proceeding was clearly likely to take a matter of months. Meanwhile it was decided that the Provisional Legislature should deal by means of Orders with all matters requiring legislative action, and that all Mandatory laws apart from those restricting immigration and land purchase should be regarded as valid. Two decades and more later, Israel was still being administered by a *mille-feuille* of Israeli, Mandatory and even Ottoman laws, the amalgam offering a rich if occasionally indigestible meal to eagerly salivating political science postgraduate students from overseas.

It was not until 25 January 1949 that 440,095 Israelis (86.8 per cent of those who, aged eighteen and over, comprised the electorate) went to the polls to elect a 120-member Constituent Assembly which never drew up a constitution but instead promptly turned itself into a national Parliament and, looking back two thousand years to the Great Synod of the Israel of the Second Temple, named itself the Knesset. Ben Gurion, however, employed this eight-month interregnum in what must be acknowledged as a constructive fashion: he began to transform a babel of discordant and in some cases warring factions into a cohesive democratic state. And since Israel was at war, he started with the army.

During the period of the Mandate the Jews of Palestine had built up their own official, underground army, the Haganah. But there were other, independent armed groups: the Palmach, the élitist crack force of the kibbutzim, the collective settlements; and two terrorist groups, the Stern Gang and the Irgun Zvai Leumi (National Military Organization) of Menachem Begin. In May 1948, Ben Gurion issued a decree forbidding anyone to hold arms in any force outside the Haganah, now the official army. The Stern Gang disbanded after the declaration of independence. Begin, a verbose fanatic who had arrived in Palestine with the Polish Army in

1942, agreed on 1 June to enrol his followers in the newly created Israel Defence Forces. But Jerusalem, under the November 1947 United Nations resolution, was still regarded as an international city rather than as part of the territory of Israel; the Irgun continued there as a separate force. And—a present to the Irgun from admiring American extremists—*en route* to Israel was steaming a ship, the *Altalena,* succulently crammed with desirable armaments.

Begin demanded twenty per cent of the cargo for his men in Jerusalem. Ben Gurion, despite a cease-fire which had come into force on 11 June, agreed to allow the *Altalena* into Israeli waters. But he insisted on taking possession himself of the ship and its contents. On 20 June the *Altalena* anchored at Kfar Vitkin, about twenty miles north of Tel Aviv. Irgun soldiers were waiting for it on the beach. But so were the soldiers of the official army. There was an armed clash—Jews fighting against Jews. A document of surrender was signed. But immigrants who were on the *Altalena* were taken off; Begin went aboard; and the ship sailed down the coast to Tel Aviv, there once again to start unloading. On 22 June the Provisional Government met and by a seven to two vote authorized Ben Gurion to take all necessary measures. Yigal Allon, Commander of the Palmach, fired on the ship, scored a direct hit, and blew her up. Begin escaped to make a fiery broadcast on his secret radio. But he advised his followers not to resist the men from the army who came to arrest and disarm them. In September, following the assassination of the United Nations mediator, Folke Bernadotte, the last remnants of the Irgun surrendered and agreed to enlist in the Israeli army.

The controversy over the *Altalena* affair continued for decades. Begin's apologists insisted that, if only Ben Gurion had been reasonable, there would have been enough arms for everyone and the whole of Jerusalem could have been taken instead of the divided city having to be shared with Jordan. Ben Gurion, who thirsted after Jerusalem more than any man in the country, believed that it was even more crucial to that country's future to rid it of rival war-lords and impose a central authority on its armed forces. For that reason, in mid-autumn, he swooped on the Palmach too, and abolished its separate command at the very moment when its men were fighting in the Negev.

Four years later Begin, now a member of the Knesset, was to clash bitterly with Ben Gurion again, this time over the acceptability of German reparations. But in 1967, with war looming and Ben Gurion in the political wilderness, Begin tried—unsuccessfully—to persuade Prime Minister Levi Eshkol to step down in favour of his old antagonist. Allon of the Palmach, on the other hand, was not to be reconciled with Ben Gurion until the by now Grand Old Man's eighty-fifth birthday celebrations in October 1971.

If the *Altalena* affair was the first test of the strength of Israeli democracy it also provided the occasion for a trial run of what was to become a favourite pastime among Israeli politicians: resignation. Two Ministers walked out of the Provisional Government because they disagreed with its course of action during this crisis. Both walked back in pretty quickly. One of them, Rabbi Fishman, found himself unable to kick the habit; a resignation of his in 1950, later withdrawn, caused a government crisis which precipitated Ben Gurion's own resignation (also rescinded).

The three contending groups involved in controversy over the unification of the army were represented in the January 1949 election by the three principal contesting parties. Ben Gurion's party, Mapai—Mifleget Poalei Israel, the Israel Labour Party—had been formed in 1930, and had dominated Jewish politics in Palestine since 1933. It was, and remained, a not very ideological, highly pragmatic socialist party. On the right was Herut (Freedom), Begin's chauvinist group which from 1955 onwards was to be the principal opposition to Mapai. The party of Palmach was Mapam—Mifleget Hapoalim Hameuchedet, the United Workers' Party—a staunchly doctrinaire and essentially humourless socialist party firmly based on the kibbutzim.

Mapam had been formed in January 1949 by the amalgamation of Hashomer Hatzair (the Young Guard), a group of militant Marxists, with Achdut Haavodah (the Union of Labour), which had itself split away from Mapai in 1944 largely because of personal differences with Ben Gurion. Together with the General Zionists (who subsequently became the Liberal Party, from which most of the Liberals later resigned to form the Independent Liberal Party), Mapai, Mapam and Herut were to be the principal secular political parties through all the seven Israeli Parliaments elected between 1949 and 1969. But over the next twenty years members of these four parties were to fight elections, and to be elected to the Knesset, under thirteen different party labels. Before a single election was even held, Israeli politicians had begun exercising their bemusing proclivity for an amoeba-like separation from their original organisms, as well as surrendering to an equally irresistible urge to associate with any conveniently adjacent amoeba.

After six uneasy years in Mapam, Achdut in 1954 tried going it alone until 1965, when it entered into an electoral alignment with Mapai. This so disgusted other members of Mapai that they broke away to set up Rafi -Reshimat Poalei Israel, the Israel Workers' List. In 1968, their differences uneasily reconciled, Achdut and Rafi joined with Mapai to form the Labour Party. But naturally some members of Rafi could not stomach this, and hived off in their turn into a new grouping called the State List. In 1971, the title being vacant, State List changed its name to Rafi.

Before its parting from Achdut, Mapam had already (in 1953) bade farewell to three others of its parliamentary representatives, who formed themselves into a Left Faction. Two of these, in 1954, joined the Israeli Communist Party, in which they found a safe haven for eleven years. But in 1965 that minute (4.1 per cent of the vote) outpost of the Soviet monolith itself split. Israel, which already had the distinction of harbouring the only legal Communist Party in the Middle East, now found itself the embarrassed host to two Communist Parties, Maki (predominantly Jewish) and Rakah (mainly Arab).

Mapam, for its part, was now to experience fifteen years of uncharacteristic tranquillity. In 1969, however, having on a number of occasions ventured its toe into the water of co-operation with Mapai by participating in the coalition government which Mapai always dominated, Mapam decided to plunge in deeper by entering into an electoral alignment with the new Labour Party. Without hesitation some of Mapam's members immediately formed a new party which, however, failed to win any seats in the subsequent election.

While the Left vainly sought to form one strong, viable Labour Party, the Right (though ready intermittently to enter into a coalition with Labour) aimed at providing unified opposition to it; but equally without success. Here too the first breakaway took place before the first election. In the beginning there were two right-wing parties: Herut, and the General Zionists, a middle-class, urban, businessmen's party. In 1948 a section of General Zionists linked up with two other groups of liberal-minded non-socialists to form the Progressive Party. This comfortably participated in a number of coalition governments; but by 1961 it was ready for bigger things. The Progressives and the General Zionists came together to form the Liberal Party. Their hope was to replace Herut as the main opposition to Mapai. But in the 1961 election Herut and the Liberals each won seventeen seats. Since Mapai had won only eight more than their joint total, these two parties hopefully went on in 1965 to form an electoral alignment. But the former Progressives in the Liberal Party could not stomach this association and took themselves off into a new Independent Liberal Party, which happily resumed its old coalition habits. Gahal, the Herut-Liberal alliance, was meanwhile (in the 1965 election) flattened by the Mapai-Achdut alignment. After this trouncing, three of Herut's members of Parliament took off into a new Free Centre group.

In January 1949 all these tergiversations and permutations were a long way away. Mapai went into the first election against 20 other parties, and came out with 35.7 per cent of the votes and 46 of the 120 Knesset seats. Ben Gurion looked around for partners with whom to form a majority. Arithmetically obvious was a joint Workers' Government with Mapam, whose compo-

nent of 19 seats would have added up to an over-all majority. "But," Mapam founder Meir Yaari later explained, "Ben Gurion preferred to strengthen Mapai's
hegemony over that of all the workers' parties." So Mapam was manoeuvred into opposition and Ben Gurion,
in addition to a handful of Arabs and other ethnic splinter groups, took into his coalition the Progressives and
the United Religious Front. Although the URF itself
was to splinter as the years went on, its nucleus, the
moderately left-wing Mizrachi groups, was never to
leave the coalition (though often to upset it and on occasion to overthrow it). The satellite fish of Mapai, the
National Religious Party was throughout to hunt with its
bigger and stronger ally, share its spoils—and impose on
it policies which helped form the character of the State.
And after the ultra-orthodox wing, which had hived off
from the URF, itself split into two in 1960, its labour
section, Poalei Agudat Israel, joined the NRP in the coalition to uphold the values of the Bible.

But, before the in-fighting got going, it was necessary
for the State to have some institutions. It had already
rather absent-mindedly provided itself with a Parliament.
The next necessity was a President. The Knesset—meeting as a symbolic act in Jerusalem, in the Jewish Agency
building (it was later to transfer to a disused cinema,
and then to a bank, in Tel Aviv, before returning permanently to Jerusalem in December)—chose Chaim
Weizmann.

Weizmann, key figure in extracting from the British
Government in 1917 the Balfour declaration, which offered a national home for the Jews in Palestine, had not
been in Israel at the time of the declaration of independence. He had not even been permitted to sign the declaration. Ben Gurion's explanation was that it only made
sense for a declaration of independence to be signed by
those present in the country at the moment of independence. Weizmann, who at that moment had been involved
in negotiations in the United States which were absolutely crucial to the future physical shape of Israel, as well
as to winning the key accolade of recognition by the
United States Government, felt that a space might have
been left on the document for his subsequent signature.

Both points of view made perfect sense. But it was well known that the two men did not get on. Both had originated from small towns in Eastern Europe. But no two men could have been more different.

Weizmann had taken up residence in England, adored that country, believed in the politics of persuasion, made his career in the World Zionist Organization, mixed naturally in the salons of international politics, was personally suave and almost ostentatiously intellectual, and in personal contacts a spellbinder. Ben Gurion, a self-taught student of ancient Greek, was nevertheless a blunt, brusque, gloves-off politician with scarcely any personal friends. "He wasn't interested in personal confidences . . . There was not much give and take between him and others," remembered Teddy Kollek, Director of the Prime Minister's Office under Ben Gurion, and later Mayor of Jerusalem. Ben Gurion had settled in Ottoman-occupied Palestine in 1916, fought his way via hard manual labour to the top position in the politics of the Yishuv—the Jewish colonial community —and, in his obsessive determination to secure an independent Israeli state, had no time for sentiment towards any country in the world. Weizmann's wife, Vera, was an elegant and ever so slightly snobbish lady who after her husband's death became known as the Queen Mother of Israel. Paula Ben Gurion was a folksy, awkward and extremely shrewd Yiddishe momma who contentedly if complainingly followed her husband wherever he went.

What was indisputable was that without these two men there would have been no Israel. Weizmann's blandishments, his negotiations and, in the final weeks, his implicit blackmail of President Truman during the run-up to a tense American presidential election campaign, had ensured that there would be a viable Israel with a secure Negev hinterland and—the sugar on the icing of independence—prompt American recognition. Weizmann, who had been offered the new State's Presidency while still in America, saw himself as an executive American-style President with power as well as ceremonial dignity. But at sixty-eight he was sick and ageing. Ben Gurion, on the other hand, at the age of sixty-two, was at the height of his powers. And, while lacking entirely Weizmann's sentimental attachment to Britain, he was peculiarly addicted to British political forms. He saw the Presidency as a constitutional monarchy, with supreme power resting in a one-chamber Parliament to which the Cabinet must be responsible. Ben Gurion, like Weizmann, was against a written constitution. He believed, too, in the British single-constituency electoral system; it was one of the failures of his Premiership that he was never able to impose this on fellow politicians brought up on the Central European game of chance known as proportional representation.

So, on 16 February 1949, Chaim Weizmann was elected by the Knesset, *née* Constituent Assembly, as first President of the State of Israel. The Knesset on the same day proceeded to pass a law setting out how the President should be elected and what his duties were, and defining its own status. This was to be the way of Israeli politics: acting first and laying down the groundrules later. When the first Knesset was elected, there were no regulations prescribing how it should be elected or what its term of life should be. The nation simply had to take Ben Gurion's word that he would not carry on for more than four years without a fresh election. In 1951, when a government crisis precipitated the country's second general election, the Parliament hurriedly passed the Second Knesset Elections Law, laying down rules and setting up machinery for voting—for that election only. It was not until 1959, after an interim measure in 1955, that a basic law was passed finalizing the country's electoral system, and including a provision that the system itself could be changed only by an absolute majority of the Knesset.

The system, as it evolved, was replete with democratic safeguards. Elections took place on a proportional basis with the country as a single 120-member constituency. Each party was allotted seats in proportion to the number of votes it received, with no party allowed representation unless it secured a minimum of one per cent of the votes. Elections were supervised, votes counted, and results certified by a Central Elections Committee, presided over by a judge of the Supreme Court who was himself chosen by the Supreme Court judges, and manned in proportion to the membership of the outgoing Knesset. Presently, under a law passed in 1969, each party was to receive from the State, to assist in its election campaigning, a financial subvention related to its Knesset strength; with an allowance on offer to any so far unrepresented party which managed to collect one per cent of the votes. The Knesset was elected for a maximum four-year period, but it was empowered to dissolve itself sooner if the government got itself into difficulties which could be disentangled in no other way.

And into difficulties Ben Gurion's first Government, which received its parliamentary vote of confidence on 10 March 1949, soon got itself. The politics of the early years of Israel's statehood were dominated by two tender, delicate issues: education, and relations with the Germany which had murdered so many Jews and caused suffering to so many citizens of the new Israeli state.

The coalition was first shaken in October 1950 by quarrels over the allocation of responsibility for education in the immigrants' camps. Education was still in the hands of the political and religious blocs which had created and dominated it under the Mandate, and there was an unedifying scramble by these pressure groups for the highly prized small bodies of immigrant children. During these coalition differences Rabbi Fishman, of course, resigned. Ben Gurion in his turn resigned, and threatened an election. Everyone returned to the position they had first thought of. The crisis went into abeyance; but only for a time. On 4 February 1951 Ben Gurion asked the Knesset for a vote of confidence on his policy of opposing Orthodox legal control over religious education of immigrant children and was beaten by forty-nine votes to forty-two. This time he had had enough, and asked for an election. On 30 July the country sent Mapai back as the largest single party, with a loss of one seat. The only sensation was provided by the General Zionists, who pushed up their Knesset total from seven seats to twenty-three and elbowed aside Mapam, the National Religious Party (the United Religious Front having split into moderate and extremist groups) and Herut to become the largest opposition party.

Ben Gurion realized that a nation which, at great risk, had managed to avoid schism into separate armed groups was now in danger of being split by pedagogic zealotry. He determined to bring all except the educational fringes under direct control of the State and, to assist him, invited the General Zionists to enter his coalition. The GZ, who wished to leaven Mapai's socialism with greater solicitude for private enterprise, expressed their delight—on condition that a member of their party should be put in charge of the key Ministry of Commerce and Industry. Ben Gurion briskly complied and then, as soon as the GZ were safely in his coalition bag, switched the basic powers of Commerce and Industry to the Mapai-held Ministry of Finance. The way was now clear to turn compulsory education into state education, and this was accomplished in a law passed by the Knesset in 1953.

However, a small and unforeseen difficulty intervened. Until the imposition of state education, the schools run by the Histadrut had been in the colourful and sonorous habit of celebrating May Day by flying the red flag and singing the Labour anthem. Mapai, seeing no reason why this tradition should be incommoded by any newfangled policy, and claiming that the parents wanted it anyhow, persisted in their flag-flying and anthem-singing. As a matter of course, the General Zionists left the coalition. Mapai, at Ben Gurion's urging, backed down; the General Zionists returned and took back their emasculated Commerce and Industry portfolio; the flurry was over. If education had not been finally taken out of politics—it was to unsettle the coalition right into the 1970s—politics had been definitively taken out of education.

The General Zionists continued in the Cabinet until, in June 1955, the Government was accused of interfering with the independence of the judiciary after the Acting Attorney-General had appealed to the Supreme Court to quash a ruling in a lower court on a libel action involving a senior civil servant who was a Mapai member. The GZ abstained in the Knesset vote, precipitating a general election in which they lost almost half their parliamentary strength. They were never to serve in a government again. But even before they first entered the Government, they had almost helped to destroy it in one of the most critical parliamentary confrontations of Israel's first quarter-century.

Ben Gurion was determined to bring about a normalization in relations between Israel and the new men of Bonn. Moreover, he far-sightedly realized that the reparations the Germans were willing to pay—mainly to Israel as custodian for the Jewish people—could play an indispensable part in building up the strength of his struggling little country. So, in January 1952, he asked the Knesset to approve the opening of negotiations for a reparations agreement with Germany.

The debate in the Knesset, from 7 to 9 January 1952, was heated and disputatious. Ranged against the Government, in addition to the General Zionists, were the Communists, Mapam and Herut. And Herut carried its opposition into the streets of Jerusalem. Demonstrations outside the Knesset placed the building under siege. All its windows were broken. The battle went on for four hours. Begin improved the occasion by informing the embattled crowd that the police, who were doing what they could to maintain order, were armed with grenades containing that same German gas which had killed their parents. Transferring his efforts to the Parliament chamber, he continued the rough house verbally, attaching to the Prime Minister the opprobrious description of "hooligan." He was very properly suspended until the Passover recess. Ben Gurion won his vote of confidence by sixty-one votes to fifty.

The German issue came up again seven years later when Ben Gurion, chancing his arm, decided to sell 250,000 flame-throwers to his West German friends. This time the General Zionists supported him. But Ministers belonging to two of his partners in the coalition, Mapam and Achdut, voted against the Government and then, arms implacably folded, refused to resign. Ben Gurion, therefore, resigned himself and called an election in which he improved his position. It caused no surprise to anyone when Mapam and Achdut joined his post-election administration.

But long before this, one of those earlier resignations, of which Ben Gurion had amassed so unrivalled a collection, brought about a situation in which there grew up a bitter feud that dominated and embittered Israeli politics for a full decade. At the end of 1953 the Prime Minister decided that he had had enough. He was, he claimed, suffering from "spiritual fatigue." And besides, he had taken a fancy to the idea of going to settle in the infant Negev kibbutz of Sde Boker. So he resigned the Premiership (while remaining in the Knesset) and, accompanied by the patient if vociferous Paula, headed south.

His successor as Prime Minister was Moshe Sharett. Born in the Ukraine, educated in Constantinople and at the London School of Economics, Sharett was everything that his predecessor was not: cosmopolitan, polished, fond of the limelight. He was not a dominating figure, and was not meant to be one; for Ben Gurion intended to come back. But meanwhile there was another vacancy to fill, for Ben Gurion had been Minister of Defence as well as Prime Minister. Chosen for this crucial appointment was a dour personage, Pinchas Lavon.

Lavon was a strong, lonely man. No one doubted his ability, and some saw him as a likely successor when Ben Gurion eventually decided to bid the Premiership his last, decisive farewell. He was, of course, from Eastern Europe: from Lvov. He had already held the post of Minister of Agriculture. He was sarcastic and arrogant and, although undeniably brilliant, was regarded by his enemies as more brilliant than was good for him—or for them. And he had a lot of enemies. In his new job he was immediately to acquire more. And they destroyed him.

The problem with Lavon as Minister of Defence was that he regarded himself as being in charge of the Ministry of Defence. And those both above him and below him did not like it. In May 1954, before what came to be known as the Lavon Affair broke out, Prime Minister Sharett wrote to him, testily: "Things are happening without my being told anything about them. I hear announcements on the radio and read them in the press, without knowing their true background." Lavon, quite simply, had an unfortunate tendency not to consult Sharett before ordering operations of which his superior was unlikely to approve; these included severe reprisal raids against the Egyptians. And the Minister won opinions no more golden from those who worked under him in his own department.

In fact Moshe Dayan, the Chief of Staff, and Shimon Peres, Director-General at the Ministry—both of them young favourites of Ben Gurion—were used to being allowed pretty well to run the shop themselves. They resented it when Lavon held meetings with senior officers without so much as letting them know. They resented it even more when Lavon stepped in and cancelled a deal they were making to buy a light tank from the French. Dayan resented it so much that he ran off to see Ben Gurion, who was in hospital at the time, and complain. Lavon, next in attendance at the bedside, contritely undertook to be more co-operative. But it was, inevitably, in an atmosphere of mistrust and suspicion, that a "security mishap" occurred in July 1954.

At this time Britain was negotiating with the Egyptians to withdraw from her Canal Zone base. It was feared in Israel that Britain's departure might tip the Middle Eastern balance Egypt's way by providing her with large additional quantities of military equipment. With the aim of shocking Britain into remaining in the Canal Zone, a decision was made to launch a campaign of sabotage against British and American property in Egypt in the hope that it would be attributed to the Moslem Brotherhood. But who gave the authorization for the operation to go ahead? It was important that this should be ascertained; because the operation failed. The Israeli network in Egypt was rounded up, two of its members were hanged, one was tortured to death, and another committed suicide.

The inquest was conducted with the secrecy appropriate to security matters in a country chronically at war. But the whispers were strident. Lavon denied that he had been involved. But Dayan, who was opposed to such an operation, and had been out of the country when it took place, on his return summoned Benjamin Gibli, his own appointment as Head of Intelligence, and asked who had given the order. Gibli replied: Lavon.

Sharett appointed an unofficial commission of inquiry, including a former Chief of Staff and a Supreme Court judge. The man responsible for carrying out the operation, known only under the code name of "Paul Frank," pointed the finger at Lavon. On 12 December the commission came to an indeterminate conclusion; it could not say for sure whether Lavon was responsible or not. But if the commission was uncertain, Lavon himself was convinced. He told Sharett that he was unable to continue working with Peres and Gibli, and asked for their removal. Sharett refused. Lavon resigned. The Affair continued to fester.

But right away it had one important consequence. The Government found it could no longer cope without Ben Gurion. Moreover, it was essential to have a new Minister of Defence who would rehabilitate the Defence establishment. A procession of leading Ministers waited upon Ben Gurion at Sde Boker. They included the Minister of Labour, Golda Meir, and ultimately Sharett himself. On 21 February 1955, David Ben Gurion returned to government office, succeeding Lavon as Minister of Defence. Following the fall of Sharett's government over the libel action issue, Ben Gurion led Mapai into the 1955 election, from which it emerged five seats lighter but still by far the largest party. Not very long after there followed an irony. Sharett, who as Prime Minister had resented Lavon's independent conduct of his office, was forced out of his new post as Foreign Minister because of Ben Gurion's insistence on personal control over foreign policy. Specifically, Ben Gurion was not going to have Sharett's misgivings hampering any plans of his for going to war. For the month was June 1956. And the Sinai invasion was only a season away.

In October 1957, on the first anniversary of the successful but politically abortive Sinai campaign, Parliament was shocked by a bomb-shell: quite literally. A mentally sick immigrant—"a person suffering from paranoia," as he was officially described—hurled a Mills grenade into the Knesset's debating chamber. Ben Gurion, Golda Meir (by now Foreign Minister), Moshe Shapira (Minister of Social Welfare) and Moshe Carmel (Minister of Communications) were all injured. It was as well that a Rothschild had left the State six million Israeli pounds (presently augmented) for the construction of a new Parliament building. The Jerusalem architect V. Klarwein's winning design was adjusted to incorporate a transparent, but bullet-proof, screen between the public gallery and the people's representatives. But ticking away was a time bomb which was to inflict more lasting injury on Ben Gurion than the wounds caused by the paranoiac's missile. The Lavon Affair was about to raise its head again.

Since giving evidence to Sharett's commission of inquiry, "Paul Frank" had been busy. It seemed he was a double agent. And in 1958 he was arrested on a charge of collecting documents to hand over to Egypt. At his trial the following year "Frank" claimed he had been asked to do this in order to exchange these documents for Israelis in Egyptian hands. He was duly found guilty of having contacts with the enemy. But at his trial he gave evidence which, while not directly relevant to the crime of which he was accused, was nevertheless undeniably interesting. Casting his mind back to the unfortunate events of 1954, he now claimed that prior to the "security mishap" he had not even been allowed to see Lavon, and had carried out the operation on other instructions altogether. He asserted further that Gibli and his assistant had persuaded him to give perjured evidence against Lavon to the commission of inquiry; and that, at a meeting with Dayan in advance of his going before the commission, Dayan had told him: "You know what to say." Following the trial, an official inquiry was set up to investigate charges against Gibli of perjury and forging documents.

"Frank's" trial had been held in secret. But the judge ensured that Lavon was acquainted with its findings. Lavon went to Ben Gurion and asked him to issue a public statement exonerating him. Ben Gurion refused: "I didn't accuse you; I don't exonerate you. Go to the courts." Instead—by now it was 1960—Lavon went to Parliament. He placed the matter before the Foreign Affairs Committee of the Knesset. The Affair, although still discussed in code terms, became a public sensation.

This was too much for the Cabinet. If there was dirty linen, it had better be got clean as privately and expeditiously as possible. On 30 October an unofficial committee of seven Ministers was set up. It was headed by Pinchas Rosen, the Minister of Justice; but its strong man was the Minister of Finance, Levi Eshkol.

Several things then happened more or less at once. Moshe Sharett issued a public statement saying that he now recognized Lavon had been misjudged. The inquiry into Gibli's conduct accused both Gibli and his assistant of having incited "Paul Frank" to commit perjury. Even so, Gibli still insisted that Lavon had given the fatal order, and Lavon's opponents declared that, although forgery might indeed have taken place, it was committed to provide convincing proof of what was in any case basically true: Lavon's guilt. Finally, reporting on 25 December, the committee of seven delivered itself of the verdict that Lavon had not given the order.

The Cabinet discussed the report and endorsed it. Ben Gurion walked out of the meeting and withdrew from all government activity. On 31 January 1961 he resigned from the Premiership because of his "profound concern for law and justice in the State." He was persuaded to return. But he refused to have any dealings with Lavon who by now, on the Old Pioneer Network, had become Secretary-General of the Histadrut. This was a post in the gift of Mapai, which controlled the labour federation. On 4 February, against Sharett's opposition, the Mapai Central Committee voted 159 to 96 to dismiss Lavon. The public career of the man who one day could have been Prime Minister was over. But the Affair to which he had given his name dragged bruisingly on.

The motives of some of those who were involved in the Lavon Affair might have been in question. Sharett might originally have behaved with hostility towards Lavon because of resentment at the manner in which his Minister of Defence had conducted himself, and might later have become his champion partly to pay off old scores against Ben Gurion. Dayan and Peres, whether or

not they were involved in any actual conspiracy against
Lavon, might have joined the pack against him in order
to rid themselves of an insensitive Minister who was in
their view damaging a Ministry to which they were devoted. Former opponents of Lavon, including members
of the Achdut, might suddenly have become his apologists in an effort to discredit Dayan and Peres, whom
they saw as potential rivals for the leadership of the Labour movement. The Affair undoubtedly developed into
a confrontation between the old ideologists and the
young pragmatists, with control of the Government of
Israel as the eventual prize. What is without doubt is
that, throughout, Ben Gurion himself pursued a course
motivated solely by a desire to see truth established and
vindicated. He was at first stubborn, and eventually obsessive. And ultimately, after the manner of the Greek
tragedies which lodged in the bookcases of his house on
Keren Kayemet Boulevard in Tel Aviv, he became im-
paled on his own obsession.

Meanwhile, however, there was an untimely election
to be fought. In 1959 Mapai had had its best result ever,
campaigning on the slogan "Say yes to the Old Man."
Now, as a result of the Lavon Affair, not one of Ma-
pai's coalition partners—Achdut, Mapam, NRP, the
Progressives—was willing to serve under the Old Man.
To sort out the mess the country was forced to the polls.
Mapai came out on top again, though with a loss of five
seats. But something rather awkward occurred. Yitzchak
Ben-Zvi, who had been elected to the Presidency after
Weizmann's death in 1952, called upon Ben Gurion, as
leader of the largest party, to form a government; and
Ben Gurion refused to form one. The awkward was then
followed by the bizarre. Ben-Zvi commissioned Eshkol
to form a government, and Eshkol did so—with Ben
Gurion as Prime Minister.

After this unique contribution to the development of
political institutions, Ben Gurion was now at liberty to
get on with a job at which he had always previously
proved himself adept: being Prime Minister. But the
Lavon Affair, like a sliver of food caught between two
teeth, irritated him to the point of distraction. The truth
simply had to be established. In 1963 he commissioned

a journalist, Chaggai Eshed of the Histadrut newspaper *Davar*, to conduct a private inquiry. On 14 June Eshed reported. Lavon, he had found, was indeed responsible for the "security mishap." He had authorized the operation retrospectively, after it had been set in train. On 16 June Ben Gurion resigned for the eighth and very last time. He was not to have nine lives; this was his positively final appearance as Prime Minister. On Ben Gurion's own recommendation, Levi Eshkol succeeded him. Yet another Eastern European immigrant, he had done all the things required to win prominence in Israeli politics. He had helped found a kibbutz, served in the Jewish Legion in the First World War, and held office in the Histadrut and the Jewish Agency. Often underestimated, and certainly found wanting in inspiration and decisiveness during the bleak period of waiting before the Six-Day War of 1967, he was, on taking office, just what the country needed: an upright machine man who set himself to heal the wounds inflicted during the final turbulent years of the Ben Gurion era. His Government was presented to Parliament as an administration of "continuation."

Inevitably continued was the Lavon Affair. Ben Gurion, still in the Knesset, demanded a judicial commission, maintaining that his new evidence cast doubt on the verdict of the committee of seven. Eshkol turned him down. And when Ben Gurion raised the issue yet again, with the Mapai Party in February 1965, he was beaten sixty-forty on a vote. In any case, the Party had other matters on its mind. Ready for the general election due that year, Mapai was moving towards an alignment with Achdut Haavodah. Long since, in 1954, the Achdut group had split away from the then pro-Soviet Mapam following the anti-Jewish show trials in Prague and Moscow. Now these righteous kibbutzniks were ready to come together again with the party from which they had split away twenty years before. And the decline of Ben Gurion, who had destroyed their beloved Palmach, and who was at the root of the original split, was far from a disincentive. The Achdut leaders stipulated that, as part of the alignment bargain, Mapai must abandon its plans for electoral reform, for so long Ben Gurion's personal objective. This was too much for Ben Gurion who, having failed by 179 to 103 votes at the Mapai Central Committee to remove Eshkol from the leadership, resigned from the party he had helped to create.

With him went Dayan, the soldier turned Minister of Agriculture, who had lost his eye fighting with the Allies in Syria in the Second World War, and become the idol of his own country as hero of the Sinai campaign. Peres, Deputy Minister of Defence, became Secretary of Rafi, the new party with which Ben Gurion was going to teach his old Mapai colleagues a lesson.

It was indeed a discouraging electoral outlook for Mapai. True, it had got its alignment with Achdut. But fighting bitterly against them, on a platform which inevitably included the reopening of the Lavon Affair, was a party whose leadership included the two most popular men in the country. Added to this, Herut and the recently created Liberal Party, whose joint representation in the outgoing Knesset was only eight seats short of Mapai's, had come together in an electoral alignment of their own, Gahal—Gush Herut Liberalim, the Herut-Liberal Bloc. But in the 1965 election the Mapai-Achdut alignment raced far ahead of the field, with forty-five seats to Gahal's twenty-six. Rafi, the party of Ben Gurion and Dayan, limped home with ten.

The Lavon Affair was over, although its final twitchings would continue for a little time yet; and an eerie coda to the entire entangled episode was to occur in 1971, when Victorine Marcelle Ninio, one of the Israeli agents imprisoned in Egypt in 1954, suddenly broke cover in Israel as an affianced Tel Aviv university student and was given away, at what was described as the "wedding of the year," by Prime Minister Golda Meir. For eleven years the Affair had poisoned Israeli politics. One man's career had been destroyed; another's had been side-tracked and eventually brought to an end, both with equally impartial finality. But the result of the second election fought over the Affair was a vindication of the maturity of an electorate which Ben Gurion had carefully nurtured and which now demonstrated that it had outgrown him. Unlike other emergent post-war democracies, Israel, together with its dominant political party, had proved that it was able to get along without, even to cope with disruption from, the apparently indispensable figure who had presided over its birth.

Israeli politics, in fact, had moved on, leaving Ben Gurion stranded on the controversies of the past. In the election on 2 November another perky little faction made its appearance—the first completely new party to gain representation in the Knesset since the foundation of the State. Since the early 1950s Israelis had half-contemptuously enjoyed reading a muck-raking weekly called *Haolam Hazeh* (This World), which developed into an incongruous but commercially highly successful combination of Britain's *Private Eye* and the old US *Confidential*. Now, fighting against a proposed tightening of the libel laws which was clearly aimed at *Haolam Hazeh* itself, the magazine turned itself into a political party and was rewarded with a seat in Parliament for its irreverent editor, Uri Avneri. Sadly for itself, Haolam Hazeh became too successful. In the 1969 election it doubled its parliamentary representation, inevitably providing the opportunity for a split, which duly occurred in 1971. Avneri was to remark pityingly of his errant colleague: "I regret that, after twenty years of friendship, Shalom Cohen's election to the Knesset has gone to his head."

Israel's new model politicians were soon to have the chance of meeting in a new model Parliament building. Ever since the early years of the State it had been planned to transfer Parliament from the inadequate makeshift building it occupied on King George V Street, in the traffic-jammed centre of Jerusalem, to a hillside outside the city where it would be flanked by a complex of three huge government offices. These buildings— Hakiryah—had been started as long ago as 1953. If they were less than distinguished architecturally, this was at least partly because funds for their construction were exceedingly hard to find. Indeed, in 1954, when the skeleton of one four-story block had been completed, together with the ground floors of the other two, all work had to stop for a time because the money had run out. But the buildings went ahead again. And across the way they were presently joined by a fortress-like pink pagoda, whose cornerstone had been laid on 15 October 1958.

The last meeting in the old Knesset building was held on 9 August 1966. The following month a Rothschild benefactress cut the entrance ribbon and the new Parliament building, equipped not only with restaurants, committee rooms, reading rooms, a Chagall tapestry and Chagall mosaics, but also with the only legislative synagogue in the world, was in business. And its first principal business was war.

On 23 May 1967 it became known that President Nasser of Egypt had placed a blockade on the Straits of Tiran, which commanded the entrance to Israel's Red Sea port of Eilat. It had long been made clear that, in the absence of a negotiated settlement, the response to such a blockade must be by force. In this crisis the need for a national coalition government was accepted. And, with confidence in Eshkol ebbing as he faced the threat of war in apparently mumbling uncertainty, a demand grew that Dayan should return to the Government as Minister of Defence, a post he had hoped for in 1963, and whose denial had been one of the factors which had prompted him to leave Eshkol's Government. Eshkol proposed Allon, as a distinguished former General, for the job. But the opposition parties would not agree. On 1 June the Mapai secretariat expressed its support for Dayan. That very same day he was appointed to the post, as member of a coalition which brought in Gahal (including a Ministry for Begin) as well as Rafi and commanded the support of 107 of the 120 Knesset members. Rafi, the party which in its 1965 election manifesto had attacked the Mapai "old-timers" who "travel in limousines yet think in terms of living in tents," moved comfortably back into sharing the back seats of the limousines with the old-timers.

In six days the war was won. But the nation's newly-found political unity proved attractive. The coalition of national unity continued. And moves began to bring Rafi and Achdut with Mapai into one unified Labour Party. With Achdut there was no problem; its leader, Allon, was already being mentioned as a possible successor to Eshkol. In December Rafi convened in conference in Jerusalem. With the support of Dayan and Peres, and against the opposition of Ben Gurion, it voted 523 to 364 in favour of merging into a new Labour Party. Ben Gurion, with a handful of ever-loyal followers, took himself off to form his own State List group. After the 1969 election, in which he and three other members of his party were elected, on a ticket which included constituency elections and universal free education, he decided in May 1970 that Knesset politics were no longer for him and retired from Parliament—and resigned from the State List—to work, as every ex-Prime Minister ought, on his memoirs. But although the State List continued as a separate group, Mapam (which long ago had become disillusioned with Communism) early in 1969 entered into an alignment with Labour—"to protect the Labour Party from Moshe Dayan"—and brought the prospect of a united Left closer than it had ever been before.

Eshkol's healing work was almost complete; on 26 February 1969, still the butt of jokes concerning his wife—a lady much younger than himself—but having achieved far more for his country than his unpretentious demeanour claimed, he suddenly died. After a period of uncertainty, in which Allon acted as Prime Minister but lacked the resolution to grasp hold of the job itself, Golda Meir, a seventy-year-old chain-smoking non-stop talker with a will of steel, went to the Premier's office in Hakiryah as Israel's Pope John. On 28 October her alignment came out top in the general election. The following year she accepted with equanimity the departure from the Government of Begin and the bellicose Gahal, consequent on Israel's decision to follow up an American peace initiative involving a cease-fire with Egypt. Lined up against an opposition of extremists was a coalition government of moderates. And the stamp was put on Pax Israelitica when, in April 1971, the first conference of the united Labour Party was attended by David Ben Gurion.

Ben Gurion had every right to survey what he had created and, past disgruntlements set aside, to tell himself that it was good. It was not simply that Israel possessed a Labour Party which, though strong enough to do without him, and which he himself declined actually to rejoin—"I will not join any party, because I wish to devote the rest of my life to one thing alone, to our youth"—was yet magnanimous and sentimental enough to turn his eighty-fifth birthday celebration into a ten-week-long national festivity. Ben Gurion had provided his country with democratic institutions which, despite imperfections, were strong enough to withstand the most testing internal dissensions.

The strains of Hatikvah played by the Israel Philharmonic Orchestra at the Dizengoff Museum nicely in time for the Sabbath on 14 May 1948 were the signal for a difficult transition. The apparatus which Palestine's Jewish community carried over from the Mandate undoubtedly assisted the new State immediately to become a going concern. All these organizations, under the Jewish Agency, had after all served them so well—and given everyone a taste of the gravy. But Ben Gurion saw that Israel must be a unitary state, not a federation of interest groups.

It was his own party, however, which was the major obstacle. With its control over a major segment of education, it was not averse to other vested interests consolidating their own share. The carve-up was epitomized by the experience described by a newcomer to a development community: "On one of my first excursions in town, I asked a child where I could find a house of prayer in the neighbourhood. She answered: "Do you want a 'Mapai synagogue' or a 'religious synagogue'?" Through the Histadrut's hold over the labour exchanges, any voter could be persuaded that the best hope of getting a job was by voting Mapai. By an Israeli paradox it was the right-wing and centre parties—the General Zionists, the Progressives, even Herut—which advocated state education, publicly run labour exchanges, and a national health service, as a way of loosening the grip on the voters of the spoils system known as *protektzia* and of curbing the power of Israel's version of Bernard Shaw's Breakages Ltd., the Histadrut. The Histadrut, founded in 1920 "to care for all the social, economic, cultural and trade union interests of the workers," was a corporate state within a state, providing not only trade union representation but also employment through the corporations it owned or part-controlled, as well as schooling, a health service. labour exchanges, wholesaling services and retail shops, banking, insurance and travel agency facilities, housing, water supplies, sea and air transport, newspapers, books, theatrical entertainment, and even football. Ben Gurion ruthlessly invoked the political leverage provided by his party's opponents in order to mitigate the worst tendencies and reduce the most oppressive powers of his own movement.

The only sectional interest which he was prepared regularly to accommodate was the religious parties. This was not because their support was indispensable to his maintaining a coalition: there would always be enough parties volunteering for that. It was because religious schism would be more difficult to cure than political schism, and in any case a spiritual basis could do the State no harm. If the army—the growing nation's other unifying force—was not to be divided against itself, it was better for all soldiers to eat kosher food than for those on different diets to be segregated at different tables in the army dining huts.

It was thus not only because he was an admirer of the British system that Ben Gurion was in no hurry to provide Israel with a written constitution; in so little haste, in fact, that after some twenty-five years of statehood and despite the specific commitment in the declaration of independence that a constitution was "to be drawn up by the Constituent Assembly not later than 1 October 1948" such a document still did not exist. The first Parliament was indeed, if a little belatedly, elected as a Constituent Assembly. It even in June 1951 got as far as voting in favour of a constitution being enacted in stages. Herut, the General Zionists, Mapam and the Communists were all in favour of this. But the religious parties would accept only a constitution based on the Jewish faith. There had already been difficulties over whether God should be mentioned in the declaration of independence—the ambiguous phrase "The Rock of Israel" was used instead—and the Mapai compromise of a constitution-by-stages, based on a series of *ad hoc* basic laws, was tacitly accepted. But, although basic laws were certainly passed, there was none which an enactment of the Knesset could not override.

The procedures laid down for the Knesset itself would have won nods of approval from the most traditionalist members of the British House of Commons. For legislation there was a first reading, a committee stage, a second reading in the full Knesset where, as with the Commons report stage, there was opportunity for further amendment, and then a third and final reading. The Bill had to receive Presidential as well as ministerial endorsement before being promulgated in the official gazette as a fully fledged law.

Ben Gurion saw, too, that government must have orderly procedures. The collective Cabinet responsibility which he gradually imposed might, even in the sophisticated state it had attained by the early 1970s, seem to more staid practitioners of Western democracy as a manifestation of the permissive society; but it was a tremendous advance on the way things had begun. It took Ben Gurion ten years and one of his own more serious resignations before, in 1958, he persuaded his naturally voluble Jewish colleagues to accept a formula for Cabinet confidentiality. And a device much favoured by certain of his coalition partners—particularly Achdut Haavodah Ministers—of bringing down governments by breaking Cabinet ranks and then flatly refusing to resign themselves, was only consigned to desuetude by the passage of the Transition (Amendment No. 6) Law in June 1962. This unfeelingly laid down that a member of the Government must resign his office if he voted against the Government or abstained from supporting it in the Knesset without prior Cabinet agreement, or if his party under certain specified circumstances either voted adversely or abstained.

The chief office in the State, the Presidency, was carefully raised above party. As Weizmann disappointedly discovered, this meant that its occupant, elected for a five-year term by secret vote of the Knesset, had no positive powers of his own. His duties, entirely formal, were to endorse laws (except those affecting his own prerogatives), sign treaties, grant pardons, commute sentences, and appoint judges, diplomats, the Governor of the

Bank of Israel and the State Comptroller. It was a post
for superannuated politicians to be courteously kicked
upstairs to, a one-man version of the House of Lords.
But in a state inherently liable to be party-ridden, it was
a post not open to manipulation by parties. This was se-
renely demonstrated by Weizmann himself who, in October 1950, on the occasion of one of Ben Gurion's very
earliest—and fairly speedily withdrawn—resignations,
called upon Pinchas Rosen, leader of the Progressive
Party, to try his hand at forming a Cabinet.

There was, as well, a wholly independent judiciary,
precluded from taking part in political activity. The
judges were appointed on the recommendation of a
nine-member Nominations Committee, five of whom
were judges and lawyers and only two government Ministers; and the Government had no power to dismiss
them. The Government reserved, and from time to time
exercised, the power to rescind by legislative action,
even retrospectively, judicial decisions of which it did
not approve; British Cabinets of both major parties had,
after all, been known to do that too. But when in 1955
the Government aroused suspicion of interference with
the judiciary it was promptly brought down and, with
the loss of five Knesset seats in the ensuing election, by
Israeli lights was taught a sharp lesson.

Not merely independent of the Government but
awarded a supervisory role over its activities, was the
State Comptroller, whose office was established by a law
passed in March 1950. Appointed for five years by the
President on the recommendation of a Knesset committee, he was assigned the role—steadily expanded by
amending legislation—of scrutinizing the activities of
every government office, every state enterprise and institution, every person or body holding state property or
managing or controlling it on behalf of the State, every
enterprise, institution, fund or other body assisted by the
government by way of grant or guarantee or with a government share in the management, every local authority,
employment exchange, and institution of higher education. The criteria of his scrutiny were not only legality,
regularity, efficiency and economy, but also ethical integrity. Year after year the State Comptroller's reports

rightly aroused from the press savage wails of self-excoriation as he remorselessly revealed examples both petty and serious of incompetence, corruption, and the devil *protektzia* itself. What, demanded shamefaced newspaper leading articles, ever had become of once idealistic Israel? But what other country, whether in the Middle East or elsewhere, so consistently flagellated itself in this annual orgy of penitent self-exposure?

Israel, quite simply, worked pretty well as a going concern. The public gallery in its Parliament might be protectively screened off from the debating chamber. But of all the States created in the aftermath of the Second World War, Israel was almost the only one which without a break possessed a democratically elected Parliament to whose debates the public were regularly admitted. It was true that coalitions sometimes took moths to form. But their evolution contributed to moderation in a nation of inherently excitable people; if government was to continue, hotheaded men knew that in the end they would have to compromise. Just as Cabinet-making sometimes required tortuous deals, so from time to time in local government the allocation to one party or another of the office of mayor required, because of the national party power structure, adjustments in the membership of the Government in Jerusalem. It happened in Nazareth, for example, in 1971. And since individual ministerial appointments were only in exceptional cases of critical importance, there was no harm in a practice which compelled politicians to adjust their ambitions to their situation.

The man who most disapproved of this system was the one who for fifteen years tried to operate it, while at the same time seeking vainly to change it. When, towards the close of his active parliamentary career, Ben Gurion created pocket parties of his own—Rafi and State List—he based them largely on the need to end proportional representation and go over to constituency election. Any Englishman who visited him was flattered with an eloquently unfavourable comparison of Israeli electoral practices with those of fortunate Britain. "The main thing," he was still saying in 1971, "is to get a true democratic regime through a proper electoral reform. There is no democracy in this country."

And it was certainly true that in Israel proportional representation on the basis of national lists did have serious disadvantages. It meant that the party machine had direct control over who was elected, since it decided the order in which candidates were inscribed on the list. This undoubtedly favoured placemen who were unlikely to give trouble, and helped to produce a Knesset largely composed of undistinguished party hacks; though really talented and independent-minded young men, such as Allon, Dayan, Peres, and the urbane Cambridge-educated South African, Abba Eban, were not noticeably disadvantaged. It also failed to provide a direct link between voters and a specific member of Parilament responsible to them in their own locality, and thus impaired the representative nature of the Parliament.

On the other hand, at a party rather than at a personal level, this system made the Israeli democracy more representative. It was calculated by wistful apparatchiks in Israel's Labour Party that, with a constituency system operating, they would regularly have won between two-thirds and three-quarters of the seats in the Knesset. It was certainly true that this would have rid them of the recurrent need to involve themselves in those demeaning coalition bargains. But it would also have imposed one-party rule in Israel for a quarter of a century; worse, by far, than a one-party state, since parties existed whose aggregate support regularly exceeded one half of the electorate, but which would never have had a hope of sharing in government. Frustration of this kind would have led to extremism. Herut, always characterized by a tendency to resort to the politics of the streets, might have been joined at the barricades by the General Zionists' bourgeois businessmen together with the Progressive Party's *gemütliche* Central European intellectuals.

As it was, with proportional representation, Mapai or its successor party always dominated the government anyhow; and this provided continuity. But Mapai had to govern by the consent of other representative elements in the country. Although no non-Labour Party ever really believed it could win an election (though intermittently the General Zionists or Herut had their hopes), almost every party knew it might have a chance of serving in a government. Indeed, during the lifetime of the first seven Israeli Knessets, every party which obtained more than five per cent of the votes did at one time or another participate in government; only the Communists were excluded. The knowledge held by almost every leading politician that he was potential ministerial material, and that some at any rate of his party's objectives might one day be enacted, was a powerful pull away from extremism.

In any case, what would Ben Gurion have been able to do with an absolute majority that he was unable to achieve through coalition manoeuvrings? He would probably have attained less of his aims than in fact he did, since he would not have been in a position to manipulate the General Zionists or the Progressives in order to reduce the powers of the Mapai-controlled Histadrut. And a huge unwieldy parliamentary caucus would either have got out of hand, inflating the *protektzia* which had so painfully been curbed, or would have required to be held in check by a strong man. As it was, the Mapai which at the start of the Lavon Affair early in 1955 was so unsure of itself that it felt it necessary to wheedle Ben Gurion back from Sde Boker, by 1963 was able with only a slight shiver to wave him good-bye.

Moreover, this system was most wonderfully adaptable. The 650,000 Jews who lived in Israel in May 1949 were during the following twenty years augmented to three times their number (in addition to natural increase) by immigrants from the most disparate lands on earth. Yet the political parties they found in Israel suited cave dwellers from North Africa as well as academics from North America, religious mystics from the Yemen as well as young Russian Jews who had known only atheistic communism. Concurrently with the first twenty years of Israeli independence, millions of submerged Americans felt it necessary to turn to the novel political solutions offered by Governor George Wallace, while in Britain frustrated ethnic minorities voted in their hundreds of thousands for Welsh and Scottish Nationalists. Yet in Israel, apart from Haolam Hazeh, which was more a wisecrack than a political party, in that same period no need manifested itself to create any new political force. Nor was this due to apathy. Israelis lamented that participation in their 1969 election was not as high as it should have been. But most Western democracies would have regarded that year's eighty-two per cent poll as an enviable example of civic consciousness.

This tiny new country, surrounded by enemies, chronically at war, and constantly beset by almost intractable problems, showed itself possessed of a staggering stability. Between 1948 and 1970 the powerful United States had five Presidents, one of whom was assassinated; and Britain got through seven Prime Ministers. In the same period the number of Israeli Prime Ministers totalled four. From 1950 to 1970 the United Kingdom, a venerable democracy whose Parliament had a maximum five-year lifespan, found it necessary to call seven general elections. During these twenty years Israel, whose Parliament (when they got around to deciding it) could run for no more than four years, also had precisely seven elections.

The judgment could not be avoided. Democracy was alive and well, and living in Israel.

2

Only in Canada

They walk through the streets in untidy, noisy, self-confident groups, even the smallest of them lugging president-sized briefcases. Prolonged parliamentary battles, occasionally fanatical, sometimes absurd, have been fought over them, causing Ministers to resign, bringing down governments, and on one occasion forcing a premature general election. The battles were justified, for their subject was important. In a State with only a particle of a past, its children's education will decide its future.

In the early 1970s Israel was spending a higher proportion of her gross national product on education than any other country in the world except Canada. Only Canada and the United States had a higher proportion of their university age-group actually studying at universities. The zeal for opening institutions of higher education in Israel's towns, comparable to the ambition of newly emerging African nations to launch their own airlines, was so great that in 1971 the Minister of Education had to introduce legislation making it a criminal offence to open a new college without a government permit. Yet when the new nation was launched in 1948, Israel had no state education system whatever, and she did not appoint her first Minister of Education until April 1949. Afterwards, it is true, some of the country's most distinguished politicians held this office: Zalman Shazar, later President of the State; David Remez, whose attempts at educational compromise led to a show-down which gave his successor, Ben-Zion Dinur, the role of architect of a state education system; Zalman

Aranne who started reform of secondary education; Abba Eban, international diplomatist extraordinary; Yigal Allon, Deputy Premier. But in the beginning there was chaos.

The trouble was not that the new Israel had no educational system; she had too many different educational systems, with each operating too independently of the others. Primary education was run in one way, secondary education in another. Two small higher educational institutions, the Hebrew University on Mount Scopus in Jerusalem and the Technion on Hadar Hacarmel in Haifa, with a total of 1,600 students, had each been in operation for nearly a quarter of a century. But under the Mandate there was no nationwide co-ordination of this system, although after more than twenty years of statehood secondary education was still to be partly governed by a Mandate Ordinance of 1933. Instead the Jewish community of Palestine was left to provide its own schooling.

In primary education it was highly successful. There was a mêlée of different segments, which took more than five years to sort out; but Zalman Shazar, when he was appointed to the Ministry, did at any rate have a basis of almost universal elementary education—ninety per cent of Palestine's Jewish children aged between six and fourteen were at school—on which to build. This made it that much easier for him and his successors to tackle the vast problems which beset them. If not painlessly, then certainly with surprising smoothness, Israel quite quickly provided her younger children with universal, free, compulsory education.

Despite the deprivation by war of the Mount Scopus site, the expansion of university education too went ahead with astonishing rapidity. In the 1950s and 1960s vast new campuses, often of notable architectural distinction, sprang up in the country's three main cities and began to spread to less developed areas. The new conscript army was developed as an educational back-stop, ready to equip the backward and the drop-outs with the elements of literacy for when they returned to civilian life. In Israel's first quarter-century, only secondary education proved too intractable to fit into the framework of the government's ambitious plans. And even in this sector, by 1971, nearly sixty per cent of the fourteen- to eighteen-year-olds were receiving some form of secondary education.

During the Mandate there had grown up a system of elementary education based on control by interest groups. Schools under the aegis of the Vaad Leumi were divided into three sections, pedantically described as "trends." There was a general trend, covering some forty per cent of pupils. Another thirty-three per cent of the children attended schools run by the Histadrut labour trend. About twenty per cent were educated by the Mizrachi orthodox religious movement. There was in addition a small number of schools and yeshivah academies in the titht, and totally independent, grip of the ultra-orthodox Agudah. There was no doubt about the ubiquitous availability of elementary education. The first need was to ensure that all those eligible availed themselves of it.

On 12 September 1949, six weeks after the final armistice at the end of the war of independence had been signed, the Compulsory Education Law came into force, aimed at taking full effect by October, 1951. It provided free and compulsory primary education, including a year of kindergarten, for all children aged between five and fourteen. Originally the Government's intention had been to apply the law only from the age of six. But turbulence in the Knesset ensued, particularly from lady members who wished the starting age to be four. One year of compulsory kindergarten was the agreed compromise.

A division of responsibility between central and local government gave the Ministry of Education the right to prescribe curricula (even down to Old Testament verses to be learned by heart and history dates to be memorized), syllabuses, timetables, textbooks and discipline, and to administer the final examination. The local authorities had the duty to construct, maintain, furnish and equip school buildings, pay teachers, and supply secretarial help, caretakers, and a school health service; certain types of areas with heavy concentrations of immigrants were exempted from this requirement. The new law also set up Schools for Working Youth, for adolescents who had not completed their primary education. These provided compulsory evening classes on five days a week in Hebrew, arithmetic, the Old Testament, social and civic studies, handicrafts and agriculture, for a catchment group consisting of new immigrants, mainly from oriental countries, and youths from deprived families. Due to shortages of accommodation, textbooks and teachers, these schools, whose number topped the two hundred mark, never made the impact they should have.

Compulsory kindergarten, too, was seen as a means of helping children from deprived homes. Increasingly successful efforts were made to include toddlers aged three or four in kindergartens maintained by women's organizations or other private sources. Below the compulsory age these kindergartens were fee-paying; but the Government provided free entry for many children from deprived homes. By the 1970s more than half the children at kindergarten were attending for two or even three years, and thirty-seven thousand were receiving their education free. Curricula developed from a complete absence of formal studies to a policy of more active teaching.

All this sounded very tidy. But at the start it was too tidy; for the trends continued. Not only were the general, labour and religious trends now enshrined in law. They were augmented by a fourth trend, the Agudah, whose political wing was represented in the government coalition. A demeaning scramble for recruits followed, particularly among the children of immigrants, with the trends sharing out localities among themselves much in the manner of transatlantic gangsters carving up territory. Although the law had specifically given parents the right to educate their children in the trend of their own choice, and even to demand the establishment of a school of their chosen trend in the area where they lived, the party carve-up in effect deprived them of this right. To cut itself in more handsomely on the deal, the labour trend even launched a religious sub-trend. Many immigrants, unable to distinguish between the trends, were in a state of complete bewilderment. Nauseated, Ben Gurion denounced what was going on as "a shameful manhunt."

The manner in which the trends were running amok was tellingly illustrated by the changes in the number of children in the schools of each trend. Between 1948 and 1950, the number of pupils at general trend schools rose only slightly, from 55,933 to 67,030. The total being educated at Mizrachi schools was up by more than half, rising from 26,621 to 40,686. The previously tiny Agudah trend more than doubled its attendance roll, from 6,957 to 14,632. The labour trend pushed up its tally at an even faster rate, from 37,304 to 82,067. Disturbed, the Government in 1950 appointed a commission of inquiry. This delivered the verdict that party representatives were indeed putting pressure on parents, whose wishes, especially on religious education, were being denied fitting consideration.

On 14 February 1951 the Knesset debated a demand by the General Zionists and Herut for the abolition of the trend system. A compromise by David Remez, who the previous year had succeeded Shazar at the Ministry, was voted down. The Government resigned and an election was called. In the campaign Mapai came down against the trend system. The Mizrachi groups agreed to enter the Government on a policy of abolishing trends but retaining a semi-autonomous religious sector in primary education. On 8 October the Knesset signified its approval of a system of state education, and the following year the Minister set up a commission to bring this about. The commission finished its preparatory work in April 1953. A draft law was laid before the Knesset in June. By August, under Ben-Zion Dinur, a State Education Law was enacted for implementation in the 1953–4 school year.

This law abolished the trends and replaced them with a dual system of state education. Parents were to be permitted to choose between state education and religious state education. Any allegiance to party politics in the organization and administration of education was banned, and to satisfy the General Zionists, following the May Day furore, political propaganda in state schools was prohibited. The trend character of teacher training colleges was also abolished, and the Ministry took over responsibility for both the training and payment of teachers in primary education.

The Ministry was reorganized, and the committee of Chief Trend Inspectors was abolished. Instead, under the Director-General, two advisory bodies were set up. Under one of these, the Council for Religious State Education, monopoly control of religious education within the state system was neatly handed over to the Mizrachi groups. At least nine of this Council's fourteen members were to be nominees of the Mizrachis. The Council had the power to disqualify a teacher or inspector on religious grounds, and to veto curricula. Its consent was required for the appointment of the Director of the Ministry of Education's Division of Religious Education. On certain issues it was even entitled to overrule ministerial decisions.

This did not, however, mean that the Mizrachi now controlled all religious education. The Agudah took the opportunity of the new law to withdraw their sixty-nine schools from the state system. But they handily availed themselves of the advantage of having their schools categorized as "recognized" institutions. In return for agreeing to a Ministry-supervised basic programme, involving at least seventy-five per cent of weekly lesson periods, the Agudah had the major part of their teachers' salaries bill covered by the Government and were in addition eligible for government development loans.

The ideals of this new state system, which was to survive unchanged for sixteen years, were enshrined in a statement of objectives which, as so often the way with Israeli official utterances, was simultaneously lofty and windy. "The object of state education is to base primary education on the values of Jewish culture and the achievements of science, love of country and loyalty to the State and the people of Israel, training in agricultural and manual work, training for pioneering, and the striving for a society based on freedom, equality, tolerance, mutual aid and love of humanity."

At first love of humanity was a little strained, because elementary education in Israel had to be carried on not

only in conditions of abject national poverty but also
with the extra burden of the mass immigration which
promptly followed the departure of the British. To begin
with, there were not enough teachers. Unqualified staff
had to be employed, and at first the proportion of these
grew frighteningly. In 1952 they accounted for forty-
four per cent of the total, and by 1956 as many as half
of all primary teachers were unqualified. Until expanded
teacher training was able to deal with this problem,
some children even had to be taught on a shift system.
But teacher training programmes gradually caught up
with needs, and by 1969–70 84.4 per cent of all teachers were qualified.

There was also a shortage of buildings. For a time
children had to be taught in temporary huts, in barracks,
in tents, and even in the open air. Supplies of equipment
were so limited that exercise books had to be rationed.
But as resources became more readily available and
conditions improved, universal primary education gradually developed from a phenomenon into a routine.

The school year was divided into three terms: early
September to the end of December; one week's holiday
and then on to Passover; and, after the Passover holiday, the summer term lasted until the end of June.
There was a six-day school week. Classes began at the
early Mediterranean time of 8 a.m. and lasted from between four to seven hours. From the age of six onwards,
homework was set. In the lowest grades the class teacher
taught the children for all subjects, but from the fourth
grade subject specialists began to take over. Manual
training was compulsory: woodwork or metalwork for
the boys, domestic science for the girls, and agriculture
for both. At the age of ten a foreign language began to
be studied, usually English, possibly French. Corporal
punishment was forbidden. Except at Agudah schools,
classes were coeducational. In the Agudah schools not
only were the sexes segregated; so were the textbooks.
Most of the normally current primers on science, history
and geography, as well as much of modern Hebrew literature, were not permitted beyond the *mezuzah*-deco-
rated doorposts.

By the beginning of the 1970s, forty per cent of children at primary schools were receiving some form of religious education. All but ten per cent were at state religious schools, which had a separate syllabus for Bible, oral law and Hebrew literature, where the day began with prayers, and whose male pupils were required to wear fringes and cover their heads. Of the pupils taught from this syllabus some seventy per cent were from families originating in oriental countries. Generally less well off and all too often less well housed than their schoolmates, these children received special help. They often lived in outlying areas or development towns, and to increase their chances of being well taught the Ministry offered bonuses to teachers willing to settle in these places for several years. Some schools improved their educational prospects by means of an extended school day, with eight to ten extra school hours each week, providing supplementary lessons in such basic subjects as Hebrew and arithmetic. There were special classes for slow learners. Some pupils received individual tuition. Homework was carried out under supervision. Also available were the facilities of an extended school year with an extra month's study in the summer, and enrichment programmes to prepare children for post-primary education. In the last two grades of some schools, additional time was provided for manual training and prevocational preparation.

Particular consideration was also given to oriental children who wished to proceed to secondary education. Until implementation of the secondary education reform was achieved, transition from primary to post-primary schools was attained by means of the survey test—the *Seker*. This test also decided whether the child was eligible for state assistance with the necessary fees. For an oriental child the qualification mark was lower than for other children. The test partly consisted of a two-hour examination in Hebrew language, arithmetic and general intelligence, and was partly decided by the teacher's assessment.

Movement from primary to secondary education involved for an Israeli fourteen-year-old leaping a chasm as wide and as awful as the English eleven-plus examination. The Israelis were simply too indigent to provide universal free secondary education as part of their state system. Right through to the 1970s, secondary education was provided by non-governmental organizations, local authorities, co-operatives, women's organizations and others, in return for the payment of fees. It was not that the Government was content with this situation. As early as 3 November 1955, the coalition programme presented to the Knesset included a pledge that "the Government . . . will endeavour to extend the applicability of the Compulsory Education Law to kindergarten age and to secondary schooling." After the 1965 election, with no progress achieved towards this objective, the new government pledged itself to the more limited objective of two extra years of free education, from ages fourteen to sixteen, during that Parliament—that is, by 1969. Nothing of the sort happened. In late 1971, after the optimistic manner of his predecessors, Yigal Allon was still hopefully forecasting the implementation of an educational master-plan by 1977.

In the meantime the Government had decided that some definite, if limited, action must serve as a temporary substitute for ambitious and grandiloquent plans. In 1957 a scheme for helping with the payment of fees for children at secondary schools, based on parents' incomes and size of family, was introduced. Benefit became available to sixteen per cent of post-primary pupils. By 1971, fifty-three per cent of secondary school children were totally exempted from fees, with another twenty-three per cent partially exempted. In 1962 the state-religious division was extended from primary to secondary education, covering all inspected post-primary schools. The Director of the Division of Religious Education was given the same authority in this field as in primary education. In 1963 an Administration of Post-Primary Education was set up to reduce the size of classes and give grants for the acquisition of library books and special equipment. In 1968 a Bill was introduced requiring all private and independent schools and their personnel—and this included secondary schools —to be licensed and supervised by the Ministry rather than simply registered with it.

Far-reaching reform was, however, on its way. In

1965 the Minister of Education had received the report of a committee recommending the raising of the compulsory school leaving age from fourteen to fifteen. The last three years of primary education were to be refashioned into the first stage of post-primary education, organized along comprehensive lines, with a common basic curriculum but gradual specialization. This teaching was to be carried on either in a separate building or as part of an existing post-primary school. The Teachers' Union demanded instead an extra year of elementary schooling, and their Secretary-General, Shalom Levin, accused the Government of placing elementary education at the bottom of its list of priorities: "Many elementary school classrooms are dark, the ceilings appear as though they are about to collapse, there is no ventilation, the furniture is unfit for use, and there aren't even enough water taps." But, all the same, the Government plumped for the committee's recommendations.

In May 1966 Zalman Aranne, as Minister, asked the Knesset to set up a parliamentary committee to study the system of elementary and secondary education in the light of developments since the passage of the Compulsory Education Law. A committee of nineteen was set up, under the chairmanship of Elimelech Rimalt of Gahal, and including four teachers' representatives. The committee approved the suggested reforms, with two modifications. First, the raising of the school leaving age should take place gradually; secondly, the "middle division" of three years should be incorporated into a six-year post-primary school, preferably comprehensive. In 1968 the Knesset voted in favour of the recommended education reforms, and the Ministry decided that they should by carried through from the school year 1969–70. In 1969 the Knesset passed the Compulsory Education (Amendment No. 6) Bill. Only the twenty-four-hour-a-day enthusiasm of Aranne had bludgeoned it through the opposition of both teachers and Labour Party.

The new law laid down that, after a year's compulsory kindergarten, the structure of education should be entirely changed. Instead of eight years of compulsory primary education, followed at the age of fourteen by four years' optional secondary education, there was to be a six-year compulsory primary stage followed by two consecutive three-year post-primary periods. The first of these was to be compulsory. The change was to be carried through gradually, with the school leaving age raised by one year by 1972 and by the second year by 1975. The school leaving age then would be sixteen.

The plan was idealistic. Neighbourhood comprehensives would help to bring about the objective, then much in vogue, of social integration. Shraga Adiel, who was for a time Chairman of the Ministry of Education's Pedagogic Secretariat, insisted: "It is an educational must for this country that children of different social backgrounds sit down together in the same classroom." But implementation of that ideal was a different matter. The plan stagnated. The reform duly began in 1969–70; but its timetable slipped. By 1971 it had been carried through in one-third of the schools in Haifa, and in one-fifth of the Tel Aviv schools. But hardly any headway had been made in Jerusalem. Altogether there were ninety-six of the planned junior high schools. And in that same year of 1971 shortage of money compelled the Ministry to concede defeat. Completion of the first stage was postponed from 1972–3 to 1973–4. The second stage was to be delayed from 1975 to 1977–8. By 1976, it was still hoped, there would be 350 junior high schools. Meanwhile priority would be given to low-income urban districts and development areas.

So twenty years on from the introduction of compulsory and universal primary education, Israel's post-primary system still resembled a somewhat tattered patchwork quilt, with shiny patches failing to conceal large threadbare corners. The new junior high schools were slowly coming into existence. At the same time the various specimens of traditional post-primary education— academic, vocational, agricultural—existed alongside them and experiments were being made in comprehensivization. Rules of payment for admission to secondary education were also complicated. Some pupils were totally exempted from paying fees; others were partially exempted. Regulations for exemption depended not only on the child's academic abilities but also on his parents' country of origin and in addition on where they had chosen to live—since all in development towns and new immigrants' settlements were exempted—and even on the date when the child had settled in the country, since all new immigrants were eligible for free secondary education in their first two years. In addition to that, there were scholarships to help with payment for transport, textbooks and school supplies if the children satisfied criteria of need. A well-motivated bureaucracy had constructed a maze.

Nevertheless, there was a way through the maze. And more and more children were finding that way. In 1948, 44 per cent of the new Israeli State's working population had benefited from at least some post-elementary education, as against only 24 per cent with no more than four years of schooling. Six years of mass immigration later, in 1954, the balance had tilted the other way. Of those of working age, 37 per cent had been at school for no more than four years, out-numbering the 32 per cent who had attended post-elementary schools. After another twelve years, in 1966, the trend had more than reversed itself. Only 20 per cent of those at work had had no more than four years at school; more than double, 47 per cent, had been at post-elementary schools. So the highly miscellaneous Israeli population of the mid-1960s was better educated than the much more homogeneous Yishuv of the immediate pre-independence period.

The brightest got to the secondary schools. Tel Aviv had twenty of these schools, all municipally owned. Jerusalem had forty-five, though only nine were owned by the city. The objective from the day the child entered was to obtain the *Bagrut*: matriculation. This was an examination taken at the end of the final year, although in 1971 the Ministry of Education announced a plan to spread it over the final three years. In the child's first two years at the school he would be in a general class. During the second and final two-year period he would specialize, with a choice of mathematics, biology, social sciences, literature or physics. The *Bagrut* qualified those who passed it to enter higher education although, if there were more candidates than places (and there almost invariably were), the university could impose a further examination. But the schools had a problem: only about thirty-five per cent of those who entered passed the *Bagrut*. So, to reduce the number of drop-outs, in 1965 an easier alternative test was introduced, a School Leaving Certificate. This involved sitting five subjects with a pass required in three. Special measures, including supervision of homework and extra instruction, were taken to reduce drop-outs among oriental pupils. The leaving certificate was also available at secondary evening classes, although here too the *Bagrut* was the longed-for objective. But with four to five lessons five nights a week, and even with a great deal of homework to top the lessons up, the pass rate was inevitably low.

If pupils at secondary schools met with by no means universal success, those at vocational and agricultural schools expected success even less, and dropped out more. They were conscious that their schools' administration was never left long enough to settle: in 1953 jurisdiction over the vocational schools was made the responsibility of the Ministry of Labour, while the agricultural schools were taken over by the Ministry of Agriculture; seven years later, the lot were handed over to the Ministry of Education. They knew, too, that the best jobs would not be available to them when they left school. For students at the vocational schools the aim —at the end of a four-year course of fifty hours a week (nine hours a day except Friday)—was to obtain a final certificate which involved passing an examination in seven subjects ranging from the Bible to a practical workshop test. Alternatively, at the end of a two- or three-year course, a leaving certificate was available. Children who had not even passed the *Seker* test at their primary school were eligible to enter the vocational schools for these shorter courses. These various certificates were recognized by the Ministry of Labour, and were a qualification for an apprenticeship at the appropriate level in the trade or craft in which the student had been trained. Selected pupils could also take additional lessons in order to be examined at *Bagrut* standard for possible admission to the Technion.

Students who entered the vocational schools did at

any rate want to learn a trade. Those at agricultural schools, on the other hand, were not necessarily interested in agriculture. Some went to them because they were the only form of post-primary education available. Others were sent by social agencies, for example the Youth Aliyah, since agricultural schools were all boarding-schools and therefore a useful depository for such children. In any case, for a long time these schools were un-attractive to talented children since they did not offer a *Bagrut* course. Later this was changed, and agriculture was even accepted—as an optional subject—for students taking the *Bagrut* at agricultural schools.

It seemed, in fact, that the fate of Israeli secondary education was incessantly to be fiddled around with, and that even by the thirtieth year of statehood the pattern would not have been satisfactorily sorted out. But other, more settled countries, with far longer records in legislation on education—Britain, for example—were during the same period not doing all that much better. And in another sphere, university education, Israel soon began racing far ahead of the field.

As Oxford and Cambridge were to England, and Harvard and Yale to the United States, so the Israelis started off with their Technion and Hebrew University. These two universities set the pattern for the Israeli university system of the 1950s and 1960s. Obtaining their funds mainly from voluntary contributions, often over-seas, they were autonomous and apolitical. Even when, by the late 1960s, they were receiving some seventy per cent of their regular budget and about forty per cent of their investment budget from public funds, this absolute independence was maintained. A legal framework was created for them in the Council for Higher Education Law of 1958, but it was a framework which consolidated their independence.

The law, it is true, regulated degree conferment by laying down that universities could only award degrees if they were recognized by a newly created Council for Higher Education, and made it an offence to award un-authorized degrees. But the Council itself was almost os-tentatiously non-partisan. Appointed by the President of the State, and under the chairmanship of the Minister of

Education, it was required by law to be composed, as to at least two-thirds of its membership, of academics of standing. The Council's functions were to recognize higher education institutions, approve which academic titles might be conferred and under what conditions, make proposals for the development of existing and new institutions, and advise the Government on financial support. Each institution had its own governing body, composed partly of academics and partly of eminent laymen. Regulation of this kind had become urgently necessary to cope with bodies, wishing to be universities, which were springing up all over the place.

It was on 14 December 1924 that Jewish university education began in Palestine with the opening at Haifa of the Technion which, as its name implied, was—and was to remain for forty years—devoted solely to the teaching of technical subjects. The Technion grew slowly. At the end of the Mandate, twenty-four years after its foundation, it had 678 students. Closed during the war of independence, it reopened in November 1949; from then on it never looked back. In 1953 it was turning so many applicants away that it began moving from its site in Haifa itself to Technion City, a 300-acre campus at Neve Shaanan on Mount Carmel. The Institute of Aeronautical Engineering was the first to be transferred. By 1956 there were 700 students at Technion City, and the move was far from completed. In 1963 the Technion expanded in two further directions. It established a Junior Technical College for training building technicians; and it launched into its first studies in the humanities ("The Classical Theories of the Stoa, Machiavelli and Hobbes","Persian, Islamic and Medieval Art"), which were to become an obligatory part of examination courses. A Technical High School was also set up.

Aided by financial help from the Jewish Agency, whose contributions were by 1971 to account for eighty-five per cent of its budget, the Technion continued to grow. It became one of the world's most important scientific and technological centres both for education and research. Virtually every discipline in engineering and the exact sciences was taught in more than twenty faculties, ranging from computer science to food technology.

Electronics, computer science and electrical engineering were going ahead fastest. But the Technion also found room, for example, for a student to submit a Master of Science thesis on ways to improve frozen concentrated orange juice. In the academic year 1971-2, with a medical school as its latest acquisition, it was bigger than Cal. Tech., and as big as Massachusetts Institute of Technology (MIT). Its academic staff alone, totalling more than 1,200, were twice as numerous as its student body in 1948. The roster of students had grown to 8,200. Yet lack of vacancies was still compelling the Technion to turn away seventy per cent of its applicants.

Even so, the Technion had a far easier passage in its new role as an Israeli university than was granted to the Hebrew University of Jerusalem.

As a result of Chaim Weizmann's drive, and in the presence of Arthur James Balfour—originator of the declaration which in 1917 promised a national home for the Jews in Palestine—the Hebrew University of Jerusalem was founded on Mount Scopus on 1 April 1925. It started life as a research institution, and did not begin awarding degrees until 1931. By 1948 it had 900 students and 190 teachers.

In the war of independence the Hebrew University suffered two serious losses. Nearly one hundred of its students were killed in action. And its lovingly developed site, including an amphitheatre in a spectacular setting, was totally surrounded by Jordanian troops. In the settlement which followed the ending of the war, the university area remained in Israeli hands; but, since it was cut off from the rest of Israeli territory, it was unusable. A demilitarized enclave, the university was guarded by caretakers and Israeli police. Every two weeks a convoy under United Nations protection was allowed up the mountain to bring provisions and change the personnel. But no students were allowed in.

Nevertheless, the Hebrew University started up again in 1949, in the Israeli-held western part of Jerusalem. Premises were everywhere. The main building, where students first settled in, was the Franciscan Boys' College of Terra Sancta. From there the improvised university spread to forty-six buildings: dwelling houses, a former police station, part of an hotel, an Arab school, half of a Christian orphanage, the former Italian consulate. In the laboratories a shift system was worked. The university's silver jubilee was celebrated in 1950 in the Jerusalem YMCA.

And the university was expanding. It acquired a law faculty, a social science faculty, a department for public administration and business administration, a school of social work, and a graduate school of librarianship. This was a particularly daring venture since, along with the university itself, its half-million-book library was marooned on Mount Scopus. By 1953 a reconstituted library had 440,000 books listed in its index. In 1953, too, a school of education was set up by agreement between the university and the Ministry of Education. A faculty of agriculture was established in the small green town of Rehovot. In May 1949, its first fifty students released soldiers, the Hadassah Medical School had been set up; the first medical graduates received their doctorates in May 1952.

Hadassah was the first to decide that new buildings must be constructed. In 1952 the ground was broken for a new medical school and teaching hospital at a hill site called Tsuba, some six miles from Jerusalem and handily near to John the Baptist's Ein Kerem. With décor by the artist whose work provided the indispensable hallmark for the most important buildings in Jerusalem— Chagall stained glass windows in the hospital's synagogue—Hadassah was opened in August 1961.

Meanwhile the university itself had decided to cut its losses and construct a new campus. On an outer Jerusalem site at Givat Ram, the first sod was cut on 2 June 1954. By 1956 the initial group of buildings had been opened, and the transfer began. By the academic year 1956–7, the bulk of the university's work was being carried out at Givat Ram, and half the students were attending classes at the new site. On 27 April 1958 the new campus was dedicated as part of the State's tenth anniversary celebrations. The notables who turned up were able to inspect twenty-five major completed buildings and a four-thousand-seat stadium. The university was also to house a white nodal synagogue.

Still the building went on and the planning went on. In March 1961, the university's board of governors approved a five-year master-plan for development. Six years later, development took on an unanticipated momentum of its own. On 8 June 1967 the Hebrew University's flag flew once again on the roof of the Jewish National and University Library on Mount Scopus. At a cost to the university of forty-one students and six teachers killed, the Six-Day War had been won and the isolation of the original Hebrew University site had been ended.

In 1961 it had been confidently asserted that the new Givat Ram buildings, planned for a university population of 10,000, "should suffice for a generation." At the opening of the academic year 1971-2 there were 18,000 students at the Hebrew University—2,000 more than it could reasonably hold, declared the University Rector. In 1971, to remedy the situation, a $100 million development plan got under way at Mount Scopus; its aim, to accommodate 14,000 students by 1976.

As it moved towards its fiftieth anniversary, the Hebrew University was responsible for more than half of all the research being carried out in Israel. At an earlier stage it had begun sinking tentative roots in Tel Aviv, with branches of its faculties of law and social sciences. But the burghers of Tel Aviv, ready to face the inevitable and accept that even half of Jerusalem must be their country's capital, were not going to be satisfied with harbouring a Jerusalem university. They set to and created one of their own.

But the new Tel Aviv university was not to be Israel's third or even fourth institute of higher education. Other educational entrepreneurs got in first. On 2 November 1949 the neglected Chaim Weizmann was given a thoughtful seventieth birthday present. Incorporating the Daniel Sieff Research Institute, founded in 1934, the Weizmann Institute was inaugurated at Rehovot. Set in vernal gardens, and of a meticulous tidiness quite unprecedented in the world's only improvised country, this science-based academic enterprise too lived in tacit rivalry with the Hebrew University. At its opening, teaching was confined to post-graduate level. A graduate school was established in October 1958, and expanded to a strength of about 500 by 1971. As the institute itself grew, it developed around faculties of biology, biophysics and biochemics, chemistry, mathematics and physics.

If science was the basis of the Weizmann Institute, Bar-Ilan University at Tel Aviv was more ethereally founded on spirit and soul. For Bar-Ilan was a religious university. Founded in the religious suburb of Bnei Brak on 20 September 1955 by the Mizrachi Organization of America, and named after the Mizrachi Rabbi Bar-Ilan, this idiosyncratic establishment's cornerstone was a "synthesis of the precepts of religion and secular technology" and its basic aim "to create a generation of men of culture and learning, who will also be versed in religious and scriptural teachings and who will preserve and continue the traditions and culture of Israel." It started with eighty students and a staff of twenty-four. It acquired four faculties, in Jewish studies, natural sciences and mathematics, social sciences, and language and literature. There were compulsory lectures in Jewish studies. By 1971 Bar-Ilan had 5,600 students and 716 staff, and was bursting at the seams. It had launched branches in the south at Ashkelon, and in the north at Safad and in the Jordan Valley. And, proudly housed in twenty-eight modern buildings on a campus at Ramat Gan, one of Tel Aviv's plushier suburbs, Bar-Ilan nevertheless had to start classes as early as 7 a.m. and go on till 10 p.m., with three shifts in laboratories, because of a shortage of space—due in its turn to a shortage of money. At the beginning of the 1971–2 academic year, 2,300 applicants were turned away. All the same, still expanding, in 1971 it opened a law faculty, established a research institute in the Old City of Jerusalem to study oriental Jewry and, in its school of education, was the first Israeli university to use closed-circuit television. As the apotheosis of that synthesis of the precepts of religion and secular technology, it was employing a computer in indexing rabbinic responsa.

Not far away from Bar-Ilan, in the north Tel Aviv district of Ramat Aviv, the new Tel Aviv university was undergoing a construction programme so massive that, along its central area in Klausner Street (at the end of which lay Israel's educational television studios, financed by the Rothschilds and opened in 1966), few of the students were entirely sure where exactly they were at any given time. It was an impressive campus, a little messy with the sand of construction, and ideally suited to conducted tours which duly took place. It was the scene of by far the biggest explosion in the history of Israeli university education.

Tel Aviv municipality established the university in 1956, bringing together the Tel Aviv Institute for Natural Sciences (founded 1953) and the Institute for Jewish Culture (1954). There were 140 students. In 1959 the Tel Aviv Academy of Music was incorporated, together with a school of law and economy; in 1962 the department of physics was opened. In 1961 the university, though still affiliated to the municipality, became an autonomous public body. Inevitably, it had a ten-year development plan for the construction of a new university campus.

This was inaugurated at Ramat Aviv in 1963. The move began. In 1964–5 there were 2,000 students and 270 staff. Still making progress the university in 1969 received full recognition from the Council for Higher Education. By 1971–2 it had as many staff as it had students six years before, and the student roster itself had orbited to a total of 14,000—a hundred-fold increase since the university's foundation only fifteen years before. Proliferating around the Klausner Street hub were 13 faculties, schools and departments, and 29 institutes. And even so, 7,000 applicants were turned away.

At about the same time that the embryonic institutions were being set up which later were to become Tel Aviv University, a similar process was taking place up the coast at Haifa. Simply to have a world-famous technical university was not enough for this busy city. In 1952 the municipality set up Haifa High School, with courses in law and economics. This was followed in 1954 by a faculty of humanities and a faculty of accounting, both set up in conjunction with the Hebrew University of Jerusalem. In 1957 they were joined by a faculty of social sciences. At the same time the original law and economics courses were placed under the supervision of the Hebrew University. In 1963 the plunge was taken and Haifa University Institute came into being, under the joint auspices of Haifa municipality (which paid the bills) and the Hebrew University. There were 675 students when it opened in 1964.

But if Tel Aviv University was to have a brand new campus, Haifa—the city which boasted that it did the work while Tel Aviv played—could not be satisfied with less. Moreover, Haifa had the advantage of one of the most stunningly beautiful sites in the Mediterranean. In October 1965, up on the heights of Mount Carmel, the cornerstone of Haifa University's new campus was laid. The designer was Oscar Niemeyer, creator both of Brasilia, brand-new capital of Brazil, and of the headquarters of the Communist Party in Paris. Two years later it was moving day. Six years later there were five thousand students and more than five hundred staff on Carmel Heights. In addition to advanced degrees, BA degrees were being offered in twenty departments. And Haifa University was about to come of age.

In January 1971 Haifa municipality handed over the key of the door, giving the university administrative self-government. It was decided that at the end of that same academic year the Hebrew University's academic responsibility should be brought to an end, sending a fully fledged Haifa University out on its own. It celebrated by launching its first post-graduate courses. But many improvements were still needed. There was a skimpy library of only seventeen thousand volumes, officially described as "still far from being able to fulfil the functions of a university library." There was no danger that this aggressively socialist city would be content with less than the best.

Haifa University's technical elder sister was meanwhile acting as foster-parent in another academic infancy. In 1965, on the fringes of the Negev wilderness at Beersheba, the Technion together with the Hebrew University and the Weizmann Institute supervised the launching of the Negev Institute of Higher Education. Growing quickly in the desert air, in 1969 it was officially recognized as the University of the Negev. Its medical school was being planned. It started the 1971–2 academic year with 3,200 students. And although its classes were still being held all over town, its new campus was approaching completion, with vividly imaginative architecture.

But if university education was more readily available in Israel than in almost any other country in the world, it was neither easily nor freely available. The tuition fees might indeed be lower than the top fees at secondary schools; and there was not only a grading system of fee reductions according to a student's economic resources, but also a special loan fund under which the government and three leading banks made finance available at a five per cent interest rate with repayments in instalments beginning one year after studies were completed. All the same, most students had to do part-time work in order to pay their way. And these students were different from, as well as proportionately more numerous than, students in other countries. Because there was compulsory military service for both young men and women, most students arrived at their university after completing their army period. They were, as a consequence, both older and more serious-minded than their foreign counterparts. They arrived at university as veteran participants in society, not applicants to join it.

But educationally that army service was not wasted. Regular army soldiers were provided with fifty per cent fee reductions at institutes of higher education. And, socially far more important, the army played its part in preparing oriental soldiers for university life, by providing a pre-academic course in their last eight months of service for such soldiers who held the *Bagrut* certificate. The army's main educational role, however, was directed to recruits who would never see the inside of a university. Its determination was to provide them with the basic elements of literacy. In a country of vast immigration, often from primitive countries, the scholarly graces were frequently not inborn. In the army's view, no soldier should be cast back adrift into civilian life without the ability to read a newspaper and a simple book, and to write a letter.

Accordingly, for those who were seen to require

them, the army provided compulsory courses in Hebrew, the Bible, Israeli and general history, geography, basic science, mathematics and civics, with the aim, if possible, of bringing every recruit up to the minimum basic elementary education standard. Its three months' course, equipped with special textbooks, provided an intensive six hundred hours of tuition in classes of ten pupils, with two teachers per class. Yigal Allon, as soldier and Education Minister, took doubled pride in praising the army as "Israel's largest and probably most successful educational institution." This was officially confirmed by the award to the Israel Defence Forces of the Israel prize for education.

But did the State of Israel itself merit a prize for educational achievement? The bare statistics were impressive. Between 1948–9 and 1970–1, the number of children at kindergartens was more than quadrupled, from 25,406 to 107,574. At elementary schools, too, the multiplication was by four: 91,133 to 369,805. Students at secondary and vocational schools increased at double this rate, from 12,689 in 1949 to 107,935 in 1970. And those 1,600 university students at the ending of the Mandate had soared to an extraordinary 45,000.

In the numbers game Israeli education was certainly winning. But literacy—and even numeracy—were more than a game of numbers. They were the basis of a society in which opportunities must be spread uniformly, in different parts of the country, among different social groups, and among children of different geographical origins. On these criteria, too, Israel had obviously come a long way. But nobody could fool themselves into thinking that there was not still a very long way to go.

3

Juggler on a Tightrope

In 1950 false teeth accounted for 2.4 per cent of Israel's export income. This fragile statistic symbolized the exiguous nature of Israel's export trade, as well as the forlorn narrowness of the new State's range of industrial manufactures. Between 1950 and 1970 the value of Israeli industrial exports exploded from $18 million to $649 million, and false teeth ceased to figure separately among the Government's fifty-two main export classifications. The expanding spectrum of the country's industries widened to include goods of bemusing variety. But two decades and more after the false-teeth era had come to an end, Israel's economic problem was even more intractable than had been apparent on independence day.

It was not that little progress had been made. Almost every year from 1948 onward offered testimony of the willingness to experiment and innovate that was prevalent among Israeli entrepreneurs. In 1951 new products included rubber soles and heels, crêpe rubber shoes, surgical gloves, typewriter assembly, and pencils. Jerusalem Pencils Ltd. was to celebrate its twentieth anniversary in 1971 with the news that it had produced its five hundred millionth pencil, as well as sundry crayons, rulers and triangles, transmitting the gift of orderly self-expression to twenty-five countries.

The following year two tyre-manufacturing factories were opened, both in partnership with American concerns. The General Tyre and Rubber Company at Kiryat Aryeh, near Petach Tikvah, was certain that it would presently meet the entire local demand and export its products as well. Its competitor, Alliance, countered with the claim that it was more up to date. Both statements were greeted with sniffs of disapproval. Demanded *Maariv,* Israel's biggest newspaper, on 27 April 1952: "Why throw away $2 million on further investment in the tyre industry? . . . Even one [tyre factory] is too much for local needs." Unperturbed, the tiny industry, employing fifty workers, went ahead. All local demand was met as soon as 1956. By 1960 Alliance had become Israel's biggest single exporter. By 1966 the two factories had a joint labour force 1,250 strong. On 3 March 1971 Alliance captured the largest single export order ever gained by an Israeli firm. Tyres worth $40 million were to be sold—to the United States. Branching out with adventurous special-purpose products while the American giants concentrated tamely on standard models, Alliance had pushed up exports to seventy-five per cent of its output, with annual sales abroad up from $1 million in 1956 to $17 million in 1971.

Still, in those early days, the innovators went ahead. By 1953 home production was meeting the entire local demand for sanitary ceramics, and exporting too. The manufacture began of ordinary and pressure piping. Nine nail factories were supplying all the country's requirements. A year later, similarly, Israel's paint industry was accounting for all local needs in paints and lacquers. Manufacture began of guillotines, stop-watches, baking ovens. It was no longer necessary to import corrugated iron for roofing. And at Hadera, American-Israel Paper Mills began to produce Israel's own paper. Progress was rapid. By 1957 newsprint was no longer being imported, and all Israel's toilet paper was being delicately made available by a plant named Supra, at Lod.

Long-playing records began to be produced; and stainless cutlery; and water tanks heated by the sun's rays; and Helena Rubinstein cosmetics; and clinical thermometers and hypodermic needles; and plastic zip-fasteners; and copper wire; and tinned gefilte fish; and instant coffee. In 1970 an entire instant coffee plant was sold for $1 million to South Korea.

The problem was, and the problem remained, that there was no co-ordinated pattern. Experiment brought success; but sometimes it also ended in failure. Enterprises were intermittently launched more in hope than by design. In 1955 in Afula, in northern Israel, a sugar refinery was insouciantly set up. The engineer in charge had never built one before, and touchingly relied on a Russian textbook. Unfortunately, too, seventy per cent of Israel's sugar beet crop lay far away in the south. After fifteen years of heavy financial loss the fact had suddenly to be faced that there was no economic justification for the refinery.

The motor car industry caused chronic headaches. Many wished that it had never been started. Its critics denounced it as a waste of resources, complaining that it did not even use a worthwhile proportion of local components. Of course, it was agreed, Israel must assemble if not manufacture its own motor cars. And at Haifa, at Ashdod, at Nazareth, the industry grew. But it kept going through crises, caused, it might be, by a steel strike in America, or simply by local tensions. Abortive, over-ambitious experiments were made. Successes, it was true, were chalked up. In January 1971 the five thousandth Ford Escort passenger car rolled off the assembly line at the Automotive Industries plant in Nazareth, only thirty months after assembly had first begun. The five-year-old plant had turned out eighteen thousand vehicles in all, and was giving employment to five hundred workers.

But another company, Autocars Ltd.—in which British Leyland was substantially involved through a maze of cross-shareholdings—was constantly in trouble. Bitter acrimony kept breaking out over its Leyland Ashdod works, which had been awarded the monopoly of bus and diesel lorry assembly in Israel, but which was alleged to have failed in fulfilling commitments over the proportion of locally manufactured parts and was warned that it would lose its monopoly. The police investigated allegations that the parent company had been selling vehicles at cut rates and on special terms to public figures. In the autumn of 1971 Autocars ran into a financial crisis and was forced into liquidation after British Leyland had failed to respond to an appeal by the Israeli Government to assume controlling responsibility;

redundancies became necessary, and a new structure for the company had to be laboriously essayed.

A cotton industry which established itself in spite of the hostility of various insects had to struggle when faced with the hard facts of international economics. An agricultural expert from California, Sam Hamburg, helped with Israel's first cotton planting in 1951; and this survived, despite determined assaults from an adversary named the spiny bolt-worm. The acreage under cultivation increased year by year: 670 acres in 1954, 12,200 in 1956. The bolt-worm, having discovered an antidote to the first exterminator which had beaten it off, rose again only to be conquered by a more fatal pesticide. By 1961 all local cotton needs were being met and exports had begun. But the trouble, really, was that the Israelis' cotton was too expensive. Low-wage, under-developed countries could under-price them every time. Only when the switch was made to sophisticated, science-based blends with synthetics did the Israeli textile industry take off.

Any poverty-stricken, tiny developing country could simply not afford mistakes and mischances such as these and others, in which incompetence, innocent hope and occasional corruption all played their part. Yet the problems of Israel were far greater than those of other impoverished new countries. For Israel had two burdens to carry which separately were potentially crushing; together were almost too much to bear; and one of which succeeded in crippling the State right through its first quarter-century of existence. The first was mass immigration. The second was the cost of defence.

The hundreds of thousands of immigrants who crowded into Israel during her first years of existence were hundreds of thousands of mouths to feed, bodies to clothe, families to house, children to educate, breadwinners to employ. The country almost suffocated under their weight, and in 1952 mass assisted free immigration was brought to an end for a time so that, given a breathing spell, this small constricted space could absorb all the disparate humans which it had ingested. Eventually immigration was to transform itself into an economic stimulant, with periodic slow-downs in entry leading to spells of economic recession. But at first it was simply too much.

The country eventually adjusted itself to the problems of immigration. Defence, however, was to remain a chronic problem. At the same time as she absorbed immigrants, built up from a false-teeth economy to mass production of manufactured exports, expanded from cottage industry to larger concerns, dispersed her population from the Tel Aviv area to the sparsely settled north and the southern Negev desert, and drew on such puny natural resources as she could find, Israel had to buy weapons from abroad and distort her industrial structure in order to secure the means of her protection. In 1971 defence was consuming ninety per cent of the country's tax income, thirty-two per cent of its imports and twenty-five per cent of its manpower, and accounting for one-quarter of its national product. That was why there was not enough money to provide free secondary education; why an incessant balance of payments deficit led to a siege economy; and why over-full employment, when it occurred between recessions, created an inflationary spiral.

Simply dispersing the population was problem enough. In 1952 sixty-two per cent of all manufacturing plants in Israel, accounting for fifty-six per cent of total industrial employment, were concentrated around Tel Aviv and Haifa. There were hardly any Jews in central Galilee or the Negev and it was necessary for security reasons to have them there. Security, too, made it undesirable for the mass of the population and the mass of industry to be concentrated in small, vulnerable areas. Development area policies, with massive incentives, achieved some success. But the central coastal strip still exerted its pull; in the 1970s Russian Jews, who had willingly undergone persecution and privation in order to escape to Israel, were still staging sit-down strikes at Lod airport rather than be housed outside the Tel Aviv district.

In a country with so small a population it was difficult to break out of the pre-independence pattern of small-scale industry. In 1947 most of the Jews employed in manufacturing worked in establishments employing less than ten people. In the textile industry's early stages its 9,000 employees worked in 1,300 different establishments. Even in the largest mills the average work-force was only 200. The Jerusalem pencil factory's saturation of the literate world with inexpensive writing implements was achieved with a staff of just 70. By 1970, only 5,734 out of 18,563 industrial establishments employed five or more people. In the whole of Israel, the number of industrial concerns with more than 300 employees was a skimpy 117. With an industry operating on this scale, mass production still had not really been given its chance.

Yet on this unstable and rickety infrastructure Israel bore the world's heaviest military load. Without external help, some of it from sources which were not only unlikely but aroused sharp internal discord, the nation would long since have totally collapsed under the dead weight. As it was, perversely, she managed to turn her need for establishing a domestic military potential into a means of creating sophisticated science-based industries. But whenever her hopes of a breakthrough to solvency looked like succeeding, renewed economic troubles deflated those hopes and left the Government with a bigger than ever problem to solve. The story of the developing first twenty-five years of Israeli industry is also a story of intermittent crisis and of the devaluation of the Israeli pound so many times that by the time of the seventh devaluation, in August 1971, its exchange rate against the dollar was one-seventeenth of what it had been at the time of independence.

It is a story, too, of how the increasing diversification of ownership of Israeli industry served different purposes; of how private enterprise involved itself in risk-taking export ventures which, if successful, brought massive rewards; of how the State itself, sometimes in partnership with private enterprise, made sure that the industries whose development was essential went ahead even if they were unlikely to bring any profit in their early years; and of how the country's whole industrial base rested on the shoulders of the Histadrut. In the 1970s as in the 1940s the Histadrut was a disproportionately strong force in a pocket economy. But if its industrial ventures were not always profitable, if it suffered financial losses and was cumbrously administered, it performed a social function of providing employment even when employing people was not the sensible thing to do.

Its own sponsors were most conscious of the Histadrut's limitations, which were inherent in the anomaly of a trade union organization also being the country's largest employer. Taking into account kibbutz industry, the Histadrut owned twenty per cent of Israel's manufacturing sector. Its employer-union dual role imposed on it an obligation for ideological reasons to outbid its private enterprise rivals. It was more generous in fringe benefits. Its wage rates were fifteen per cent higher, but not its production. It pervaded such disparate fields as metals, chemicals, electronics, ceramics, plywood, rubber, fire bricks. Its industrial holding company, Koor, which had started in 1944 with two plants—Vulcan Foundries and Phoenicia Glass, with 500 workers—became the largest industrial body in Israel, by 1971 employing 17,000 workers in 44 industrial plants. It accounted for six per cent of the country's industrial manpower, eight per cent of its industrial output (valued at 700 million Israeli pounds—$166 million) and ten per cent of its exports. In association with foreign partnership, it jointly owned Alliance Tyres. Its metal interests varied from building cranes to cutlery, the output of its electric and electronic plants from batteries to telecommunications instruments.

The Histadrut was Israel's leviathan. But other sectors of industry had their part to play. Loans and grants from abroad came most naturally to the Government, which accordingly gained control over vast resources for investment and consequently over considerable sectors of economic activity. In 1969, 9.8 per cent of employees in industry worked in the public sector, whose task was often to launch hazardous and initially unprofitable enterprises. The government developed a growing tendency to found factories and then to sell them either to the Histadrut or to private enterprise. The Histadrut itself was partial to entering into business with private partners who could provide necessary know-how. And private enterprise itself started up in business on its own initiative.

Between 1960 and 1970 the number of employees in private industry rose from 125,000 to 208,000. By 1970 it accounted for 75 per cent of total industrial manpower and 70 per cent of total industrial output. In the food processing and canning industry, 80 per cent was privately owned. In textiles, most go-ahead of all Israeli industries, 98 per cent was in private hands. In the years from 1960 to 1969, exports as a whole quadrupled; private industry's share of this fourfold total went up from 58 per cent to 74 per cent. There was a great deal of grumbling from the Manufacturers' Association about the strangulating effect of governmental bureaucracy; and the hindrances this raised could certainly not be discounted. All the same, private enterprise in Israel did not seem to be doing too badly for itself, or for its country.

Yet it was the Histadrut which remained the stable base and the pace-maker. Its advantages were economies of scale, ease in changing technologies, and ability to complement different functions such as manufacturing and marketing. A disadvantage was that its lumbering structure prevented it from acting quickly. It was that much more difficult for it to close a factory or place one of its firms in bankruptcy. When the recession of the mid-1960s got under way, its inflexibility prevented it from acting quickly enough to shed redundant manpower. By the time it was ready to act the recession was over. This meant, at a time when construction was down 50 per cent, that the Histadrut's construction company, Solel Boneh, lost some 60 million Israeli pounds ($17 million) because only 7 per cent of its workers were laid off when it should have shed 35 per cent. By those very inherent defects it helped to stop heavy unemployment turning into mass unemployment. A counterbalancing advantage was that, having held on to the manpower, it had the workers ready in employment available for the boom which followed in 1967.

That 1965–7 recession was a dread time in Israel; a time when relief works were so prevalent that elderly bearded men could be seen all over the country engaged in the elementary Keynesian process of building roads. But if that was the worst recession it was not the first.

In the early years of the State the most rudimentary tasks imposed themselves: absorbing the immigrants and organizing an economic system for an independent state rather than a colonial community hived off into its pioneering ghetto. Once this was achieved, partly by sending immigrants off to agricultural settlements to grow food for themselves and the nation, partly by starting off labour-intensive manufacturing enterprises, unemployment fell. But inflation imposed restrictive policies and, by 1953, unemployment was up again. Two years later the country had settled down into a period of growth. Construction gave way to production. Agricultural self-sufficiency led to an emphasis on industrial development. Jobs in the paper, motor, tyre and chemical industries, among others, from 1955 pushed unemployment farther and farther down until by 1959 a period of comfortable prosperity had been reached.

But during this period the balance of payments deteriorated. An economic policy based on emphasizing exports failed. The high employment of 1964 gave way, with restraint policies, to the very high unemployment of 1966–7. It took a war—the Six-Day War of 1967—to bring about the biggest boom Israel had ever known. But the brim-full employment accompanying it led to inflation. The export rise tailed off. A further dose of heavy taxes failed to help. President Nixon's dollar-protection measures of August 1971 were seized on as a subterfuge for devaluing the Israeli pound yet again. And still the experts warned that the devaluation was too small and had come too late. David Horowitz, Governor of the Bank of Israel at the time, made it known that he had recommended devaluation two years earlier.

In the primitive days of 1948 such sophisticated crises would have seemed enviable status symbols to those attempting to operate Israel's primitive economy. Instead of almost uncontrollable inflation, there was stringent price control, accompanied by the rationing of food and basic necessities. Only fifty to sixty thousand Jews were in industrial employment. Some industries had been established during the war, when Israel was needed as a quartermaster's store and larder to British forces in the Middle East. Haifa Bay had already become the heavy industrial area, with Phoenicia Glass, Vulcan Foundries, Nesher Cement and Shemen soap and oils. The food companies of Elite, Lieber and Assis were established in the Tel Aviv district. But industry was backward technologically. Not only were the units small, but the equipment was outdated. Of the major industries which in the future were to provide the bulk of Israel's employment and foreign exchange income, at this stage only two, diamonds and chemicals, were very much in evidence.

As early as 1949 diamonds accounted for half of Israel's industrial exports: $5,200,000 out of a total of $10,400,000. It was in the late 1930s that Jews had first begun coming to Palestine from Antwerp and Amsterdam in the Low Countries to establish diamond cutting and polishing plants. During the war these refugees were given their opportunity to break into the world diamond market when the Belgian and Dutch industries were closed down. The end of the war, and renewed activity in Europe, pushed the Israelis into a less crowded sector of the market. They became predominant in the supply of smaller and medium-sized stones, in the jewels used in engagement rings known as melees; and eventually they were to produce and sell as much as eighty-five per cent of the world's supply of such stones.

It was a convenient industry, which relied on easily transportable imported materials and could be established anywhere in the country. The Israeli Government encouraged the dispersal of the industry to development areas as well as the main centres, such as Tel Aviv, Netanya, Petach Tikvah and Bnei Brak, and encouraged the training of workers. By the end of 1969 employees, including administrative and clerical staff, numbered 12,400, in 468 enterprises. They were still being added to by an intake of Jewish diamond workers immigrating from Belgium. The industry was Israel's highest single source of foreign revenue. It accounted for one out of every three diamonds sold anywhere. In 1969 exports totalled $215,907,316—35 per cent of total Israeli exports. In 1970 a weakening in world markets caused sales to fall back to $202 million. But in 1971 record sales—$265 million—were achieved once again. Markets were expanding from North America and Europe to include the Far East. The industry was being diversified to include fine jewellery production.

With that amiable Israeli tendency to jump the gun, Moshe Schnitzer, President of the Israel Diamond Exchange, was by June 1971 claiming that Ramat Gan, outside Tel Aviv, had taken away from Antwerp the title of diamond capital of the world. Certainly Ramat Gan was a pardonable cause for pride. For here was the heart of Israel's diamond industry. Almost half of the country's diamond establishment—201—were sited there. And sparkling over them was the new marble-faced, 28-storey, $5 million diamond centre completed in 1968. Rough stones and polished diamonds were stored in its electronically controlled vaults. In its diamond exchange more than $1 million worth of diamonds changed hands every day. Even Mr. Schnitzer could in 1971 have cited with reasonable satisfaction a tribute paid by *International Diamond Annual:* "The rise of the Israeli diamond-cutting industry to the point where it approaches Antwerp in world importance has been one of the most significant single events in the sphere of diamonds during the past decade."

Diamonds had to be imported in their rough state. A lack of local raw materials was indeed one of Israeli industry's major handicaps. But even in the undeveloped days of 1948 it was clear that, among the new State's few natural resources, chemicals at least were plain to see. They were often of poor quality, and exploiting them presented great difficulties, as the history of the tribulations of the Negev makes plain. But at least they were there. The Palestine Potash Company existed in Mandate times. So, too, did the Fertilizers and Chemicals Company in Haifa Bay, which was founded in 1946; although the first of its installations did not begin until 1949. In 1955 three new plants—for potassium sulphate, di-calcium phosphate, and phosphoric acid—came into operation. Enough superphosphates were being produced to supply all Israeli demand and leave a little over for export too. From 1952 Negev phosphate rock was being used, instead of imports from North Africa and the United States. A giant plant was completed for production of ammonia, and another for ammonium sulphate. By 1958 Fertilizers and Chemicals was supplying domestic agriculture with all the fertilizers it needed. It was also producing such basic industrial materials as sulphuric acid, ammonia, hydrochloric acid and phosphoric acid.

The Haifa-Acre area became a chemical enclave, with companies like Chemicals and Phosphates Ltd., New Haifa Chemicals Ltd., Israel Petrochemical Enterprises, Electrochemical Industries Ltd. Their noxious but necessary products ranged from sulphuric acid to ammonium nitrate, from nitric acid to domestic detergents, from PVC to carbon black. The chemical industry's work-force multiplied more than six times, from 1,900 in 1948 to 12,000 in 1971. Its exports were up more than two hundred fold, from $400,000 in 1949 to $97 million in 1970. It began to concentrate upon the production of disinfection materials, industrial chemicals and pesticides; in 1970 pesticide exports for the first time exceeded home sales. And yet this was still an industry with problems.

In 1967 and 1968 attempts were made to bring about a fully integrated Israeli chemical industry. A committee of economic ministers decided to merge all chemical, petrochemical and oil refinery plants into a single undertaking. It never happened. In 1971 a much less ambitious project was embarked upon: not integration into one company but the collection under one institutional roof —to be called the Israel Chemicals Company—of a group of only the inorganic chemical companies, which would individually retain complete independence. But regardless of the outcome of this venture, the industry had for too long been held back by the very basis on which it operated. For twenty years the idea had been to operate small-scale units aimed at meeting local needs and exporting any excess production, below cost if necessary. The industry's twelve thousand employees worked in two hundred companies; and Dr. Yael Ben-Tovim, chairman of the chemistry committee of the Jerusalem Economic Conference, highlighted the absurd situation which had been reached when he pointed out:

"We have the raw materials here, yet we export them in bulk, instead of trying to sell refined chemicals." The 1970s witnessed an attempt to restructure the industry into large-scale units based on sales abroad, with the Israeli market just a component of the over-all market. A five-year investment plan, valued at $595 million, was launched. Time had been wasted, and there was a lot of catching up to do.

Israel had a socialist government. But like socialist governments in other countries, it found economic planning very difficult to implement. From time to time it would set up grand-sounding inter-ministerial committees, made grander-sounding still by massed ranks of auxiliary sub-committees (thirteen at one count, in 1956) to prepare plans for the customary five-year period so beloved of economic planners. But, Israel being a democracy, these were indicative plans, not prescriptive instructions. And anyhow they were never carried out. Throughout, in fact, the Israeli economy had to be moulded by regulations affecting foreign trade and by one basic item of economic legislation, passed first on 29 March 1950 and periodically amended over the next two decades, the Law for the Encouragement of Capital Investments.

The aims of this law were comprehensive. They were to attract foreign capital, increase exports, reduce reliance on imports, absorb immigrants, and populate underdeveloped areas. As it evolved, by means of the original law itself, through subsequent sweeping amendments, and together with ancillary legislation dealing with parallel subjects, this legislation was to offer some of the most attractive incentives—compulsion was not attempted—available to industrial investors in any country. It depended on two fundamental bases: approved status, decided by an Investment Centre, and area of location. Israel was sliced up into three different layers: "A" Development Zones, covering most of the Negev and Eastern Galilee, where enticements were juiciest; the rather less attractive "B" Development Zones, which took in all the rest of southern Israel up to a line stretching from Jerusalem to the coast, together with two small areas in the north of the country; and central Israel, in which some incentives were not available at all, and others were scaled down.

A lucky or provident entrepreneur would receive Approved Enterprise status for creating or enlarging an enterprise or part of an enterprise if he established it in an "A" Development Zone and met certain other requirements; or if he went to a "B" zone and exported a certain proportion of his output; or anywhere at all in the country if he exported the major part of his output. Benefits included cash grants, graded according to area, for building and site development, as well as for machinery and equipment. There was also an accountant's dream of tax concessions: on income tax, profit tax, property tax, customs duties and purchase tax. Special inducements were held out to foreigners making investments in foreign currency.

Those willing to import their precious hard currencies into Israel were eligible for concessions on investments in projects which were not even granted Approved Enterprise status. Both principal and profits were permitted to be repatriated in the currency in which the investment had been made—a miraculous loop-hole in Israel's obsessively stringent exchange control laws. There were special benefits for Approved Loans, with extra-special benefits for loans made in a foreign currency. And a foreign investor received concessions on an Approved Property if he created, enlarged or acquired it, or even part of it, with his treasured foreign currency. There were, too, exemptions from capital gains tax, income tax concessions, and the right to repatriate capital, dividends, and interest on bonds for those investing foreign currency in Israeli securities.

There were various other apples of the Government's eye. Science-based industries sited in "industrial parks" near academic research institutes received grants for land development and building, as well as additional loans. If Approved Enterprise status were conferred on them, then they were eligible for additional grants for training of graduate employees. And if an approved research and development project resulted in a product for export, a joyful government was ready to share half of the R and D cost.

Tourist projects were eligible for Approved Enterprise status, with special grants for land development in connection with enterprises in the "A" zone, and long-term loans for construction of new hotels, graded according to area. Construction of tourist parking lots, restaurants, clubs and shops also attracted loans, as did the renovation of Israel's unusually ample stock of seedy hotels.

The status of Approved Property was available for constructors of rented housing. Property tax concessions, accelerated depreciation and other income tax benefits were available in the case of buildings of which two-thirds were intended to be rented for housing purposes. And—the attraction of immigrants being always a high priority—special preference, including subsidies and guarantees of full occupancy, was available for projects designed for newcomers to the country.

So much of what went on in Israel seemed like something out of an old Ealing Studios film that it appeared a good idea to offer incentives to film makers. If the enthusiasts at the Ministry of Commerce and Industry were excited more by the idea of large quantities of films being made in their country than by any great solicitude concerning the quality of such films, the incentives they offered were certainly worth having. Approved Enterprise status was available if the film met minimum financial investment criteria, if a minimum foreign currency investment was made, or if at least one-third of the film's income was derived from abroad. There was an export premium for services bought within the country and paid for in foreign currency. Entertainment tax was refunded to all Israeli film producers, and foreign producers could get a refund too if they left all the local income from their locally produced pictures inside the country, and if at least twenty-five per cent of their technical staff were Israelis. One cinematic Approved Enterprise, given the go-ahead by the Investment Centre in 1971, was for construction of a million-pound "Wild West" city in central Israel, where foreign film companies might with as little inconvenience as possible manufacture Middle Eastern Westerns.

Determination to bring work to the development zones was backed up with special incentives additional to those provided by the Approved Enterprise rules. These included reduced rental fees for industrial buildings, low interest loans for their construction and purchase, grants for site development, loans for working capital, grants for on-the-job training of workers and for transfer of existing enterprises to development areas, and even preference in respect of government tenders.

These incentives worked. At times they worked so well as to cause controversy, when approved enterprises earned larger profits for themselves than some go-it-alone projects. In the very first year of the working of the law, 426 undertakings were awarded Approved Enterprise status, and another 271 were found eligible for concessions. By 1955 establishments approved by the Investment Centre were manufacturing pistons, refrigerators, telephones, penicillin, detergents, flutes, rubber boots, typewriters and clocks. An amendment to the law in 1969 introduced an entirely new category of project eligible for aid: Recognized Enterprise. The French arms embargo following the Six-Day War had hit Israel badly, and scared her even more. Incentives were offered to ventures which produced defence material that otherwise had to be imported. But this was far from the beginning of Israel's defence industries. These had been growing for almost twenty years, and by the 1970s included Israel's largest single industrial enterprise.

Jewish arms manufacture in Palestine started long before independence. Underground workshops began producing three-inch mortars, ammunition for small arms, and hand grenades. The organization known as Military Industry was brought together in 1950 from several independent and overlapping workshops. By 1954 it was a fully integrated organization and had already begun to plan for manufacture of what was to be its most famous product, the Uzi sub-machine gun. Some five years after coming into existence the impertinent little Israeli state had begun its first military exports. Military Industry was soon producing regular and adequate supplies of smoke bombs and incendiary bombs, as well as the Uzi, which in its turn was added to the country's export catalogue. The stock list was regularly growing, additional items including bazookas and bombs for jet aircraft. By 1958, thirty separate items were in production for home and export markets.

The next stage was diversification. In 1959 Military Industry began producing non-military products. As the years went by these included hoisting cranes, cogwheels, chemicals for agricultural use, and automatic trunk telephone systems. Some ten years after the enterprise had been founded it was exporting to fifteen countries. By 1962, forty-five per cent of its output was being sold abroad. For the first time it held a display of its products, with demonstration firing of its newly developed artillery and mortar shells. It played its part in bringing work to the development zones. It opened its own technical school.

In the three years after the Six-Day War, Military Industry's activity was greater than in all the rest of the years it had existed. The number of its employees doubled; its production quadrupled. In 1971 its work-force increased by eighteen per cent, while productive capacity was up by fifty per cent. Rifles, machine guns, bazookas, recoil-less guns, anti-aircraft guns, hand grenades, shells, tank cannons, anti-tank guns, and detachable fuel tanks were among its most successful products. Exports were reaching fifty countries. And Israeli-made flares lighting up foreign skies were an unanticipated variant of the Hebrew greeting. "Shalom."

Even more of a phenomenon was the Israel Aircraft Industry Ltd. Originally named Bedek, this was established by American Jews who had fought in the war of independence. It began in 1953 as an aircraft maintenance unit. After foreign experts had been engaged for a short period, all key positions were taken over by Israeli personnel. Gradually the company progressed from repair and maintenance of aircraft and engines to production of engine replacement parts and ground equipment. It took over the overhaul of E1 A1 planes, previously carried out in Britain. It overhauled, repaired and exported old aircraft which had been written off as scrap.

In 1959 Israel Aircraft Industry went over to manufacture, completing preparations for the production of the Fouga Magister jet trainer, known in Hebrew as Senunit, the Swallow. Manufacture of the Fouga Magister was based on technical knowledge obtained from the French parent plant. At the time, this aircraft was described as the company's "crowning achievement." The first series involved the assembly by local workers of imported prefabricated parts. The next series, begun in 1962, was all Israel's own work, apart from the engine and navigation instruments. The first batch for Israel's air force came off the assembly line in 1965.

Having borrowed from the French, the company now proceeded to improve on the Americans. Rights to manufacture a version of the Commander jet executive aircraft were obtained from the United States. But the Israelis were not satisfied simply to produce a copy. They expanded the seating capacity of the original, extended its range to two thousand miles, and promoted it to the rank of Commodore. The first test flight took place in 1971.

Even so, no one at Israel Aircraft was going to be content until the appearance of the world's first all-Jewish aircraft. Planning had begun on a twin turbo-prop short take-off and landing passenger/cargo transport plane, the Aravah. This machine, able to carry twenty passengers or two tons of cargo, and with a range of over eight hundred miles, was conceived, planned and developed in its entirety by the company. Its maiden flight took place on 9 April 1970. And even though the first flying model crashed in a test flight, with three killed, in November 1970, the Aravah was able six months later to make a triumphant appearance at the Paris Air Show in May 1971. True, President Pompidou, visiting the show, huffily gave the Aravah the cold shoulder. But his irritable remark, "Yes, I know you make planes," was in itself almost as much a tribute to the existence of an Israeli aircraft industry as an award made that same month in Geneva by the International Institute of Promotion and Prestige, which celebrated Israel Aircraft's "advance to the first rank of aeronautical firms in the Middle East in spite of singularly difficult conditions."

Yet the company's activities were far from confined to the overhaul, repair and manufacture of aircraft, or even production of the comfortingly named Gabriel sea-to-sea missile, first publicly displayed on the eve of Israel's twenty-second anniversary of independence. For this enterprise, even though its shares were all held by the Ministry of Defence, had diversified into variegated civilian production. One of its subsidiaries, Elta, in addition to winning the contract to install new radar facilities at Lod Airport against international competition, specialized in complex electronic equipment, including an appliance for reviving heartbeats. Another made precision instruments, yet another plastic materials, and a fourth produced systems working by compressed air. In fair exchange for the rights to the Fouga, special tools were being manufactured for a French aircraft-engine firm. Israel Aircraft Industry's payroll had increased from 70 workers in 1953 to 13,500 in 1971. Its turnover had risen from $2,300,000 in 1960 to $100 million ten years later. It could and did claim to be able to make "practically any part needed for the construction or repair of aircraft."

But while these and other industries established the framework of an Israeli industrial economy, and while the Law for the Encouragement of Capital Investments made that framework more orderly, the young State's problems became less and less manageable. Unemployment was high. Shortages were so great that in 1951 spinning mills working for home production were idle for four months due to lack of foreign exchange to buy raw materials. As much as twenty per cent of the increasingly glum population lived in poor temporary housing. It was time for a turning-point. The year 1952 provided two.

In February of that year a New Economic Policy was unveiled, aimed at halting inflation and reducing the balance of payments deficit. It involved the devaluation of the Israeli pound from a rate of 0.357 to the United States dollar to three official but separate rates: for diamonds, for citrus, and for all other exports. Restrictive economic measures accompanied the devaluation. Credit was restricted. The expansion of the money supply was slowed down. At first the medicine worked, and exports rose. But demand fell, economic growth tailed off, unemployment went up, domestic prices increased relative to foreign prices, and further adjustments to the exchange rate culminated in a straight devaluation to 1.80 Israeli pounds to the dollar. Meanwhile, however, another event had occurred which was to give Israeli economic development a boost that helped to carry it over the hard times and on to more than ten years of consistent prosperity.

David Horowitz, Director-General of the Treasury, had dreamed up the chimerical idea of persuading the Germans to pay Israel hundreds of millions of dollars as compensation for damage done to the life and property of Jews in Europe. The West Germans actually accepted the proposal, and it was clinched at a secret meeting between Horowitz and Chancellor Konrad Adenauer at the Crillon Hotel in Paris in 1951. On 10 September 1952, the reparations agreement with Germany was signed by Moshe Sharett in Luxembourg. The Federal Republic agreed to pay compensation worth more than $800 million over a period of fourteen years. Seven-eighths of these reparations were to be paid to Israel, the remainder to Jewish institutions. Between 1953 and 1965 what was literally a lifesaver was to finance between a quarter and a third of Israel's import surplus. In the year 1960 alone, more than half the import surplus was covered. The compensation was paid in kind. It included 59 ships, machinery for 1,500 factories, equipment for the expansion of the railways and the electrical grid. To these it added fuel, raw materials, industrial and agricultural products. It enabled the development of new industries, the replacement of obsolete equipment, the go-ahead for government development projects. It was worth every imprecation Menachem Begin could mouth.

The bottom of the slump was hit in 1953. But the corner was being turned. The plastics industry was expanding; and manufacture began of polystyrene resins and phenol formaldehyde, previously imported. The Nesher cement works near Haifa, polluting the bay for miles around, was supplemented by another at Ramleh, with a third almost ready to come into operation. A boom was on its way.

A period of sustained growth began in 1954. It was to lead to an increase in the gross national product averaging ten per cent a year. The strength of the chemical industry increased to seven thousand workers in five hundred plants. Hosiery exports were up sixfold on the year before. In June unemployment was down by more than a third compared with January. Public investment rose, encouraging private investment to pluck up courage too. Consumption started perking up as well. Spending power was given a huge boost by the injection into the economy over the next decade and more of $1,000 million in individual restitution payments from Germany. These were eventually to cause inflation by pumping up the money supply, and to damage exports by encouraging local manufacturers to go for the easy home market. While, between 1955 and 1959, the nineteen per cent annual average rise in exports was more than double the eight per cent rise in imports, between 1960 and 1964 they levelled out respectively at fourteen and twelve per cent. But meanwhile restitution was helping to lift the Israeli economy off the ground.

In September optimism was encouraged further when a small strike of oil was made at Cheletz, near Ashkelon. Later there were other strikes. And in 1958 a field of natural gas was found at Rosh Zohar near the Dead Sea. Eventually Israeli domestic oil production would yield an annual total of 115,000 tons of crude oil, while gas would contribute the thermal equivalent of 127,000 tons of fuel oil. With Israeli annual oil consumption at six million tons, these were modest but helpful aids to the economy and to import saving.

It was 1956 and things now were really on the move. The textile industry spread from the Tel Aviv area south to Kiryat Gat, east to Jerusalem, and north to Nazareth, Caesarea and Safad. Woollen yarn spinning was introduced. Electrochemical Industries' Frutarom plant began to produce chloro products, caustic soda and insecticides. Glass output was meeting all local demand. Military Industry now began selling the Uzi sub-machine gun abroad as well as producing TNT at home. Nesher became the country's greatest single exporter. And, pushing Israel ahead in technology, a "swimming pool" atomic reactor was bought from the United States. But if the peaceful uses of atomic energy were Israel's path for the future, the use of conventional weapons in the Sinai peninsula precipitated new economic opportunity. The Sinai war of October 1956, by opening the port of Eilat, opened as well new export markets in Africa and the Far East. And the arrival of more immigrants in 1957 than in any year since 1951 boosted demand and employment still further.

The opening of one blockaded port was not, however, enough for the Israeli government. A calculation had been made that by 1965 the country's ports would have to handle 4,150,000 tons of cargo, and that there was existing capacity for only 3,250,000 tons. Neither Jaffa nor Tel Aviv were capable of being turned into deep waters harbours with the potential to meet the expected increase in goods traffic. To the single-minded Israelis there was only one course open: the third port would have to be built from scratch. French and American experts carried out preliminary surveys. And in 1957 it was decided to go ahead with the construction of an entirely new harbour, on the Mediterranean coast twenty miles south of Tel Aviv, at Ashdod. Alongside the port would be an industrial city.

In that very same year Ashdod's first permanent houses were built, and seventeen families had moved in. A contract for building the port was awarded in March 1961 to three French firms in conjunction with Solel Boneh Overseas Ports Company. The cornerstone was laid. And it July work on the port began, building out to sea. It was not an undeviatingly triumphant progress. Work fell behind. In 1963 a report by the State Comptroller found that cumulative arrears in construction had been due to an unrealistic timetable, to defective preparatory organization, and to a serious lag in the supply of materials. It had been planned that the initial part of the new port—for citrus and bulk loading—would come into operation in May 1965. In fact the first ship sailed in on 21 November of that year. Running-in of the port began. By 1971 it was handling thirty per cent of the tonnage of all Israel's ports. It also became noted for its industrial disputes. Visitors taken to witness Israel's magnificent engineering achievement would have the privilege of viewing ships standing gracefully out at sea waiting for the current strike to be settled.

Meanwhile Ashdod's industrial city had been taking shape. In 1962 regular production began in the Leyland assembly plant, destined to have its own troubles but at any rate providing work for the new population. Twelve diamond polishing factories were established. Israel's only nylon spinning plant was busily spinning. A rice-husking plant was in business. And in 1971 Sunfrost, the largest and most modern frozen food plant in the country, set up shop with a $5 million investment. Moreover, there were people there to do the work (when not in a disputatious mood). The few dozen families of 1957 had grown, by 1972, to a population of 40,500.

The period from 1957 to 1959 was one of growing national wealth and declining unemployment. Inflation was brought much more under control. The emphasis of investment switched from agriculture to manufacturing, and at the same time industrial policy, together with housing, was used for population dispersal. New development towns were founded, and industries were established in development areas. A pipeline was laid from Eilat to Beersheba. A steel mill began operating in Acre and Acre's Steel City was producing 125,000 tons a year by 1971.

In 1959 every economic indicator pointed to "Fair." Expansion was going steadily ahead. Prices were reasonably stable. There was an encouraging improvement in the balance of payments. The standard of living was rising. Employment was well up. So was productivity. In 1960, 150,000 were at work in Israel's industry. But before long, clouds were to overshadow Israel's place in the economic sun.

Unemployment had virtually disappeared. But the import surplus was uncomfortably large. The time had accordingly come for the introduction of yet another New Economic Policy. This one, launched on 9 February 1962, was drastic. It included a further devaluation, to three Israeli pounds to the dollar, and a decision to replace with protective tarriffs the existing administrative protection of Israeli production from outside competition. Up to this time the aim had been to safeguard almost all the country's industrial output by administrative controls. One of the consequences was inefficiency of home production and a distortion of the spread and growth of industry. Not only was this protective mechanism to be replaced by tariffs—low on investment goods, high on consumption goods—but the tariffs themselves were to be progressively reduced. By the end of 1966 administrative protection had been replaced by tariffs in respect of eighty-five per cent of local output, and it was time for phase two: the gradual lowering of tariffs. When, at the beginning of the process on 1 June 1962, the first list of unlicensed imports, valued at $120 million, was published, it laid down that cereals, sugar, soya beans and other essential foodstuffs were from now on to be admitted freely. The Second New Economic Policy was under way.

It did not work. Inflation continued. A wage freeze, with built-in cost of living allowance, negotiated with the Histadrut failed because wage drift took over. Industrial exports did not grow fast enough. The balance of payments went on deteriorating. The Government took what action it could. It was dismayed in 1965 to be excluded—for political reasons, it was convinced—from the European Economic Community's newly created system of tariff preferences for developing countries. But on 4 July in that year a breakthrough was achieved with the EEC on another front when a trade agreement was signed in Brussels. Valid for three years, and renewable for a fourth, it brought about a lowering of tariffs and eased the import into the EEC countries of such Israeli goods as farm produce, chemicals, textiles, asbestos, glass—mirrors were becoming a large Israeli export, and production of car windscreens had begun—and aluminium. The agreement was particularly helpful for citrus, processed agricultural products and asbestos fibre.

The trade deficit increased remorselessly, reaching a peak of $570 million. A new policy of restriction of home demand and consumption was tried. Export incentives were added to improve the mix. But the worst recession in Israeli history was at hand. Each ingredient fed on the others to multiply the effects. The cutback policies held back the increase in the gross national product, and resulted in less investment and less consumption. A slump in immigration (only 15,000 in 1966 compared with 30,000 in 1965 and an average of over 50,000 in the four preceding years) brought about less demand for housing. Investment in the building sector, running at fourteen per cent a year between 1961 and 1964, fell to a mere one per cent in 1965. One-tenth of the labour force was in the building and ancillary trades, so that the fall in construction worked its way through the cement and housing supply industries and infected the whole economy. A classic stagnation was reached. Stability in prices and wages was achieved. But the price was high—tripled unemployment.

On 9 May 1966 the Minister of Labour went to the rostrum in the Knesset and reported that unemployment and economic recession were abroad in the land. Certain development towns had been especially hard hit. There was particular concern about redundancies in Ashkelon and the bright new hope of Ashdod. It was decided to offer extra incentives to factories in the development towns, with emphasis on the diamond industry—which had run into its own difficulties—and clothing. It was a joyless picture. A period of exuberant expansion had come to a full stop. Simultaneously with the petering out of the catalyst of immigration, labour-intensive projects such as new port works at Ashdod and Eilat, the construction of the national water carrier, new power stations, expansion at the Dead Sea Works, had all reached their end. Increased mechanization and factory efficiency—in other circumstances an occasion for modest pleasure—had reduced employment opportunities still further. The growth of the national product was down from an average rise of ten to twelve per cent in earlier years, and from eight per cent even in 1965, to a 1966 flickering increase of only one per cent. The trade deficit was down to $450 million. But Israel had ground to a halt.

The trough was reached in the first half of 1967. In April production was fifteen per cent down on the previous year. The daily average of registered unemployed was seven times the level of two years before. It got worse in May. Between March and August there was a daily average of twenty thousand on temporary relief work. Haifa, Tel Aviv and the central districts were now the worst hit. It took a war to put things right.

The quick blitz victory of the Six-Day War of June 1967 did not simply save Israel from destruction. It did not only result in a mass shopping and sightseeing invasion of the newly occupied territories by a penned-in population. It also set the productive adrenalin flowing through the nation's economic system. Euphoric psychology affected economic physiology. But it was more than that. Not only was there a will to produce. There was soon, also, and equally an outcome of the war, a need to produce.

France, sidling up coquettishly to the Arab countries, imposed her embargo on the sale of arms to Israel. The shock was enormous; its effects permanent. Israel was suddenly deprived of further supplies of the aircraft which had helped her to win the Six-Day War. And although she immediately began to look around for—and eventually received—other supplies from elsewhere, an uncomfortable thought began to nag. When next might a friendly government, on whom Israel relied absolutely, abruptly decide to cut off an essential commodity? The answer was ineluctable: Israel must start to make herself as self-sufficient as she could possibly be.

This motivation led not only to the massive development of the military and aircraft industries, but to advances in other basic sectors, too: metals and electronics, in particular. But it had an effect on the quality of Israeli industry, as well as the nature of its output. It was necessary to build up more sophisticated enterprises. And it was necessary to make them larger. Efficiency, productivity and quality control were all given top priority. One outcome was the extension of mass production.

Although it was remote in kind from the armaments-based heavy industries which this new outlook nurtured, one industry in particular suddenly began to display a remarkable potential for expansion. The textile industry had grown, in the early years of independence, from a need to create labour-intensive industry in new towns. At first production was limited to thick cotton and wool yarn, white cloth, khaki cloth and knitted goods. Exports in 1948 were valued at $300,000. As the industry painfully fought for life it was plagued by inefficient production and, at the same time, by over-production. Cotton spinning and weaving mills opened, and then proved uneconomic. Progress was made, with the aid of equipment acquired through German reparations, when a decision was made to move away from the standard products which low-wage underdeveloped countries could produce more competitively, to quality products based on knitted synthetics. After the Six-Day War one especially noteworthy firm showed exactly what enterprise could achieve.

The Gibor textile company was set up with the simple aim of making panty-hose. Its founders applied for, and received, the benefits which went along with Approved Enterprise status. They then proceeded to outrage those who felt that Approved Enterprises ought not to be profitable enterprises, by swiftly making themselves—and, in foreign exchange terms, their country too—a small fortune. Gibor had a payroll of 3,300, including Druse ladies busily manufacturing panty-hose in a village on Mount Carmel. Its exports rose from $1 million between May and December 1967 to $20 million in 1970. It accounted for more than twenty-five per cent of Israel's textile exports and became the country's biggest exporter. The following year, despite a fall in world prices, and a sag in demand for its specialized product, it went on increasing its sales and keeping its scattered enterprises on the job for a steady twenty-four hours each working day.

Gibor's success was part of a general advance in the textile and clothing industries. Nether apparel was especially seductive to Western customers. In 1970, its first year in operation, the Triumph-International company, securely based in the Holy City of Jerusalem, exported $330,000-worth of foundation garments. Beged-Or, countering strongly, proved that high quality outer clothing in leather had international appeal. In fact before long no clothes-conscious Western capital could hold up its head unless it was host to an Israel Week or fashion show. At home, "vertical concerns" grew, covering every process of production from the spinning of raw fibres and yarns to making-up and even retailing the finished garments. The industry, like Israeli industry in general, continued to operate on too small and fragmented a scale: in 1969 there were still more than 2,000 small units in the knitwear and clothing industries, with more than 80 per cent employing 20 workers or even fewer. All the same, in 15 years they increased their share of national exports from 6 per cent in 1955 to 14 per cent in 1970. In that period total national exports rose from $89 million to $776 million, and textile exports went up from $5,500,000 to $108 million. In 20 years the exports of the textile industry had multiplied a cool 360 times.

By 1969, then, Israel was booming again and full employment was back. Further to safeguard her trading position, her Government opened negotiations with the European Economic Community in October 1969 for a comprehensive preferential agreement. On 24 June 1970 a five-year agreement was signed under which a mutual lowering of tariffs was agreed. In return for Israel undertaking to lower her tariffs to the Community according to an itemized list, the Common Market countries decided on a fifty per cent reduction in customs duty for most Israeli industrial exports and a forty per cent cut for citrus and several sub-tropical fruits. It was further agreed that at the end of 1973 negotiations would be reopened in order to achieve a progressive removal of barriers to substantially all trade between the parties. The ultimate aim was a customs union or free trade area.

But even while this negotiation, with its eventually happy outcome, was taking place, less felicitous events were putting it in a sombre setting. The boom was running out of steam, and the balance of payments was going wrong. In 1968 the increase in the gross national product was 14 per cent. The next year it subsided to 10.5 per cent. Exports were up in 1969 by 14 per cent. But at the same time a huge import surplus—$880 million—was piling up. And 1970 was worse. The gross product was up by 8.5 per cent—little more than half the rate of two years before. Exports rose by only eight per cent: imports had increased by a whopping 21 per cent. The balance of payments deficit was terrifying. But it was not yet at its worst. On 21 August 1971 when Pinchas Sapir took cover under the world financial fog created by President Nixon's measures to protect the US economy and devalued the Israeli pound by a flat 20 per cent to 4.20 to the dollar, Israel's trade deficit, double the pre-1967 rate, was running at the grotesque level of $1,400 million.

With strikes, poverty protests, and discord between the Government and the Histadrut, had the painstaking efforts to industrialize Israel failed? The balance had to be weighed.

Anyone who got into a motor car and drove anywhere in Israel—even to the most remote locations—could not fail to see signs of a single-minded determination to develop anything which gave even a hint of being capable of development. The result had been a growth of industry from a crude and unsophisticated level to a stage of remarkably complex development.

The country originally concentrated on the food, clothing and footwear sectors. These were industries aimed at providing consumer products for the local market. They were succeeded by expansion based on science, defence and export potential. From the mid-1950s emphasis was on larger-scale production in metal, electrical goods, rubber, plastic, paper, wood, chemicals, food processing, refrigerators and washing machines. During the 1960s, as the Israelis saw more clearly what they could do best, fashion goods, metals, chemicals and electronics emerged as the most favoured products. The State was forced to discover, often by expensive mistakes, which industries were, in her peculiar circumstances, the best on which to concentrate. She found that it paid her most to exploit such raw materials as she could locate; to foster industries which were little dependent on raw materials—rayon, plastics, pharmaceuticals; and to try to develop industries where the raw materials were, if not indigenously available, then at any rate cheaply transported, and where the cost of bringing them in was far more than counterbalanced by the value added by local skill and know-how. It was on this basis that the diamond, paper, tyre and fashion goods industries grew.

In her first two decades of independence Israel created for herself major new industries based on polished diamonds, textiles, mining products, light machinery, and canned foodstuffs. Her three major industries, classified by share of output and of labour force, were foods, beverages and tobacco; textiles and clothing; and chemicals and petroleum refining. Her fastest growing industry was electronics. In 1970 the output of its labour force of 9,000 was valued at 420 million Israeli pounds ($120 million) compared with five million 10 years before. Companies such as Tadiran and Motorola were producing communications systems, mini-computers and digital instrumentation. The growth of Tadiran was astonishing. Its ownership split three ways between Koor (50 per cent), an American company (35 per cent) and the Israeli Ministry of Defence (15 per cent), Tadiran had between 1961 and 1971 increased its work-force from 350 to 3,000 and its turnover from 1,900,000 Israeli pounds to 148 million. Its ground-to-air system was thought to be the best in the world.

In the metals, electricity and electronics industries as a whole, employment had risen between 1967 and 1970 from 65,000 to 100,000. There was still a shortage of skilled manpower. Yet more manpower was likely to be needed. In its 1971 economic forecast, the Ministry of Commerce and Industry saw the major share of industrial investment going to metals—especially precision instruments—and chemicals, particularly basic chemicals and pesticides.

The growth of industry was paralleled by the growth of exports. In 1968 industrial exports accounted for 81 per cent of all exports; in 1950 the percentage had been 58.1. The main export burden in the early years of the

State was carried by the diamond, foodstuffs, textile, clothing and motor car industries. Then more newly developed industries took over: tyres, plywood—half the output of Israel's five plywood plants was being sold abroad—cement, chemicals and metal products. After twenty years Israel's industrial export drive mainly depended on diamonds, fruit preserves and juices, textiles and clothing, fertilizers, mineral products, tyres and tubes, machinery, plywood, pharmaceuticals, pipes, cement, books and religious articles. The highest export growth rate was in the metal industries, ranging from metal pipes to electronic equipment stimulated by the defence industries.

In its first quarter-century the record of achievement of Israeli industry was one to bring a blush of pride to every Jewish mother's cheek. The industrial labour force had risen from less than 70,000 to 275,000. Although the country was prevented from exporting to any of its immediate—Arab—neighbours, its exports as a proportion of imports, only 5.8 per cent in 1948, had risen to 21 per cent in 1953 and 70.2 per cent in 1967. By 1970 this ratio had slipped back to 55.7 per cent, but was still nearly ten times better than 21 years before.

Israel had no need to flinch from comparison with all except the most advanced and prosperous industrial countries. By 1969 her industrial production was 17 per cent ahead of that of Egypt—a country with 10 times the population—and in 1971 the Israeli gross national product was already 87 per cent of the Egyptians'. It was greater than Portugal's, having grown annually between 1950 and 1969 by an average of 10.5 per cent. In 1971 *per capita* income in Israel was higher than in Austria, Italy or even Japan. This affluence was demonstrated by widening ownership of consumer goods. Throughout her existence Israel had consistently levied very high taxes on cars and household equipment. Yet between 1953 and 1966 the percentage of Israelis owning a radio rose from 46.9 to 90.9. Refrigerator ownership increased from 12.4 to 80.1 per cent. At the beginning of the period there was one private car between every 138 Israelis; by the end the proportion had fallen to one car for every 29.

These would have been remarkable achievements in a country which had been able to plan its industrial expansion free of any outside or internal distractions. But to begin with Israel had not really sought to plan its industrial production at all. Industry was orginally far from high on the Government's list of priorities. In the early years of the State, mass immigration and its consequent food shortage concentrated attention on agriculture. Capital investment and technical progress boosted food production until it could cope with most national needs. But at the same time as the need was met, employment potentialities were reduced by the very technical advances which had provided one of the world's most snack-happy nations with more than enough provender to supply not only three square meals a day but to satisfy between-meals cravings too. Stomachs grew contentedly fuller, but from 1962 employment in agriculture began to fall both absolutely and as a proportion of total population. In the twelve years to 1971 Israel's farm production doubled, with manpower down about twenty per cent. The need to create jobs, the need to disperse the population to areas where agriculture on a large scale was not possible, and above all the need to export, tilted the balance to expansion of industry. The proportion of the labour force in manufacturing began gradually to rise and so did the proportion of the national income devoted to manufacturing.

But if the structure of the economy was, to begin with, loaded against industrial expansion, so too was the structure of the expanding population. Before independence only one group of immigrants had come to the country as refugees: those from Germany, in the 1930s. And in their case the standard of skill and education was very high. Now, driven by oppression in their native countries, or by a simple faith which itself signified a lack of sophistication, immigrants from primitive lands were arriving who lacked skills and even the elements of education, whose absorption was a poser in itself, who were not immediately capable of complicated production processes, and who added to the new nation's problems by increasing inequality of incomes and wealth and so helped to create social differences which had not existed previously.

Over the years much progress was made. But other problems replaced those which were solved. Even by 1968 the components of Israel's work-force were notably unsuitable to a country with Israel's difficulties. Less than half the workers were actually engaged in production or else in creating the nation's infrastructure: 27 per cent worked in manufacturing or in mining, 9.2 per cent in agriculture, and 7 per cent in construction. Against these, 21 per cent were involved in trade, transport or commerce, and a huge 33.6 per cent in services —administration, education and health. This service sector was much more typical of a wealthy, developed country than of the struggling urchin among nations which Israel too often forgot that she was.

One reason for this forgetfulness was that the urchin's rich uncles were very generous with pocket money. Between 1950 and 1967, Israel benefited from a monumental net capital import surplus of $7,400 million. Institutional remittances—mainly from American Jews —together with personal remittances, German reparations and personal restitution, and US Government grants-in-aid totalled up to a whopping dole of unilateral transfer payments. To these were added the proceeds from Independence and Development Loan Bonds, loans from the United States, the World Bank and other institutions, and private foreign investment. Such payments helped Israel to accumulate foreign currency reserves, and also to offset her massive aggregate import surplus.

They were a tranquillizer which eased pain and anxiety. But by doing so they dulled the contented addict's realization of the ills which beset him. Between 1949 and 1968, Israel accumulated an aggregate import surplus of $7,700 million. Without the contributions she received from overseas—after fund-raising drives which often involved all her leading governmental figures—she could not have survived. They covered seventy per cent of her deficit. But they also deceived her citizens into believing that their country really could afford to provide them with all those television sets, electric mixers, foreign cars and overseas trips. Israel was living not up to her own means but on the generous hearts of American Jews and the guilty consciences of post-war Germans.

One of the earliest films made in Israel was called *The Juggler*. It was a sentimentally heroic melodrama, featuring Kirk Douglas. But, for getting on for a quarter of a century, the real-life history of Israel was itself frequently a sentimentally heroic melodrama, and Kirk Douglas often seemed to have a feature part to play in it. And it was undeniably a juggling act. The balls which had to be kept in the air were the cost of financing mass immigration, the need for constantly increasing expenditure on social services, and the ever louder demand for higher living standards. This alone was a feat requiring consummate skill. But there was something more. The juggling act had to be performed on a tightrope.

The tightrope was the insatiable demands on Israel's economy made by defence. Any one of a number of statistics encapsulated it: the $825 million bill for defence imports in 1970, which crippled and distorted the country's entire economy, would do as well as any. The juggler balanced precariously on the tightrope, occasionally clinging on by the toes of one foot. If it came to it, one, two, or even all three of the juggler's balls could be dropped and the act could still go on—though to catcalls instead of the desired applause. But once the grip on the tightrope was lost, the curtain would have to come down; because the only safety net was the tightrope itself.

Energetic Ministers of Finance like Pinchas Sapir, sage Governors of the Bank of Israel like David Horowitz, could sigh and warn their fellow-countrymen that this was a foolhardy performance. But all were agreed that without the foolhardiness there would have been no performance at all.

4

A Pillar of Sand

On the night of 9 March 1971, Miriam Baibus presented her husband Shmuel with a baby son. The new arrival was the couple's tenth child. He was a big, bouncing
baby, weighing over twelve pounds. He was also, immediately, rather a well-off baby, since one of his birthday
presents was a savings certificate valued at one thousand
Israeli pounds—almost £120 sterling. The presentation
was made on behalf of the municipality of Eilat, Israel's
port and seaside resort at the tip of that northern arm of
the Red Sea known to Israelis as the Gulf of Eilat and to
others as the Gulf of Akaba. On the eve of the twenty-
second anniversary of the capture of Eilat on 10 March
1949, the Baibus baby was entered into the records as
the town's fifteen thousandth inhabitant.

The Eilat into which the child was born was untidy,
sprawling, polluted, increasingly the object of criticism.
But, on the day that Israeli independence was declared,
it did not exist at all. There had been an ancient site,
mentioned in the First Book of Kings in the Bible:
"And King Solomon made a navy of ships in Ezion-ge-
ber, which is beside Eloth, on the shore of the Red Sea,
in the land of Edom." But when the Negev Brigade arrived at the Gulf in 1949 all they found was a control
point and police station named Um Rashrash. That in
that spot there was eventually not simply a booming
town where the Baibus family could make their home,
but a town which was the lively terminal point of a settled Israeli Negev, was due to three men. Chaim Weizmann had connived and blackmailed for the Negev in
New York and Washington. Ben Gurion, his iron will

overriding the objections and timidities of others, had insisted that it be seized hold of by military force. Yigal Allon, Commander of the Southern Front, had gone down and taken it.

For Weizmann and Ben Gurion the Negev was a dream in the mind that would not stop nagging until it came true. Weizmann, the man of negotiation and compromise, militantly insisted: "The Jews will never surrender the Negev; everyone there will die first." Ben Gurion described this southern land as "Israel's greatest hope for the future," and mystically affirmed: "Just as the Negev contains hidden resources so does man; but it is in the Negev that man can become conscious of his hidden powers, arousing him to tap them and put them to creative use." Nor was this simply empty rhetoric on his part. In 1953, surrendering the Premiership and departing to settle in a primitive Negev kibbutz, he gave up his role as his country's Churchill and instead became its Horace Greeley, urging Israel's youth to follow him south.

Weizmann and Ben Gurion showed not only courage and determination; they demonstrated imagination too. For in 1948 the Negev they were so obsessed with possessing was no land of riches and resources. It was an empty, barren, unsettled wilderness. Buried in the sand which made this scrub desert depressing to the spirit, and mostly uncultivable too, were ancient ruined Nabatean cities: Avdat, Shivta. Creating vast gaps in the scrub were monstrous craters and canyons, their geological strata gaping open in almost vulgar colours like mottled intestines. At its northern fringes a small Beduin town, Beersheba, ruffled the untouched surface. There were no roads; archaeological knowledge had had to be brought into play by Yigael Yadin, Chief of Operations of the Israel Defence Forces and subsequent excavator of Herod's Dead Sea stronghold of Massada, in order to find tracks over which the Negev Brigade could advance south from Beersheba. Apart from the installations of the Palestine Potash Company, mainly at the northern end of the Dead Sea, there were no known natural resources. Above all, in a territory which made up sixty per cent of the new State's land surface, there were hardly any people. Nomad Beduin, searching for pasture for pasture for their flocks, had roamed over Palestine's frontiers with Transjordan and Egypt, crossing traditional smugglers' tracks—and on occasion utilizing them for their intended purpose. There was a minimal sprinkling of Jewish settlements, which since 1939 the British Government's White Paper had effectively ruled out. In September 1948 there were only 14,200 people living in the Negev: 1.7 per cent of Israel's population. The number of Jews was 1,200, two out of every thousand Jews in the new Jewish State.

A couple of decades later there were half a dozen towns and cities in the Negev, together with six collective kibbutzim and three co-operative moshavim. The Nabatean ruins had been restored and were regularly visited by tourists. First-rate roads criss-crossed the territory, and the railway had come quite far south. There was a thriving and busy airport at Eilat. Ambitious industrial and scientific enterprises were scattered over the wilderness like so much expensive litter. Weizmann, with all his hopes for it, might never have thought it possible. At the age of eighty-five Ben Gurion paternally surveyed it from Sde Boker, to which the President of the State and the Cabinet trooped down in October 1971 to offer their birthday congratulations and to see a little of what had been achieved.

Development began at the northern and southern ends. When Israeli troops took Beersheba on 21 October 1948, they found a Beduin town from which the two thousand or so inhabitants had fled. Beersheba, where the Bible records that Abraham lived in his latest years, had in modern times been established by German army engineers as a Turkish administrative centre for the Negev's Beduin tribes. In the First World War General Allenby had taken it on his march north, and a British military cemetery commemorated his campaign. For Allenby, Beersheba had been the gateway to Jerusalem. To the Israelis it was to be the gateway to the south.

At first Beersheba housed an army camp. That meant a need for coffee houses and restaurants. Families joined the men from the army. The Beduin came back into the town to buy supplies. More people from the north arrived to service those who lived in the town or relied on it. They were followed by immigrants from refugee camps in Poland and from North Africa. There was no selection; the people just came. And this haphazard growth was to leave in the town, even when it had grown vastly, a wide-open, frontier atmosphere. A visitor on arrival got the feeling that he ought to find out what time the rodeo began.

The population never stopped growing: 1,800 by the end of 1949, 8,300 in 1950, 13,500 by the end of 1951, 45,000 in 1960, 55,000 in 1963. At the outset of the State an ultimate population of 60,000 had been envisaged. In 1970 there were already 77,400 inhabitants in Beersheba. They lived in a town which provided them with work, with education and with leisure facilities. There were factories for chemicals, ceramics, textiles, industrial diamonds, tiles, metal goods, refractory bricks, aircraft components, agricultural machinery. In 1961 a 300-bed Kupat Holim central hospital for the Negev was opened. In Beersheba on 31 October 1957 there was established the Negev Institute for Arid Zone Research, a combined enterprise of the Hebrew University of Jerusalem and UNESCO. Its regional and environmental studies included work on the desalination of sea-water, environmental physiology—including study of the blood-pressure of the workers at the Dead Sea Company at Sodom—and agricultural-biological research. In 1965 Beersheba's place as an academic centre was assured by the opening there of the University of the Negev. The town had a music conservatory. It had nine cinemas. It had a television transmitter. It had a semi-luxurious hotel, the Desert Inn, with its own night-club and swimming-pool. Every Thursday morning tourists came to gaze entranced at the Beduin camel market. Beersheba was also noted for the best ice-cream in Israel. The seal was set on the State's pride in what had been accomplished there by the decision to hold the national independence day parade in Beersheba in 1964.

Beersheba had become the fourth city of Israel, after Tel Aviv, Jerusalem and Haifa. But it was not an attractive town. At first it was supervised by a military governor. By the time administration had passed to a mayor and an elected council, who had the right and the power to plan, there was already too much on the ground that could not be changed. And local government itself was not trouble free. In 1963 what were described as "local tensions" led to the displacement for a time of the elected council, which was only restored in the autumn. Meanwhile, Beersheba had grown up in confused and illogical fashion. If the establishment there of large chemical enterprises—the factory which refined Dead Sea bromine, the insecticide works of Makhteshim Chemicals (exports to all five continents)—symbolized its increasing wealth and importance, these installations also highlighted Beersheba's problems.

Beersheba was proud of its planned industrial zone. But in February 1971 there were protests against the pollution caused in this zone by the Makhteshim works, the Dead Sea bromine plant—and the municipal compost works. There were complaints of headaches and even vomiting. The mayor appointed a commission of investigation. The judgment of an expert from the Hebrew University was that the industrial centre should have been sited not in the town's north-east but to the south-east instead. The mayor promised action. So did the Minister of Health. Meanwhile a new unit for the production of bromides was opened, increasing production capacity from 4,500 to 6,000 tons a year. The town's rubbish continued to be carted three miles from its centre, to be dumped there, and to be left untreated. The most prominent monument in Beersheba remained an imposing synagogue, begun without sufficient money, and left unfinished as a brand-new ruin.

Almost exactly due south of Beersheba, and 155 miles away, lay Um Rashrash. To begin with, land communication between the two places was possible only by camel or Land Rover. But communication soon became necessary because, in addition to its military garrison, the newly-named Eilat was fast getting ready for its first civilian inhabitants. In 1950 construction began on the settlement's first twenty houses. The next year, together with a further fifty wooden hutments, they were com-

pleted. The nucleus for a residential zone was taking
shape. Making its first tenuous beginnings, also, was a
botanical garden. Israelis like to surround themselves
with something green. In Eilat the prevailing wind from
the east ensured that anything that grew tall enough
soon bent sideways. Visitors had to accustom themselves
not only to the great heat—which reached 104 degrees
Fahrenheit in August—and to the very dry climate—
less than an inch of rain a year—but to the constant
mournful keening of the wind and to the disconcerting
sight of palm trees listing westward in unison.

And visitors there soon were. In 1951 the army's engineering corps completed a road from Beersheba to Eilat, its surface mostly un-asphalted. In the same year the
engineering corps also built a landing strip. In 1951 too
—in April—a cargo steamer called there, and construction of a lighter basin began. Eilat port, however, was
for the time being prevented from becoming a going
concern. In 1950 Egypt had seized the islands of Tiran
and Sanafir which dominated the Straits of Tiran at the
southern end of the Gulf of Akaba (or Eilat) and
placed a blockade on Israeli ships attempting to sail to
Eilat. Following his arms agreement with Czechoslovakia in 1955, President Nasser extended this blockade
to the ships of all nations.

These actions stopped the growth of the town's sea-
faring trade, but not the growth of the town. Its water
supplies were assured when water was found at Beer
Ora, some twelve miles to the north, and a pipeline for
regular supplies was laid. Water came also from Yotvata, twenty-five miles northwards. The population of Eilat grew to 375 in 1952. The following year saw forty
more apartments under construction as well as a hotel.
A dispensary and a dental clinic tended bodily ills. Asphalt roads were being built. Communications were also
improved by the erection of a central building at the
aerodrome. In 1953 Eilat was granted local council status.

By the next year a jetty had been constructed. The
growing number of local inhabitants and visitors now
had a restaurant at which they could eat. And the food
available at the restaurant included freshly caught fish.

Five fishing crews had begun trawling at Eilat, and the
various transport facilities now available made it possible for such of the catch as was not consumed on the
spot to be transported by air to Tel Aviv. Expansion
proceeded. A pier and mooring wharf were completed.
A diamond polishing plant and a locksmiths' workshop
were established. Two hotels, one with nine rooms and a
second with twelve, were opened for business. For the
benefit of their patrons, a net was put up to protect
bathers against sharks.

But even though the Ministry of Finance had offered
to grant permanent residents remission of income tax
and exemptions from customs dues and luxury tax on
such essential items as refrigerators and air-conditioners,
Eilat's growth was still constrained. In mid-1956 fewer
than one thousand people were living there. The autumn
of that year provided the event which was to transform
both Eilat itself and the role of the town in the life of Israel. The Suez war of October 1956 resulted in the conquest of the Sinai peninsula by Israeli forces. Even when
the Israelis withdrew the following year, United Nations
troops remained at Sharm el Sheikh on the Straits of Tiran. The blockade of Eilat had been lifted, and the Negev itself opened up.

In nearly eight years, between the raising of the Star
of David over the Um Rashrash police station in 1949
and 15 November 1956, 10 ships had docked at Eilat
carrying 6,800 tons of imports and exports. In little
more than eight months, between 15 November 1956
and 31 July 1957, 27 ships carrying 32,569 tons called
at the port. Trade brought people. In the year 1956–7,
400 more housing units were erected. By mid-1957
2,500 people were living in Eilat. As part of Israel's
tenth anniversary celebrations, in 1958, the harbour was
ceremonially reopened. In that year it handled 50,000
tons.

Tanker jetties were built. A new jetty for mooring six-
to seven-thousand-ton vessels—twice the previous tonnage capacity—was completed. Part of the sea-shore
was filled in, and the port area was asphalted for use as
an open-air store. There was a fish-canning factory. By
1960 a southern jetty had been completed and a lighter

quay built. A quay for fishing vessels in 1963 was followed in 1964 by the first stage of a new Eilat port, including a 590-yard jetty and mechanical loading of bulk cargo. On 29 January 1971 the first container ship—from Japan and Hong Kong—docked at Eilat. Use of the port of Eilat was stimulated by incentives which included refunds of added transport costs of goods exported from it.

Now Eilat was going ahead. Its population was 5,702 by 1961, 10,000 by 1963, 12,000 by 1964. In 1960 it had been linked to the power station at Timna copper works, fifteen miles or so to the north; in 1968 it was connected to the national electricity grid. But the most significant technological development in the town had to do with water. In October 1959 Israel's Ministry of Development and the Fairbanks Whitney Corporation of New York signed an agreement forming a company to exploit and develop an invention by one Alexander Zarchin. The aim: to purify sea-water. The objective: four working units to be ready in Eilat by 1962.

The Zarchin desalination method was based on the principle that salts separate out from sea-water when the water is frozen. Rather late, construction began on the Eilat experimental plant in April 1963. Running-in started in June 1964. But technical costs made the method so expensive that the installation had to be closed down. The determination to supply Eilat with desalinated water was not, however, abandoned. The cheaper evaporation method was decided on instead. If a desalination station was combined with a steam power station, the surplus energy used in producing electricity could be used for desalination as well. By March 1965 a single unit plant of this kind was supplying Eilat with drinking water and electricity. In 1970 a second unit—captured from Egypt in the Six-Day War and transported from Sinai in piece-meal chunks—was added. This unit was put out of action for a time by a strike of opportunist shift workers, taking advantage of an overhaul on the first unit. But the two together—when eventually operating—supplied one third of Eilat's water.

Improvisation could rescue the town. But improvisation was also ruining it. The trouble with Eilat was that it grew up just anyhow. This was not because of any lack of intention to plan. To begin with a managerial team was sent in, responsible to an inter-ministerial committee. In June 1957 a Company for the Development of Eilat was formed by the Ministry of Development and an investors' group from South Africa. In 1963 an official committee laid down in detail a list of desirable developments. But matters did not work out satisfactorily.

While the town was small, its development remained orderly. Opposite the airport a modern commercial centre was built, with thirty-two shops, a bank, a post office, a town hall, a club house and a cinema. Accompanying these was a cultural centre named after Philip Murray, the American labour leader; this had a concert hall, a library and a restaurant. A 750,000-Israeli pounds 28-bedroom grade "A" hotel was completed by 1958. Glass-bottomed boats, plying the bay, enabled tourists to view the coloured fishes flashing by amid the luminous Red Sea coral. In April 1962 Eilat was firmly placed on the tourist map with a Red Sea Festival, whose pageantry and performances were attended by fifteen thousand visitors.

Things then proceeded to get out of hand. In one of those unfulfilled anticipatory announcements so characteristic of Israelis at their most appealingly optimistic, a statement was made in 1964 that "in order to improve nature the Government and municipality plan to undertake the digging of canals and artificial lakes on a big scale, thus changing the town to a small Venice." The aspiration was attractive. Its realization was described in a lacerating report from the State Comptroller in January 1971. A programme approved by the local town planning council in 1965 had included hotels, rest houses for day-trippers, restaurants, souvenir shops, entertainment facilities, beach services and installations for water sports. Six years later the outcome of these hopes was just two further hotels and a night-club. A bridge over the Venetian canal was planned in 1964, ordered in 1967, but not completed by 1971. A planned promenade had not been finished because there was no bridge to link the two sections of the sea front, because there were no buildings to line the promenade and because, in any case, money had run out.

Even so, visitors increasingly crowded the town. They found hippies soiling its beaches, which were littered with stones and broken glass and black with oil slick. The glowing coral was also endangered by pollution. Protection rackets had arrived. There were fist fights at night-clubs. Prostitution was on the increase. Jobless youths were coming in, setting up house on the beach, and proceeding to pilfer and steal. The stage had been reached where local residents were volunteering to help the police in dealing with an abnormally high crime rate. Moshe Kol, the Minister of Tourism, told the Knesset in March 1971 that the Eilat beaches were neglected, its hotels were providing inferior service, and its restaurants charging ridiculous prices. In the same year Murray Koffler, Vice-President of a Canadian hotel company, made a horrified inspection of the town and commented: "I couldn't ever possibly recommend people either to invest there or even to visit it." And he delivered the verdict. "Eilat is a disaster area."

Miriam and Shmuel Baibus were bringing up their ample family in a coastal resort that had degenerated into a seaside slum. That, with determination, could be put right. In any case, they could comfort themselves with the knowledge that they were living in one of the most prosperous ports on the Red Sea, with promising potential for growth. They also lived with the awareness that they were part of history. For they were citizens of a town whose freedom to trade without hindrance had been established by a war in 1956 and had been the cause of an even greater war in June 1967. Eilat's resemblance to Venice might so far be limited to their shared pollution problem. But Eilat's tiny history already had its moments of pride. And in commerce its future was assured.

With a first primitive link established between Beer-sheba and Eilat, the Israelis in the early 1950s began to take a closer look at the resources available in the territory between these two growing towns. A company was formed to prospect and promote the processing of minerals, of which three already had been found: kaolin, phosphates and manganese. In the Makhtesh Gadol, the Great Crater fissuring the Negev, production began of clay for the ceramic industry and quartz sand for the glass industry. Farther west, in the Makhtesh Ramon, flint clay was found, for use in making bricks. More and better quality quartz sand was discovered near Eilat.

Now, too, a start was made in settling the area between the Negev's northern and southern towns. In 1951 the first major agricultural settlement was founded in the Aravah valley, part of the Great Rift Valley, running down the Jordanian frontier. Based on the wells there, and on a climate good for winter export crops, Yotvata produced vegetables, flowers, early grapes and melons. Its most astonishing phenomenon was its dairy produce, with herds maintained on feed supplies. Their yield was even made available to supermarket shoppers in aerosol cans of whipping cream labelled "Reddi-Whip." Meanwhile, farther north, about twenty miles south of Beersheba, a start was being made on a more urban development.

Yerucham was intended as a link between Beersheba and Eilat and was, indeed, a staging post on the first main road south when this was eventually built. But it never had a chance. Its development was blighted when the much more advantageously situated town of Dimona was founded, a dozen miles to the north-east, in the following year. And later on a diversion eastwards of the main road south bypassed Yerucham completely. The town had been founded in 1951. It was established near to a *tel,* or ancient mound, and it was hoped that a possible link with history would act as a stimulant; but, with its many disadvantages, it merely faltered forwards.

By 1952 only 173 people were living there, mainly immigrants from Romania. Gradually Yerucham acquired a little industry. By 1955 there was a bakery, a salt plant and an ice factory. In 1957 a diamond polishing plant began work. But even local council status, conferred in 1960, was not enough to stave off the unemployment which afflicted the town in 1962. A knitwear enterprise was established there later. But such activity as Yerucham had came mainly to depend on the glass industry, manufacturing bottles both for soft drinks and medicines, and exploiting available sand deposits. By 1970 the population had increased to 5,400. But when Arad, founded twenty-five miles to the north-east ten years later, had to cope with a manpower shortage, Yerucham suffered from a jobs shortage and relied disproportionately on welfare payments. There it sat, in the middle of the desert, patronizingly described as a "forlorn hamlet" and acknowledged as an urban mistake.

Mistakes were inevitable in the opening up of the Negev. But plans for discovering and making use of the desert's resources went ahead. A start in a new direction was made in 1951. Near Timna, north of Eilat, it was known that in ancient times there had been extensive copper mines in the area. Great natural sandstone column formations loomed over the site of what were popularly, if erroneously, known as King Solomon's mines. The modern Israelis wanted to find out whether there were any copper deposits that they could exploit. In 1948 copper ore resources had been discovered. In 1951 the Timna Copper Mining Company was established. Exploration work was begun in the early 1950s and was completed in 1953 by Belgian engineers, acting in an advisory capacity. On the strength of demonstrated ore deposits of seven million tons, with an average copper content of 1.5 per cent, it was decided to start a plant. Preparation of the site for a copper works began in June 1955. The plant was ready in 1958.

Production began on 1 April 1959, and the plant passed from running-in to regular working the next year. But soon there was trouble. There were hitches in developing the underground shaft, and geological information was unsatisfactory. In October 1963 the Minister of Development announced that all expansion at Timna would be frozen until further checks had been conducted. The cause of this painful decision was a severe report from the State Comptroller. This criticized production losses at Timna, in contradiction to forecasts. It complained that the gap between prediction and planning on the one hand, and tangible results on the other, was far too wide with regard to physical conditions at the site, the pace of construction, the first cost of production, and underwriting. The company, quite simply, had failed to solve all the technical problems of underground mining; more thorough checks were required before fresh developments could be risked.

These strictures were treated very seriously. Between 1963 and 1966, improvements took place. The operation was reorganized; surplus workers were shed; the company's headquarters were moved to Timna itself. Modifications to the production process doubled capacity. Output rose. The corner was turned in 1964, when for the first time profits began to be earned.

Like every similar project undertaken in the Negev, Timna had been a difficult undertaking with only flimsy prospects of success. The copper deposits themselves were of poor quality. The working conditions were almost literally hellish, in the vicious heat of the Southern Negev. In the first twelve years five workers were killed. Only extra-special incentives ensured that the labour force would remain. Pay was higher than for similar jobs in the north. A round trip flight to the north was provided every sixty days, and annual holidays varied between eighteen and twenty-eight days. There was a company hotel for unmarried employees.

Yet, painfully, the company prospered. Output of copper ore rose to a million tons a year. Further copper deposits were found, estimated to last for another twenty years. Plans were made to sink a second underground mine as companion to the first three-shaft underground mine and to a surface operation. The number of workers grew to 1,050, including miners, engineers and maintenance men. And plans were made to diversify the company's activities. These, originally, had been based on mining and processing the copper ore to produce copper cement. The total output was then sold through the London Metal Exchange. The value of exports had risen between 1962–3 and 1969–70 from $2,800,000 to $16,000,000. But, ludicrously, Israel then was itself obliged to import the finished product for local manufacture. So, in December 1970, the company was empowered to buy up Zion Cables Ltd., a copper wire plant at Rishon Lezion. This would be the first step in converting the Timna Copper Mines from a small producer of raw materials into an integrated industrial complex.

Eighty miles or so farther north, the first gingerly efforts had been made to tap another Negev resource at about the same time as the Timna company was first established. Here too the raw material was of low quality. Here too the teething troubles were bothersome. But here too obstinacy met with success. At Oron, not far from the ruins of Shivta and Avdat, phosphate rock was discovered. The deposits were part of the great North African-Middle East phosphate belt, stretching from Morocco to Turkey. Phosphates were very useful for producing phosphoric acid, a raw material for the chemical fertilizer and food industries. Here, accordingly, was an asset worth exploiting. A company called Negev Phosphates (later to be merged with the Chemicals and Fertilizers Company into a chemicals and phosphates conglomerate) was registered on 22 April 1952. The erection of the first plants was begun, and trial production started.

The quality of the rock was low. To begin with, it was crushed but not enriched. Enrichment installations were erected; but at first the required quality was not reached. Gradually enrichment methods were developed by selective quarrying and improvements in the installations. By 1956 satisfactory and consistent production was being obtained. But even so the product was not yet up to the best international standards. A major expansion project was launched in 1962, and a calcination kiln built. But once more there were problems. Output did not rise as much as had been hoped. The level of investment, together with technical problems, led to losses. Labour was also a problem. Costs were high because working conditions were difficult. At first the workers had to live in a camp, though later they moved to Yerucham and the new town of Dimona.

Very gradually Oron pulled through. The 69,000 tons of rock worked in 1952–3 rose to 115,000 in 1956 and to over one million in 1970. By 1964 the entire local demand for fertilizers was being met. By 1970 export trade accounted for most of Oron's output. That same year the arrival of the railway, whose Oron spur brought trains farther south than anywhere else in Israel, demonstrated the importance to the State of an enterprise which had tremulously justified itself.

All the time, thirty miles to the north-east, was waiting Israel's most capacious treasure chest: the Dead Sea. A long pool of sparkling turquoise water, into which the River Jordan flowed from the north; against which nestled at one end Kumran, cache of the Dead Sea Scrolls; and over whose southern shore towered the pillars of salt among which Lot's wife was said to be concealed, this was known to the Jews as Yam Hamelach, the sea of salt. Its contents were amazing. There were twenty-two billion tons of magnesium chloride, twelve billion tons of common salt, six billion tons of calcium chloride, two billion tons of potassium chloride, a billion tons of magnesium bromide. Calculations of how long these deposits would last were of astronomical magnitudes—two thousand years, twenty thousand years, sixty thousand years. For practical purposes the resources of the Dead Sea were limitless. There were additional quantities of sulphates, cesium, cobalt, lithium, rubidium, manganese. The task was to tap them. A start was made at Sodom.

No one knew whether this spot at the south-western corner of the lake had really been the site of the damned city of the plain, whose sinful men had sought to rape an angel of the Lord. But the place, remote, arid, forbidding, monumental with its towering salt rocks, was certainly godforsaken. It was the ideal location for a nationalized industry, and the Israelis after due deliberation established one there. Exploitation of the Dead Sea's resources had begun as long ago as 1929, when the Palestine Potash Company was awarded a concession. Extraction began in 1932, and the company's products first reached world markets in the Second World War. It had based its operations on the northern shore of the sea which, after the war of independence, fell into Jordanian hands. The Dead Sea Works, registered on 26 June 1952, took over such assets and installations as were available.

First, there had to be a way to get there. In 1951, the course of a road from Beersheba to Sodom had been laid. Construction went ahead. It was an assignment which only madmen or ignoramuses would have attempted; 290,000 cubic yards of rock had to be blasted, 785,000 cubic yards of earth to be excavated. The first major engineering feat of independent Israel, which took two years to achieve, was pronounced completed on 26 March 1953 when the Beersheba-Sodom road was opened to traffic.

The early years were very hard. A camp was established on site for six to seven hundred workers, and it took on the atmosphere of a gold-rush town in a less than veracious Hollywood knockabout adventure film. The work-force was not stable, its simple hobbies ranging from drugs to prostitutes. Two decades later, long after the camp was gone, a suggestion to a young lady of a night trip down to Sodom still had unequivocal implications.

But all Israeli enterprises in remote areas, right through to exploitation of the captured Sinai oilfields in the late 1960s, were conducted in this rough-edged fashion (even though generally with less basic pastimes). In any case, the enterprise went ahead. The foundations of the new Dead Sea Works factory were laid on 12 February 1955; the installations were brought into initial operation the following June. The factory building was completed in March 1956; running-in tests followed, with regular production under way in the following financial year. Inevitably these preliminary activities did not go smoothly. Faults were found both in construction and production. Foreign experts were brought in. The Minister of Development appointed a committee of inquiry to discover the reasons why the enterprise had so far failed to come up to expectations. By the end of 1956 improvements had been achieved. But as late as 1958 it was being stated officially: "Many have become doubtful whether the enterprise can ever prove successful."

For what was being attempted at Sodom was being achieved hardly anywhere else on earth. Apart from the Dead Sea Works, only one small American company was producing potash from water; everywhere else it was mined. The main use for potassium chloride was as an agricultural fertilizer. It was also a raw material from which other potassium compounds could be obtained for use in such industries as soap, glass, textiles and dyeing. The Israelis were producing it by harnessing the energy of the sun. The salts of the sea, which was very shallow at this southern point, were evaporated in pans. The carnallite thus precipitated was decomposed and washed, and potash was then separated from the other salts, dried and stored. At the beginning, things went very slowly. By 1955 the plant's capacity was only 135,000 tons a year.

The first real token of progress was the dismantling of the camp. It was closed in 1957. Now workers were taken on more selectively; transients gave place to family men, for whom a housing project was launched in the new town of Dimona, twenty-five miles to the west; absenteeism fell to a very low level. At one time a committee had been set up with a view to establishing a town at Sodom itself. But the project never got anywhere. The Dead Sea was a place where the work had to be done because the raw materials were there. No one, however, could be expected to make a permanent life in that furnace. But at least the furnace had started producing the goods.

In 1961 the Dead Sea Works became Israel's biggest exporting producer. Very heavy investment began to expand the installations. A crash development programme was instituted in 1962. Financial aid was provided by the Government and by loans from, among others, the World Bank. A power plant was built to supply electricity and steam for the production processes. It was powered by natural gas through a pipeline from Rosh Zohar (where Lot took refuge), seventeen miles away. All water requirements were met by a desalination unit. By 1964 a new plant, with dykes in the sea, had been completed, output was up to 320,000 tons, and production was now possible in various crystal sizes. That same year, all the company's production was sold in advance. Then, however, plans for further progress got stuck.

To expand capacity, it had been decided to convert the southern segment of the Dead Sea, thirty thousand acres in area, into a gigantic evaporation basin. A Dutch firm planned the operation. Then an American contractor, hopefully described as "knowledgeable and experienced," took over. The work began; and abruptly stopped. The contractor insisted that the specifications were impracticable, that the job itself was technically impossible. Hands were wrung. The pan area could not be fully exploited; the quantities of raw material produced must inevitably be less; the full production system could not be brought into use. Riding to the rescue, equipped not with knowledge or experience but with impudence, came the Israelis. They set to work. By 26 June 1968 the large wall of the new dam was ready, and productive capacity had been raised to 1,200,000 tons a year.

So eventually the Dead Sea Works was a success. Between 1956 and 1966 its work-force had fallen from 1,200 to 600 men. Yet its output was up eightfold, from 48,857 to 415,044 tons of potash. Between 1958 and 1968 exports quadrupled, from 80,000 to 320,000 tons. Destinations abroad of Israeli potash increased in this period from 10 countries to 34. In 1960–1, a profit was achieved for the first time. The production target set for 1970 was one million tons, and that target was reached. Four-fifths of the million tons was exported. And then a day came which publicly and officially certified the Dead Sea Works as a going concern. The day was 19 October 1971. The place was Jerusalem. The participants were Arye Shahar, chairman of the Dead Sea Works, and Chaim Gvati, Minister of Development. Following a cutback in potash production in Canada, world prices had risen and enabled the Dead Sea Works to make a more than comfortable profit. Out of that profit Arye Shahar had deducted a cheque for 4,400,000 Israeli pounds (just over $1 million), which he now handed over to Chaim Gvati as his company's first ever payment of royalties to the Government for the right to exploit the Dead Sea's resources.

Not only potash was being sieved from the Dead Sea. In 1963 a table salt factory was completed. Previously this salt had been a by-product of other processes, most of it going to waste. But it was 99.9 per cent pure, and worth salvaging. In 1971 a plant was being set up for the production of magnesia, in the hope of presently obtaining magnesium metal, for which there was a substantial world demand. The production of bromine had already been regarded as worth a company all to itself.

Bromine, a reddish-brown liquid with a pungent, choking smell, was obtained by extraction from the concentrated solution of Dead Sea brine which contained fifty to sixty times as much bromine as open sea waters. Its main use was in the form of bromine compounds in the petroleum, photographic and pharmaceutical industries, and for space and soil fumigation in agriculture. One compound, ethylene dibromide, was added to tetraethyl lead to produce ethyl, an anti-knock compound for petrol. On 16 June 1955 the Dead Sea Bromine Company was established for the production of this useful if nasty material. Preparation of the area and erection of buildings began in August 1955.

The first machinery was installed at the beginning of 1956, and the main plant started work at the end of the year. In mid-1957 an installation for ethylene dibromide came into operation. By 1970, nine thousand tons of bromine and bromine products were ready for world markets. The Dead Sea, so inhospitable that no fish could live in it, so noxious that humans who swam in it had to wash as soon as they came out of the water, was grudgingly but surely yielding up its harvest.

It was also providing prosperity for the top right-hand corner of the Negev. And it helped to bring life to a new town which, founded after the backwater of Yerucham, was soon to outstrip it. It was claimed that the planning of Dimona began as early as 1952. But when the first house was actually built there, in 1955, no carefully worked-out plan could be discerned. Water was brought by tanker. People were brought, too, and in effect were told: Build something and stay. Many, however, did not want to stay in this remote desert habitation. Some of them refused to get off the bus which brought them, and demanded to be sent back to Beersheba. Teachers and nurses preferred to make their homes in Beersheba and travel in daily to their work.

The town had been planned as a half-way link between Beersheba, twenty-five miles to the north-west, and Sodom. It was hoped that Dimona and Yerucham would give each other support for purposes of security; but, in fact, Dimona sucked the life out of Yerucham. Dimona itself was not so close to the big town of Beersheba that its own development would be stunted, and was therefore itself able to become an economic centre. Its situation 1,970 feet above sea level gave it a tolerable climate. It was stategically placed where agricultural land met the desert.

It started slowly and not very well. But despite itself it was a runaway success. Intended to have a maximum population of five thousand, and starting with only 311 inhabitants, it was soon submerged with would-be citizens and passed the five thousand mark in 1961. By 1972 Dimona was home to twenty-four thousand. The first of these were Moroccans, and other immigrants from French North Africa followed. The town became famous, and preened itself with civic pride, when Israel was conquered by a pop song called "Simona from Dimona."

It acquired a water pipeline (in 1957) and a power station. In 1960 it received the accolade of a status symbol more impressive even than a pop song. Israel already had one atomic reactor, at Nachal Sorek. Now a second was sited on the road running past Dimona; and it was larger, with a capacity of twenty-six megawatts. Its activities, about which large rumours were immediately current, included research into desalination. Rather more mundane was its preservation of onions and potatoes by the agency of isotopes. It was also provided with an industrial school for apprentices.

Tourist guides, wishing to impart an air of mystery to a rather dull ride, would tease their charges with the false information that the dome behind the threatening-looking fence was in fact a textile factory. This was highly credible, since Dimona soon added to its scientific qualifications a national reputation as a textile centre. In 1961 a textile plant representing an investment of 14 million Israeli pounds ($4 million) came into operation. The next year a dye works opened. Dimona's output included both synthetic fibres and cotton yarn. Those of its workers who were not employed in textiles, at the reactor, or down at the Dead Sea, could work in the metal industry or in a diamond polishing factory. All told, they had 325 manufacturing establishments from which to choose.

Dimona was a busy town. It was a town where people could spend their leisure at three cinemas, a swimming-pool and a sports stadium, and where there was a hotel at which such visitors as it had could stay. It was a town full of children, who could be seen streaming to forty-six kindergartens, ten elementary schools, and two high schools—one religious, one secular. It was a lively town. It may have grown up haphazardly. But it had grown cheerfully. On a warm Saturday afternoon it had an air almost of subdued carnival as its population promenaded through the civic centre gazing at the cookers and television sets in the windows of the closed shops, and clustered around the open cafeteria to consume fattening *pita* sandwiches.

Very different and much tinier was the settlement which had meanwhile been planted twenty miles to the south-west. Sde Boker would never approach the size of Dimona but, because David Ben Gurion had lived there, it would forever be much more famous. This desert kibbutz had been founded on 15 May 1952 by ex-soldiers who had taken part in the conquest of the Negev. Their aim was to breed cattle and sheep on natural pasture, grown from Sudanese grass. They also grew plums, grapes, apples and peaches, which, steaming a little, they sold at the roadside to wayfarers in air-conditioned buses. They also, in rather a big way, produced education. There was a secondary school which educated three hundred students from Yerucham, Mitzpeh Ramon and Negev moshavim. There was a teachers' college. There was an Ulpan, where Hebrew was taught to immigrants. There was a field study school, where children learned about the flora, fauna, rocks, ores, soils, history, archaeology, meteorology, physiology and climate of the desert. All these together made up the Sde Boker Midrasha, which Ben Gurion dreamed might one day become a "combination of Oxford and MIT."

To the south and the east the Negev was being farmed. The Negev Ceramic Materials Company was exploiting clay and glass sand in the Great Makhtesh and near Eilat. Glass sand deposits were found at Dimona. The Palestine Salt Works was mining salt from Mount Sodom, and the Aravah Salt Works was mining rock salt there. Gypsum for cement was being quarried in Makhtesh Ramon, and dark marble of the finest quality had been found in that vast crater as well. At Sodom asphalt was discovered. South of Eilat there was granite. And it was now possible to travel from Tel Aviv to Eilat by bus. On that road south, the time had come to found another town.

It did not grow very big. Mitzpeh Ramon was established in the wrong place. Sensationally sited, on the lip of the Makhtesh Ramon, it was ideal as a half-way stop on the main road from Tel Aviv to Eilat. But before very long the main road moved east, while the town stayed put and stagnated. At least, though, it had another reason for being there, as a centre for military units which patrolled and manoeuvred in the desert. It was in fact started by the Ministry of Defence, which had been given the assignment of co-ordinating its construction in co-operation with that favourite Israeli institution, an inter-ministerial committee. Water was provided by pipeline. Work opportunities were to be based on the raw materials available—ball clay and marble—in the crater down below.

Mitzpeh Ramon was founded in 1954, and became a permanent settlement on 25 May 1956. Settled initially from the north of Israel, it had fifty-five families living there by 1959. The population grew to six hundred by 1962, with the men fully employed at the local quarries. Their families were provided with every convenience that could be devised. They had a kindergarten and a primary school, a doctor and nurse and a pharmacy to service them, a post office, a youth hostel, a football pitch, a park and a thousand trees. There was also a supermarket. Varied employment was introduced with a glove factory and a factory for making plastic cases and containers. On the cliff overlooking the canyon was built a road house, the Nevatim Inn. To cheer up the residents and astonish wayfarers, eleven pieces of modern statuary, carved from the living rock, were one day put on show. Gaudily coloured, and not too much out of place, they gave a touch of life to a tentative little town where the population topped a thousand, but where houses were often empty and people seemed to leave as often as they arrived.

In its early years the Negev was very slow in coming alive. By the end of 1955 there were still only 2,500 Jews living there. But 1956 saw three great developments which brought new activity to the wasteland. The central road from Beersheba to Eilat was opened, cutting down the journey from ten hours to four. An oil pipeline was built from Eilat to Beersheba; the oil began to flow through it in 1957, and in 1958 it was extended to Haifa. And on 29 March a decision made in August 1952—by a Cabinet committee, inevitably—was turned into spectacular reality. The railway at last touched Beersheba. It had been pushed south fifty miles from Na'an, a little south of Tel Aviv, at a cost of 10,500,000 Israeli pounds. Its construction had begun with the excavation of 650,000 cubic yards of earth and the building of nine bridges. Much of the material had been supplied from German reparations.

The impatient Israelis were not going to stop there. If the railway could not immediately be extended to Eilat it must at least be pushed on to Dimona. Work on the extension began in 1958; but in 1960 it was held up by a humiliating shortage of funds. Only in 1965 did the trains at last reach Dimona. The previous year it had been officially announced: "In the very near future Eilat is to have a railway link to Beersheba." By 1970 the line had got as far as the Oron phosphate works, but there were still nearly a hundred miles to go to Eilat and so far only that unvanquishable optimism to bridge them.

Even so, the Negev was becoming a busy kind of desert. As though it itched them intolerably, the Israelis could not long refrain from scratching it. In March 1959 a natural gas field had been discovered at Rosh Zohar, near the Dead Sea, with reserves equivalent to at least a million tons of oil. Later, smaller quantities were to be found near Arad. In 1960 the Eilat-Beersheba pipeline became fully operational and the national electricity grid was extended to Sodom and Oron. Among the increasing number of settlements, two in particular stood out.

In the Aravah rift just south of Sodom, a moshav was founded named Neot Hakikar. It was not a very promising location. The summer temperature might rise as high as 50 degrees centigrade—more than 120 degrees Fahrenheit. There was no vegetation except salt shrubs growing in a salty soil. But pioneers came down and built themselves a settlement. They placed their dwellings round an internal countryard, partly as a protection against the heat, partly as a protection against the Jordanians: for Neot Hakikar was a gunshot from the frontier.

Then the settlers got to work. They washed the salt out of the soil. They cleared the scrub. And they began to plant. There were date palms. There were winter crops of onions, eggplants, melons and tomatoes, the earliest in Israel. Livestock was brought in too. A herd of 350 cattle fed on forage grass. Neot Hakikar even had its own fish-ponds. Drinking water was brought in daily from Sodom. This frontier colony was vestigial. In the winter the population might be as high as seventy. In the summer there was a skeleton crew of eighteen. Neot Hakikar was just one of a series of settlements scattered thinly down the Aravah rift, and along the unmarked desert frontier. But it was a phenomenon in its own right.

And then town planning came to the Negev. In Beersheba, Dimona, Mitzpeh Ramon, families had been shoved in and shacks run up. The first roads were makeshift and so were the schools. In Arad it was all going to be different. Instead of this latest new town being filled with unwilling immigrants, Arad was going to be a place which would actively attract newcomers; and those newcomers would be Israelis educated and trained to make the town work, not reluctant wards of the State. The population, in fact, would be selected, on criteria of job suitability, age and health.

The site was chosen, some twenty-five miles east of Beersheba and ten miles west of the Dead Sea. It opened up a completely new area on unsettled Beduin

land, and on a smugglers' line. It was an immediately indispensable new link with the remote kibbutz of Ein
Gedi, eighteen miles away to the north-east overlooking
the Dead Sea and just on the 1949 armistice line with
Jordan. Its livelihood would be securely based on local
natural resources: rich phosphates, marble deposits, natural gas, cement, the Dead Sea minerals, and industry
drawing on these local assets. It was also handily near to
the ruined fortress of Massada, at the town's outset not
yet excavated and restored but already on objective for
militant pilgrims.

So in 1961 Arad was started off with a unique document: a master-plan. A team from the Haifa Technion
supervised the architectural preparation. The intention
was that the basic elements of the master-plan—roads,
commercial centres, schools, the water supply, electricity, sewage—would all have been provided before the
first permanent residents moved in. And in this town
basic facilities would be available on the spot at the
start, so that people did not have to travel to get them.
Even the streets were to have names. The Ministry of
Labour was in charge of development. Steadily the work
progressed.

In 1961 administrative and planning units moved in.
In January 1962 residential, industrial and tourist zones
were marked out, and the first sixty single-storey asbestos houses began to go up. They were simple, mass-pro-
duced houses, the work of the Ministry of Housing. But
demand for them was to be so great that at one stage
1,500 families were applying for 170 homes. Arad was
ready for its formal inauguration, and this took place on
21 November 1962 with Minister of Finance Levi Eshkol in attendance.

The place started to grow. In 1963 the first stage of
asbestos housing was completed and the population had
reached five hundred. A school, kindergarten, restaurant, clinic, post office and bank were operating. There
were shops. A pine grove was planted and a children's
playing field laid out. There was even a dusty little park.
More amenities followed. Arad acquired a library, a petrol pump, a hundred-bed youth hostel, a music room,
and a draughty barn of a cinema where sophisticated

French films issued their sound-track to a desert air which had never heard anything like that before. Work began on a road down to the Dead Sea, a spectacular drive which provided a startling view of a deserted but still sturdy Roman strongpoint.

The town was gradually acquiring an identity of its own; but so slowly, to the disappointment of those Israeli planners who were always in a hurry. A mass of civic organizations sprang up. A large population to man those organizations was, for the time being, lacking. The plan had allowed for six hundred dwelling units to be added each year. The rate, however, stuck at around 250. Developments in the town's economy had not moved as fast as was hoped for, and this reduction in scope cut down the number of settlers. The economic plan was not being fulfilled quickly enough. Apart from other factors there was simply not enough money. Because fewer factories came in than was hoped for, local taxes were not bringing in sufficient revenue. The target of a population of ten thousand in five years was not reached.

All the same, Arad did begin to attract industry. A prefabricated building plant was established in 1966; following the failure of one knitted goods factory, another knitwear enterprise, nothing daunted, moved in during 1968. Hopes for giving the town a boost, which would help to push its five thousand population up to the take-off point of twenty to twenty-five thousand, most particularly rested in the plans for a massive chemical complex to be set up nearby. There were to be two major companies, both based on Dead Sea chemicals.

Construction began in 1968 of the Arad Chemical Industries centre at Tzefa, north of Sodom. Its basis was Dead Sea brine and local phosphate rock. The idea was to pump the brine from the sea in a 16-inch pipe. From this was to be produced 400,000 tons a year of hydrochloric acid. This, in gaseous form, would acidulate the phosphate rock to produce 230,000 tons a year of phosphoric acid, for chemical fertilizer. Natural gas was to be used as fuel. Quite apart from outlay by the State on infrastructure, the installation meant a massive investment of over 130 million Israeli pounds—nearly $40 million—by the two partners, the Israeli State and the American company Madera (which in 1971, because of its own internal problems, pulled out). The other plant belonged to the Dead Sea Periclase Company, one of whose end products, again using local materials, was a high grade fire resistant intended for lining steel furnaces. This was a joint venture of the Israeli Government with Grefco, an American firm.

So at last Arad was to have a core around which it could grow. Some of the town's ventures had been disappointing. It had hoped that its fine climate, brought about by its height of more than two thousand feet above sea level, would make it a health and holiday resort. It certainly was healthy for sufferers from asthma, and an institution for asthmatic children did beneficial work. And its advertising copy to attract tourists painted an idyllic picture: "Arad—blessed with ideal natural conditions for those seeking perfect rest and relaxation . . . the Mountains of Moab with their ever-changing colours mirrored in the blue waters down below . . . the place where you find modern, fully air-conditioned hotels, lawns and swimming pools." The trouble was, however, that by the side of the waters down below a string of equally modern hotels had sprung up, following the opening up for industry of the Dead Sea shore; and that was where the tourists preferred to be. Even its advantageous siting near the less sheer side of the Massada rock was nullified by the construction of a cable car route on the steep seaward approach.

All the same, Arad was on balance a success. It had had a fortunate start with a distinguished first administrator, Arie Elav, who later became Secretary-General of the Labour Party. It had achieved local council status and progressed to party politics. If it was not warm and jolly, like Dimona, it was remarkably efficient, orderly, and even clean. And whatever its future—whether or not it ever reached its programmed population of fifty thousand—Arad had progressed so notably in its early years that in his 1972 report the State Comptroller praised it as the "epitome of a model and modern development town."

The new town's road link with Sodom—involving a

descent from 2,060 feet above sea level to 1,288 feet below sea level—was opened in 1964, and in that same year the new highway south from Sodom was completed, linking up with the central Negev road twenty-five miles north of Eilat. The journey to the Red Sea from the Dead Sea was now cut to three hours. A gas pipeline was laid to Dimona and to the phosphate works at Oron. The extension of the railway from Beersheba to Dimona was followed by the spur to Oron. And opportunism added to military victory inspired the most ambitious trans-Negev communications scheme of all.

The Six-Day War of 1967 closed the Suez Canal. Oil for Europe had to go the long way round the Cape of Good Hope. The Israelis, almost the moment the war was over—in fact that very same month—began preparing plans for a land canal: an oil pipeline from the Red Sea to the Mediterranean. To those who argued that such a vast capital expenditure was pointless to replace a sea route which might be closed for only a short time, their answer came pat. This was the age of the giant oil tanker. The Suez Canal was, in any case, too shallow to take such monsters. But Eilat harbour was deep enough for them; and therefore the new pipeline would always be needed. Foreign governments were sceptical. But the Israelis went stubbornly ahead. In 1970 the 42-inch, 160-mile-long pipeline from Eilat to Ashkelon, the Philistine ruin on the Mediterranean which was now a garden colony of South African Jews, was completed. Soon eleven million tons of oil were being shipped through it. This was less than the planned target of fourteen million tons; delays in starting operations and a shortage of tankers were the reason for that. But, for a project which knowledgeable overseas statesmen insisted was hardly worth looking at, it was not too bad a start.

If atmospheric conditions were right, a man driving through the Negev desert could occasionally see, and even photograph, a strange and slightly frightening sight: a moving pillar of sand. Like that pillar of sand, the progress of the modern Israelis in the Negev could be regarded either as something merely mundane and evanescent, or else as a miraculous phenomenon. There was evidence for either view. The attempts at exploiting the local resources had been expensive, difficult, and often unsuccessful; the craters of the central desert were littered like Brobdingnagian rubbish dumps with doleful, abandoned workings; yet there, in the middle of the most inhospitable territory on earth, some of these industries survived, even prospered, and made their proud if occasionally astonished contribution to the country's export trade.

None of the six Negev towns could be exhibited as a showplace. Beersheba was littered and polluted. Eilat was a thriving scab festering on the shore of the Red Sea. Yerucham and Mitzpeh Ramon were stunted stepchildren, almost written off by their disappointed ministerial progenitors. Dimona was a cheerful improvisation. Orderly, civilized Arad, the apple of its parents' eye, was a slow developer. And the Government, surveying the progress so far of these urban experiments, had no plans whatever for further desert cities. Yet there these six were, with tens of thousands of people living busy, industrious and certainly eventful lives, in places where a quarter of a century ago there were only rock, wind, and the camels of transitory Beduin. Pencilled-in target populations for 1982 were thirty-two thousand each in Eilat and Dimona, and a cool two hundred thousand for Beersheba.

It was true that the Negev was still by far the emptiest part of Israel. Nevertheless it was the land of multiplication. In 1970 its population density was fourteen times greater than in 1948. Its proportion of Israel's total population was nearly four times as great as twenty-one years before, and its proportion of Jews had increased thirty fold. There were now 138,000 people in towns and urban settlements, 160,600 Jews and a total population of 189,000 living in this barren dagger pointing south.

The Israelis expected so much of themselves that they aroused expectations in others which were unfair and beyond fulfilment. Anyone flying in a helicopter over its surface could turn up his lip in scorn at the environmental horror comic which the Negev had become. But the traveller on his way south by land, who stopped off at the kiosk outside Yotvata to cool his parched throat

with a carton of chocolate-flavored milk, could pause
for a moment in wonder as he all of a sudden realized
the extraordinary human achievement involved in what
he was doing, in the place where he was doing it. In an
Israel which was too much in a hurry for religion, a pillar of sand could still mean a miracle.

5

Interlude with the Landed Aristocracy

As Eton College is to the British Conservative Party and the National Union of Mineworkers to the Labour Party, the kibbutz is to the State of Israel. There was a time when Old Etonians dominated Conservative Cabinets and accounted for an almost indecent proportion of Conservative members of Parliament; when, however small the Parliamentary Labour Party might be in its worst electoral years, the mining areas would ensure that a militant, utterly loyal cadre of Labour members would be returned to Parliament and have a strong say in the leadership. Now, as other less socially defined forces have come to preponderate in each party, the numerical strength of Eton and the NUM has waned; but their charisma remains, ensuring that their sons are still over-represented at the top of their parties and continue to be regarded with solemn respect. So it is with the kibbutzim.

Just as the NUM was one union among hundreds, just as Eton was one good school among dozens, so the kibbutzim always accounted for only a small proportion of the Jewish population in Palestine. At their zenith, at the time of independence, only 7.1 per cent of the Yishuv lived in them. But this seven per cent was the seven per cent. These were the people who provided the impetus which brought about the new State; the people whose courage and panache created the military *élan* of the Haganah and most particularly the Palmach; the people who gave a country without religion a stern, al-

119

most Spartan, but astonishingly pure ideology as its motivation. These pioneers, often of middle-class origin, who deliberately set themselves to till the soil as a tangible link with their land, became that land's landed aristocracy.

The kibbutz was a collective, and every member owned the estate. It was not equally shared between them, like a co-operative. Each owned all of it at the same time. To enter a kibbutz and watch its members going about their occasions was to see a group of people at perfect ease with their property: helping themselves to what was needed from kitchen or garden in the instinctive knowledge that it was theirs; moving from building to building with a proprietorship all the more confident for being entirely unspoken. Their apartments were simple, in the younger or more penurious settlements even makeshift; but no lord of a stately home could have had a more expansive sense of privilege.

Like aristocrats they carried very little money; in their case they simply did not have it, but in both cases it was rarely needed. The man with a title could run up a credit account; the kibbutznik at home got the best of everything free. He ate free. He got the certainty of the best available medical help free. His children were the only children in the country who received free education right up to university age, in classes whose size was comparable with those at the best British public schools. A totally classless group within their own communities, and proletarians by deliberate decision, the kibbutzniks nevertheless formed their country's officer class and its governing class.

Their children were not a burden to them. Like the children of the British upper class they were looked after during the day by capable, trained and reliable persons, and then at a suitable hour of leisure presented to their parents in circumstances most conducive to displays of mutual affection. Their parents lived a rustic, even parochial life, but provided themselves with facilities—concert halls, libraries—far superior to those available to any surrounding peasantry. A selected few —but a high proportion in relation to the population as a whole—would leave their estates for a few days in the middle of the week to go up to the capital and see to the affairs in the country. Just as some European aristocrats lived in castles which had once been strongpoints against outside attack, so certain of the kibbutzim were established in frontier locations for the express purpose of warding off marauders.

In the days before independence, no kibbutznik felt required to prove himself. His existence as a kibbutznik was proof in itself of everything that might need to be proved. But independence changed everything. Suddenly there were institutions to fulfil the functions which had been the peculiar responsibility of the kibbutzim. There was an army to defend the border. There were government departments to organize settlement. There was no need for anyone to embody and safeguard the Zionist ideology because that ideology had been consummated in an announcement (by an ex- and future kibbutznik) at a museum in Tel Aviv. And there was a totally new kind of immigrant.

So many of these latest immigrants were not just opposed to or uninterested in the Zionist, socialist, collectivist ideology. They had grown up simply unaware of it. They had not been members of ideological youth movements. They had not come to Palestine as young idealists, leaving their parents behind in a discarded Diaspora. They were, in the main, refugees from European camps or from North African or Middle Eastern ghettos. They were not intellectuals to whom the simple agricultural life made a cerebral appeal. They were often hawkers or petty traders. The collectivist principle had no meaning for them. Nor, to people whose whole lives revolved around the patriarchal family unit, did the kibbutz attitude to family life arouse anything except uncomprehending antipathy. They simply did not want to live on the kibbutzim.

The first kibbutz, Degania, was founded on the eastern shore of the Sea of Galilee in 1909. Its structure did not evolve from a carefully thought-out theory, but grew organically in response to need. Because those involved were socialists, a collective response came more naturally to them when faced with material and physical problems which individual effort was not strong enough to solve. So there grew up a collective, communistic society in which everyone was equal, whether man or woman, and whatever task they were assigned. They were equal in wealth because none of them received any pay. Instead all shared in what was produced: not by having equal shares, which could be withdrawn and cashed, but by being fed, housed and clothed, and by holding all property in common. Each married couple lived privately in their small apartment. But that apartment was theirs only so long as they lived in it. It belonged to the kibbutz—to everybody.

The kibbutz provided them with their clothes, their furniture and their food, which they ate communally in a village dining hall. They had limited private possessions, and were allotted small sums of money with which to buy them. Some kibbutzim had their own internal money, for use only at the kibbutz store. Not only was food provided by all for all. So were medical care, laundry facilities, cigarettes, and education. Children lived separately from their parents, freeing them for full-time work and being looked after by experienced personnel from among the membership. But family ties were very strong. Children spent the late afternoon hours with their parents when they were at leisure after their work, and also the Sabbath week-end. During week-days they were at school, whose classrooms were generally situated in the houses where they lived.

The kibbutz was one of the world's few living systems of direct democracy. All important decisions were taken at weekly meetings, which every member was entitled to attend and at which each had an equal voice. Not only were the affairs of the settlement discussed at these assemblies, but so were the personal circumstances of individual members. If a member wished to go to a university, wanted leave to go on an outside mission for the army, needed to take a trip abroad, it was for the meeting to agree, and if necessary to provide the finance. But no member was there against his will. He could leave whenever he liked. And just as he could be admitted to membership and joint ownership of the kibbutz while bringing nothing but himself to it, so, if he left, all he had the right to take away was himself. The kibbutz would probably help a member who decided to leave and try his luck in the world outside; but it had no obligation to do so. The property of the kibbutz belonged to the kibbutz, not to anyone who belonged to it at a particular time.

To most of the new post-war immigrants, all these notions were baffling. If they had to feed their families by growing the food themselves, then the alternative principles of the moshav village settlements—family unity, private property and co-operative effort—were much more attractive. In the first two years of the State only 16,000 out of 393,000 immigrants settled in kibbutzim, half as many as went to the moshavim. At the end of 1970, there were 85,100 people living in 229 kibbutzim: 61,200 in 133 pre-independence settlements, 23,600 in 96 founded since independence. Between the end of the Mandate and 1970, the number of moshavim, on the other hand, increased from 58 to 382. The proportion of Israel's population living in kibbutzim slid from the 7.1 per cent of 1948 to 4.2 per cent in 1961, 3.9 percent in 1967, 3.3 per cent in 1970. -

In an outside society where class distinctions were gradually becoming more apparent and more important, a consciously proletarian system whose participants regarded everyone else in their enclosed community as absolutely equal with themselves began to seem outdated and even a little amusing. Moreover the kibbutzniks' often almost fanatical obsession with the forms of ideology, and the disputes which stemmed from it, gave outsiders—busy with finding a place in life and making some kind of living—an impression of antiquated irrelevance.

Kibbutzim were not simply idealistic socialist societies: something dreamed up on a wet day by William Morris, or even Samuel Butler. They were tightly organized political entities, almost all of them members of three main kibbutz caucuses. There was a small number of what might be termed non-denominational settlements, and a handful belonging to the religious sector, Hadati. But 208 of the kibbutzim belonged—moving leftwards—to the Ichud (Union), Hameuchad (United) and Haartzi (Nationwide) organizations. Ichud Hakibuttzim ve Hakvutzot, with 76 kibbutzim inhabited by

26,500 members and their children, was linked with the old Mapai party. Hakibbutz Hameuchad—56 kibbutzim, 22,800 population—was the kibbutz branch of Achdut Haavodah. Hakibbutz Haartzi, whose 76 kibbutzim with 29,700 inhabitants made it the strongest of the three, was also the most intensely ideological. Each of its kibbutzim was a branch of Mapam, and any Haartzi kibbutz where 15 per cent of the membership rejected this political alignment was extruded from its affiliation.

Haartzi regarded itself as a distinct cut above the others. It scorned them for surrendering to the heresy of hiring labour for their factories—which it did itself, though on a lesser scale—and for a tendency to weakness with respect to enforcing the principle of children living in separate houses from their parents. But although Ichud and Hameuchad were both since 1968 linked with the same Labour party, there was if anything a greater bitterness between them than between either of them and Haartzi. A member of a Hameuchad kibbutz learning that a foreign visitor was engaged in a programme of visiting a series of Ichud kibbutzim would suspect some recondite plot on the part of the Labour Party (Mapai-dominated) and even of the Government. The reason inevitably was that there had been a nasty split between Ichud and Hameuchad, which at one time were both part of the Hameuchad movement.

Just as Achdut had broken away from Mapai in the 1940s, so, for the same reasons, but after a decent interval, part of the Hameuchad sector hived off in the 1950s and linked with a group called Chever Hakvutzot (Society of Kibbutzim) to form Ichud. This involved not simply the resignation of a clutch of settlements from the parent body; in some cases the acrimony was so great that individual kibbutzim themselves sundered in two. Old friends would not speak to each other. Work came to a halt. Partisan cronies would send their *chaverim*—comrades—to Coventry and take their meals cocooned in mutual antipathy at different ends of the communal dining hall. Sometimes whole groups moved out into other kibbutzim, perhaps distantly situated but of a more agreeable political leaning. In other cases a kibbutz would just crack into two halves, both remain-

ing geographically contiguous, side by side, each obsti-
nately retaining the same name and assisting a desperate
postman by adding an A or a B to their titles. Even after
the quarrel between Mapai and Achdut Haavodah was
settled after twenty years, Ichud and Hameuchad continued as separate and not entirely amicable entities.

This did not mean that there was no contact between
the different organizations. All were members of the
Histadrut. All, together with the moshavim, were represented on the Histadrut subsidiary marketing and wholesale organizations, Tnuva and Hamashbir Hamerkazi.
They participated in a joint teachers' training college.
They had even, in 1963, set up an over-all loose federa-
tive body, Brith Hatnuat Hakibbutzit, the National Union of Kibbutzim. But decisions of this kibbutz convention were operative only if all the separate kibbutz
movements gave their assent. And these movements
each possessed their own organizational machinery.

Haartzi, as might have been expected, had a tidy internal structure. The 500-member *Moetza* (Council)
met annually. The *Vaad* (Board) with 150 members,
convened at two-monthly intervals. The *Mazkirut* (Secretariat) called its thirteen-man committee together once
a week. The Ichud was by contrast considerably more
casual. It had a smaller assembly which gathered every
four to six weeks, and a larger body which could get
along without consulting more frequently than once every four years.

Set in this institutional pattern, and left behind by a
changing society which was creating for itself a new social structure, the kibbutzim were in danger of becoming
completely ossified. That they did not; that, while
losing a loftily elevated place in Israeli life they
nevertheless remained a living part of a living State, was
evidence of their adaptability and capacity to survive. If
the kibbutzniks were no longer the automatically accepted leaders of Israel, they were ready to show their fellow-countrymen that they could remain pace-makers in
whatever game anyone cared to play. Israel decided to
industrialize. So did the kibbutzim; and, what is more,
they made the decision ahead of the country. Having so
decided, they excelled. The first industrial kibbutz was

Givat Brenner, which in 1930 began to manufacture products such as non-ferrous castings. By independence there were thirty-two kibbutz industrial establishments. And every single year after independence more were started. Between 1960 and 1968 the number of workers in kibbutz industry doubled. By 1971 they numbered 9,200.

Curiously, most of the kibbutz industrial enterprises were not started for purely economic motives. Sometimes, for reasons of security, or to establish Jews in a sparsely populated area, a settlement would be planted in a district where agricultural development was unsuitable. Sometimes there were kibbutzniks who simply wanted to do a job other than farming. Sometimes the mechanization of agriculture increased productivity so much that even the most willing manpower was not required. In all of these cases industry was the answer.

The variety was remarkable. They made metal and metal products, electric and electronic products, wood products and furniture, plastic and leather goods, foodstuffs, pharmaceutical and chemical products, building materials, printed matter, decorative products and leatherware. They helped to establish the canning industry. They accounted for some forty per cent of the nation's plastics production. It seemed there was nothing they could not make, whether it might be thermostats or anodized aluminium, diamond tools or control panels. Kibbutz Hafetz Chaim, in partnership with private investors, established a frozen food factory, specializing in frozen kosher meals. These were supplied to the airport at Lod. A variant was heat-and-eat kosher meals prepared expressly for export. Up near the Lebanese border, kibbutz Dafna had a footwear factory, employing a hundred men. Their brand product was seamless, completely waterproof boots. They made half a million of them a year, and exported ninety per cent.

It went without saying that these activities engendered an ideological problem. An agricultural kibbutz could organize its activities to suit its membership. During the heavy summer fruit season, everyone whatever their job could pitch in and, for example, help to pick the pears. If there were still not enough hands, overseas students could be taken on as temporary volunteers. But a factory could not operate that way. A factory had an assembly line which needed to be kept moving. A factory had orders, often from overseas, to fulfil. A factory was often set up in association with foreign businessmen, who explicably wished to safeguard and augment their investment. Instead of the machines suiting the workers, the workers had to suit the machines. Kibbutzim could sometimes not supply the right number of workers, or workers with the right kind of skill. Reluctantly, and wringing their ideological hands, they had to hire labour from outside their settlement.

This went against the whole ideal of the kibbutz. It violated the notion of a self-sufficient community doing all its own work. It went against one of the basic aims of the founders of the first kibbutzim, who had rebelled against prosperous Jews hiring more needy Jews—or, even worse, because colonialist, hiring Arabs—to do heavy manual work that was socially beneath them. And, because if a man was hired by other men he could not claim equality with them, it for the first time introduced social inequality into the kibbutz framework. All the same, it had to be done.

There were kibbutzim which tried to find a solution compatible with their ideology. Hamadiya, which manufactured 100,000 wooden doors a year, approached the problem by organizing hired labour from the near-by town of Beisan into a co-operative group. This group was given a share of the profits as well as wages earned, and its members were eligible for co-option to management jobs. But, if they had equality, it was conferred on them as a gift, not theirs by right. The Haartizi movement found the very notion of hired labour repugnant, and derided its counterparts for surrendering their purity. But Haartzi, too, could not refrain from partaking in this sin, even if it erred less than others. Ichud, the least ideological, manned up to seventy-four per cent of its industrial needs with hired help. Haartzi, and Hameuchad too, held the level down to thirty-five per cent.

Only fifty-four kibbutzim were able to keep their industrial projects operative without taking on outside labour. By 1971, four thousand of the 9,200 kibbutz industrial workers were hired hands. The agonizing continued. Shlomo Stanger, Secretary of the National Union of Kibbutzim, said in March 1971 that the problem of hired labour still weighed heavily on their conscience. But conscience, however bowed down, had still to come to terms with the practical world.

Kibbutz industry may have been less pure than it would have liked. But it was undeniably successful. By 1972 there were 203 industrial plants in the kibbutzim. One kibbutznik in every four was working in a factory. His output was about one-quarter higher than that of other industrial workers. He produced one-third of the total income of the kibbutzim. While these settlements accounted for less than four per cent of the country's population, their share by 1971 in its industrial output was up from 3.1 per cent in 1951 to about seven per cent, and in industrial investment they accounted for ten per cent. They had also conferred on their country an environmental discovery: the knowledge that it was possible to have industrialization without urbanization.

One reason why kibbutz industry was relatively more successful than the nation's industry as a whole lay in the nature and quality of kibbutz manpower. There was an impressive kind of independence and sturdiness about kibbutzniks, the result of an upbringing which provided total security and which yet inculcated self-reliance. It was also the outcome of the best education that the country could provide. The kibbutzim provided their own teachers, trained at their own training college, the largest in Israel. Seminar Hakbibutzim had branches at Tel Aviv and Beit Berl. Its main centre, however, was Oranim, near Kiryat Tivon, outside Haifa. Oranim had six hundred students on its books. In June 1971 it became part of Haifa University and its graduates accordingly were eligible for BA degrees.

Kibbutz teachers were not only trained well. After their training they were able to concentrate on their teaching. Unlike teachers outside they did not have to campaign for pay increases. Unlike those outside teachers who regarded their pay as inadequate, they did not have to divert their energies to additional jobs in order to make ends meet. The classes they taught were small and more easy to handle. The curriculum, laid down by the education committee of each kibbutz group, was not single-mindedly directed to passage of the *Bagrut,* since kibbutz children generally did not sit for this examination. In fact they did not sit for any examinations, were not graded by marks, were not penalized by punishments.

In the ample kibbutz evenings, with no long journey home, they did, however, have time for the substantial amounts of homework they were assigned. And this homework went on for many years, since these children, alone in the country, were all guaranteed education up to the age of eighteen. The outcome was not simply that there was no illiteracy in the kibbutzim. It was also that kibbutz children were over-represented among the secondary-school age group. In 1961 the average length of a boy's education in Israel was 8.9 years. In the kibbutzim the average was eleven years.

No kibbutz was typical; for these, to the surprise of outsiders who came and saw them with preconceived notions soon discarded, were the most individualistic communities in the country. But it was possible to pick out certain kibbutzim whose histories embodied most aspects of the post-independence history of the movement as a whole. One was Givat Chaim, not a very long drive out of Tel Aviv. There were two kibbutzim of that name. For Givat Chaim had been fissured by the great 1952 split. The new, Ichud, settlement was set up by part of the original membership together with others who came down from another kibbutz, Kfar Szold.

More than five hundred lived there at the beginning: 280 adult members and more than 250 children. They started with essentials and no more. They had a barracks for accommodation, houses for the children (always over-privileged in any kibbutz) and a dining hall. They participated in the canning factory which Givat Chaim had started up when an undivided community. Their livestock included cows, ducks and poultry. They had citrus plantations and vineyards and also grew apples, alfalfa and vegetables.

Their progress was not painless They began to keep sheep, but had not sufficient land for them and were forced to give them up. They gave up growing cereals after a while. They gave up the vineyard, as well, because the price of grapes was too low for the effort to be economically worth while. An attempt at cultivating avocado pears went wrong, and a banana plantation also failed. They abandoned all vegetable crops and concentrated on fruit. Of the poultry with which they had experimented, chickens and ducks were discarded, leaving them with turkeys, a particularly popular Israeli fowl

Givat Chaim prospered. When it started only about twenty per cent of its land was irrigated. By the 1970s, irrigation covered all the settlement's 900 acres. The kibbutzniks had about 180 acres of citrus plantations. They were also, by now, growing cotton. They were helped along with loans for agricultural development and building. Some of the money had been paid off, but other loans had had to be extended. After twenty years Givat Chaim was not only a thriving, busy community but also a very attractive place to live.

The settlement had been connected to the electricity supply after six months. It got a hospital after two years. Its health needs were attended to by three nurses, a physiotherapist, a child psychologist, a social worker, a non-member dentist, and a doctor shared with another kibbutz. Education began with the baby house, where children remained until they were three years old. They then moved on to kindergarten until the age of six. Next came eight years at elementary school, followed by a four-year spell at secondary school from the ages of fourteen to eighteen. The secondary school was a district school for several kibbutzim, but it was there in Givat Chaim. From the late 1950s there had also been a special school for disturbed or retarded children, attended by 160 pupils from Givat Chaim and other kibbutzim. The kibbutz had thirty of its members engaged in adult study, at university, at the Rehovot agricultural college, and at technical courses.

The most minute details of daily life were carefully worked out. Cigarettes were free. There was a budget for clothing. Everyone got an allocation for basic furniture. Each member received about 200 Israeli pounds in pocket money, and there was a shop where small items could be bought. Everyone was allocated a radio, within two or three years of membership, and in addition a refrigerator. For the women there was a beauty parlour, and for the men a barber came every month for about ten days. Leisure facilities included a swimming-pool, a tennis court, a library and—the supreme achievement after eight years of anticipation—an assembly hall. This was a vast and spacious building, with an ample stage on which adolescents enthusiastically performed folk dances and tiny children shyly lisped songs, while even smaller tots eating large handfuls of sustaining carbohydrate constantly plunged in towards the attractive light and colour, and then out again into the black cricket-rustling night.

As in most kibbutzim, leisure was regarded as highly important. Everyone had between ten and sixteen days off work each year, depending on age, and was entitled to spend seven days away. The kibbutz also provided a special holiday for its members every second year. For the older members this was made an annual event—first for the over-60s, then for the over-55s. Givat Chaim was, in fact, ageing.

In its first twenty years population increased by less than 200. The number of members was up, to a total of 470. But the total of children was only 160. Partly this was because the settlement's first generation was all more or less of the same age, so that parent age groups were getting beyond the child-bearing age. Partly it was due to a departure rate of about thirty per cent among the second generation. This loss was not made good by restocking from new immigrants. Some Poles and Hungarians did arrive in 1957, but most of them did not settle.

Like many established kibbutzim, Givat Chaim was secure and a little stolid. As a place to live, and in which to bring up children, it was seductively pretty, none of its problems apparent to a casual visitor who in working hours saw a harmoniously operative mechanism and, if invited to a celebration, was bewitched, almost transported, by the sight of white-clothed tables, full of food and coloured soft-drink bottles, stretching endlessly over a rolling green while dogs ecstatically yapped and children rolled over and over down a slight but sufficient incline.

So many of Israel's kibbutzim presented an idyllic picture to the passing stranger. At Ein Gedi, immaculate in its isolation, gramophone records of 1930's Broadway musicals floated out over the impassive waters of the Dead Sea. Ayelet Hashachar was so trim that even the lawns seemed to have been freshly painted the previous day. Tiny Maggal, not many yards from the pre-1967 Jordanian border, had a club-house which looked as though Heals had equipped it. Yagur claimed the best iced soda-water in the country, available on tap at a special installation behind the dining hall. The buzz of the tractors from Sdot Yam hovered complacently over the ruins of Caesarea. But not one of these or any of the others was free from the problems with which the kibbutzim of the 1970s had, by no means entirely successfully, constantly to cope.

The founders of the kibbutzim paradoxically had it very easy. For them life was hard but simple. Either the kibbutz survived or it did not. If it did not, that was that. If it did, then strenuous physical work had justified deeply held ideology in a practical manner. But the children of the first generation were born with the ideological silver spoon in their mouth. Because they did not have to toil to fulfil their beliefs, but instead had the fruit of the toil passed on to them, the beliefs they inherited could not be held in the same passionate way They had a very different and difficult task: to maintain the momentum of a going concern.

What is more, they had to do this in a country on the move. It was not too difficult to be an agricultural pioneer in a colonial territory with sketchy living standards, few opportunities to become rich or famous, little industry to provide attractive alternative occupations, and a structure of society in which the kibbutznik was more independent than the town-dweller directly subject to the Mandatory government But, with national independence and growing prosperity, the kibbutznik could see others no more talented than he doing exciting work, owning their own car, going on foreign trips, making themselves reputations He felt he must leave the kibbutz if he was not granted the education to which his IQ entitled him; but if he was provided with this higher education, he might leave the kibbutz because it gave him no scope for the skills he had learned. He had to be a highly motivated socialist not to be tempted. And his wife would often feel the temptation even if he did not.

On the one hand the kibbutz women complained that their work was not as interesting as the men's; that they were too often compelled to look after the children's houses or content themselves with simple clerical occupations, while their husbands were technologically involved in complex industries. But, deploying entirely contrary arguments, they also demanded the right to a home of their own with their children living with them while they attended to their housewifely tasks. It was its inherent truth that made kibbutzniks smile wryly at the saying: A man leaves the kibbutz either because he hasn't a wife or because he has.

The strains of living, eating, spending leisure hours with the same small number of people were more difficult to bear for those younger members who could not look around their settlement in the knowledge that without the work of all of them it would not have been there. It was natural for a man to see the defects of what he himself had not created but instead took simply for granted. However affluent a kibbutz became, even if, like Shefayim, it went so far as to provide a television set for every family, it could in the end promise no more than a simple life; and to be a kibbutznik was not necessarily to be an ascetic. Again, in an uncomplicated agricultural community, where everyone understood what everyone else was doing, it was easy to maintain the cohesion of this small society. But in a large settlement, where people were involved in many occupations, often of a highly skilled nature, interests were not only different: they diverged, and resulted in some kind of fragmentation.

Beyond the spongy lawns and twirling irrigation taps there was often neurosis, sometimes the worse for a lack of realization of the different, but often more serious, problems with which town-dwellers had to cope. Yet in most comparisons the kibbutzniks had the best of it. The standard of living in the kibbutzim rose steadily, and kept pace with that of working people in the towns. Not only was their education better: so were their social services, so was their provision for old age. And although they often were not able to realize it themselves, simple statistics measured their more secure life. In 1969 the marriage rate for kibbutz men was 12.7 per thousand, and for women 11.5, compared with national rates of 9.4 and 9.5 In 1970 the kibbutz birth rate was 117 per cent of the national average, the infant death rate 46 per cent, the over-all death rate 67 per cent.

These healthy, long-lived villagers had excelled at their new industrial skills, and at the same time they continued to lead the country in agriculture. Farming still provided 40 per cent of kibbutz jobs, the rest being divided between industry and services. At first, after independence, the farming sector was given the unaccustomed duty—previously shared with Arab farmers, the majority of whom had now left the country—of feeding not only the existing population but the hundreds of thousands of new immigrants too. More land was available, both where Arabs had left it and not returned, and where irrigation had been introduced. Mechanization was made necessary not only by the size of the job but also because of the shortage of manpower.

At first the need to regenerate impoverished Arab land and to train new immigrants led to a fall in output per acre. But gradually progress was made. The kibbutzim were to lag behind the agricultural sector as a whole in citrus and vegetable growing. But it was they who launched cotton and sugar-beet. Other innovations were ground-nuts and tobacco. Between 1956–7 and 1964–5, there was a 50 per cent rise in the over-all agricultural output of the kibbutzim, and between 1957 and 1966 productivity per worker was doubled. Output was increasing while manpower was not. By the early 1970s these settlements, with 32 per cent of the rural population, and cultivating 42 per cent of all available land, were producing 60 per cent of the country's apples and pears, 69 per cent of its cereals, and half of all its agricultural output. Moreover, they were more prosperous than ever. In the 1930s the kibbutzim had been in deficit. From the 1950s they were profit makers.

And they continued to produce the country's leadership in industry, in institutions of higher learning, and right at the very top. Ben Gurion was a kibbutznik and Golda Meir, though no longer one herself, had a daughter in the Negev kibbutz of Revivim to which she liked to go to spend her holidays. Kibbutzniks were over-represented in government, with such Cabinet Ministers as Yigal Allon, Chaim Gvati and Israel Galili; and in Parliament, most notably by a Speaker of the Knesset, Kaddish Luz. Mordechai Hod, Commander of the Air Force during the Six-Day War, was born in kibbutz Degania. And in that war, 200 of the 778 fatal casualties were from the kibbutzim. Israeli officers, of course, were accustomed to lead their men into battle with the cry: "Follow me." Of the officers in the Israeli army, 22 per cent were from kibbutzim, which also provided a disproportionately large number of air force pilots.

But these were not simply solemn Spartans. They added by their existence to the nation's vivacity and variety. Just as the English stately homes sought to attract paying visitors with zoos, nudist colonies, or vintage cars, so the kibbutzim became part of the tourist and entertainment business. Kibbutz Dalia was known for its dancing festival; Ein Gev for its Passover music week; Ein Harod, Hazorea, Ashdot Yaacov, for their art galleries. Hazorea, as well, advertised itself in the newspapers as "Israel's largest and finest furniture manufacturers." Ginossar advertised not only in the press, but also by means of radio commercials, the attractions of its guest house by the Sea of Galilee. Eilon had a mosaic works, Yotvata its milk bar, Givat Brenner a travelling band. The history of the country and of the Jews was commemorated in a starkly moving museum at Lochamei Hagetaot in the north and in open-air tableaux at Yad Mordechai, near the Gaza Strip.

The kibbutzim still meant much to the country. They were no longer, perhaps, the epitome of its values. But they were still, although sometimes it would not admit it, what it would most like to be even though it knew it no longer ever would. In *The Highway Queen,* one of the most popular Israeli films of 1971, the only generous and good-hearted character in an otherwise squalid story was a lorry driver from a kibbutz. To a national audience this symbol of purity was immediately meaningful.

In the first two years of the 1970s four out of five children born on the kibbutzim were staying. Moreover, a significant number of the more idealistically motivated immigrants who came to the country after 1967 were making their way to these curiously magnetic settlements. During 1970, 1,850 moved in. Kibbutzniks, landed aristocrats similar in many ways to the gentry of wealth and breeding in monarchies abroad, were very different from them and very special in their attitude to work, to politics, to society. They were an aristocracy which, like some religious order, required a man to make if not a vow of poverty then at any rate a decision about what life meant. And on this basis they were an aristocracy that anybody could join.

6

The Garden Suburb

It took half an hour or so for Tel Aviv to achieve its apotheosis. That was the duration of the declaration of independence ceremony which, on the afternoon of 14 May 1948, conferred on Palestine's all-Jewish city the most supreme moment it could ever know. Tel Aviv was not born great. It had greatness briefly thrust upon it, and then seemed fated to live in perpetual anticlimax. The capital of the new country was to be Jerusalem. Tel Aviv was too young to have any great shrines for pilgrims to visit. It had no historic buildings, indeed hardly any buildings of more than passing interest. It was a dull eastern Mediterranean town, an Athens without the Parthenon, the Roman ruins or the hills, cluttered with square, cream-coloured dwellings and edged by a rather mangy sea front.

As the years of statehood went by it grew. Although the main institution of government were transferred to Jerusalem, so many national activities remained centred on Tel Aviv that the city gradually took on the role of a New York to Jerusalem's Washington. But the only characteristic which in 1948 it shared with New York was intolerable humidity. There were no soaring skyscrapers to give it excitement, no large open spaces to lend it charm. Some of those who lived there defiantly professed to like it. But a tourist who arrived in Tel Aviv after first having tasted the dramatic beauty of Haifa's panorama would be disappointedly depressed. And Tel Aviv got more and more scruffy. The traffic jams were increasingly intolerable. The facilities were inadequate. It was even difficult to get a glass of fresh orange juice at the height of the citrus season. Residents and frequent visitors were resigned to putting up with a place which work obliged them to live in, or necessity to pass through. Then, very suddenly, in the early 1970s, they all woke up to the startling realization that this unpromising duckling had stealthily but steadily been transforming itself. If parts of the place were as bad as they had ever been, others had acquired a remarkable appeal and even distinction. Tel Aviv, like New York, was on its way to becoming a wonderful town.

It had been founded in 1909 as a Jewish garden suburb north of the venerable Arab city of Jaffa (as mentioned in the Bible). Jaffa hugged the curve of the bay. The Hill of the Spring, as the suburb's founders called it, was established on unenticing sand dunes, ever encroaching inland after having been brought from the delta of the Nile and deposited on the coast of Palestine. It was the first all-Jewish town in the modern world, and by the time of Israel's independence it had acquired a population of almost a quarter of a million, more than three times the size of neighbouring Jaffa. Following the passing of the United Nations resolution, in November 1947, Tel Aviv swallowed up the old German colony of Sarona, which had earlier been taken over for use by the British Army and police. When independence itself came, Jaffa was snapped up too. The duckling had become a cuckoo and taken over the nest.

Sarona, with its neat, regular streets lined with farmhouses, was what made post-independence Tel Aviv really important. It was renamed Hakiryah (the city) and turned into the new Government's headquarters. Gradually most of the ministries moved to Jerusalem. But they left outposts at Hakiryah; and the Ministry of Defence for security reasons still had its headquarters there. An integral part of the expanding city of Tel Aviv, yet carefully cordoned off from it, Hakiryah became a purposive government compound. Actual access was not difficult. Sooner rather than later, however, an intruder was bound to be stopped and his business ascertained. People in uniform were everywhere: burly and heavily moustached personages, devotedly got up to resemble caricatures of British sergeant-majors, being much in evidence as gruff but kindly sentries. Khaki-coloured cars and military motor scooters chugged busily around.

The Kafkaesque sense of alienation which a visitor could feel within moments of penetrating Hakiryah was increased by the baffling inability of its denizens to direct anyone to the simplest destination. One street away from the Prime Minister's office, they would deny that any such office existed except in Jerusalem. The labelling of most of the thoroughfares with letters of the (Hebrew) alphabet rather than with names was another barrier to clarification. Yet amid all this confusion, and with an appointment with a totally untraced Cabinet Minister only seconds away, the outsider was still aware that all around him essential work was being performed with great efficiency.

While Sarona was to be a centre of activity, Jaffa had become derelict. Of the 70,000 Arabs who had lived there, only 5,000 remained when the town surrendered to the Jews on 13 May 1948. The rest of the place was taken over by new immigrants, even though large tracts of it were no more than slums. It was to be another ten years before new life came to Jaffa. Meanwhile Tel Aviv needed all the living accommodation it could find. Between November 1948 and the end of 1952 its population grew by more than 100,000, from 248,300 to 350,000. Four years' growth had already taken the city near to what was to be its maximum size.

It was not, however, until the mid-1950s that Tel Aviv began to take on the aspect of a city of consequence. After only a few months as host to the Knesset, which met in a reconditioned cinema on the sea front, it had lost the country's Parliament to Jerusalem. In 1955, however, Tel Aviv's skyline was pierced by the city's first tall office building. This was, naturally, the new headquarters of the Histadrut. And, equally inevitably, the building became known locally as the Kremlin. Slowly, gradually, other imposing landmarks were added. October 1957 witnessed the inaugural concert—with Leonard Bernstein, Artur Rubinstein, Isaac Stern and Paul Tortellier—of the new 2,900-seat Frederic R. Mann concert hall. Reminiscent in its squat, glass-bedecked style of the Royal Festival Hall in London, this Mann Auditorium was sited in a square where, in 1958, it was joined by the Helena Rubinstein Art Museum. The Habimah Theatre made the square a three-arts centre. But plans for further expansion of the museum by the addition of several other pavilions were thwarted by two ancient sycamore trees. The people of Tel Aviv refused to allow them to be uprooted, and the painter Nahum Gutman declared that the bulldozers would have to roll over his dead body. The trees remained and the new museum had to be sited somewhere else.

Conservationists, in fact, were winning everywhere. For now there was a slum clearance scheme to demolish Jaffa. A "Save Old Jaffa" campaign was launched in response; and the campaign was successful. In 1960 the Old City of Jaffa Development Corporation was founded as a fifty-fifty concern by the Tel Aviv-Jaffa municipality with the Government Tourist Corporation and other government institutions. The first task in renovating the area was to persuade the existing inhabitants to leave. Of 250 families, only eleven in the end wished to remain. The others accepted financial compensation or else new homes. Work then began on remodelling the homes they had left.

The chosen buildings, 150 to 200 years old, lined twelve narrow cobble-stoned lanes. The main object of the Corporation was to maintain these buildings' characteristic style without attempting an exact restoration. Stone-masons from Jerusalem succeeded in maintaining a harmonious general scheme after learning from local Arabs a Roman method of producing pigment from crushed brick. This was then used for wall coloration and for overpainting cement patching which would otherwise have been unsightly.

Running water and electricity were installed in the houses. But all piping and wiring, as well as mechanical equipment and refuse bins, were concealed inside walls and behind unobtrusive covers. All sign-writing was controlled, the street names being uniformly posted in ceramic, in signs of the zodiac. In total one hundred separate units were created. They were sold for between

7,000 and 40,000 Israeli pounds, plus the cost of repair, and the Artists' Association was asked to buy some flats for letting to struggling artists. Altogether sixty of the units which had been created went to artists as studios, workplaces and dwellings. A special committee examined applicants both for those places and for small shops, restaurants and three night-clubs. The final plan produced a long central garden and piazza, approached by a massive flight of hand-hewn steps, and a built-up area with narrow alleys leading to small incidental piazzas. The precinct was confined to pedestrians.

The effect was enchanting. Tel Aviv's publicists proudly described the area as a "modernized Montmartre." But the Old Jaffa so superbly brought back to life was not a second anything. It was unique—and a success. There had always been the danger that deliberately creating an artists' quarter might result in something chic and artificial. Instead this small area was novel and genuine. During the day a saunter through its narrow passages brought the delight of sudden beguiling vistas: Jaffa lighthouse, perhaps, framed against a cerulean blue sky. At night, with the district carefully and unobtrusively lit, it was time for the small antique shops, still open at midnight, to offer the chance of some small but delectable *trouvaille*. A special walled-off excavation area politely hinted at Jaffa's ancient past. And to sit eating ice-cream or water melon in an open-air café with a sea view made the present very pleasant.

With Jaffa so skilfully preserved, the expansion of Tel Aviv itself was also under way. In 1961 a huge city hospital with 330 beds was opened, named after Moshe Ichilov, a former Deputy Mayor of the town. And in 1962 work began on what was to be the tallest building between Milan and Tokyo. To make way for the Shalom Tower, in the centre of the city, just off Allenby Street, two long-established buildings had to be demolished. Learning and culture, in the shape of the central library and the famous Herzlia Gymnasia high school, gave way to commerce.

Although the symbolism of the tower's name—"Shalom" (peace)—was much emphasized, this label in fact derived from the name of Shalom Mayer, who had been a Tel Aviv businessman and civic leader. The building was erected by a corporation of Wolfson, Clore and Mayer in partnership with the Rassco company. Rising thirty-four storeys above ground, and with four underground floors, the tower housed offices, Israel's first department store (forty-five departments) and an underground car park. Later a hotel was added.

The tower took four years to build. Its twin elevator shafts were completed first, and long before the building was finished a vertiginous ride to the 420-feet-high top of the tower provided a queasy tourist attraction. During the 500,000 man-days of construction, not a single worker was injured. Materials used included 4,000 tons of steel reinforcement and 1,750,000 cubic feet of concrete. A mosaic by Italian craftsmen depicted the history of Tel Aviv in 50,000 separate stones. This was eventually secluded from the people of Tel Aviv themselves, and became part of the lounge of the new Tower Hotel. At the top of the building the view was amazing. To the south Ashdod and Gaza could be seen; to the north, Haifa and sometimes even Mount Hermon, where the Lebanon met Syria. And it was possible, looking out to the west, to spot an airliner flying into Israel and then, turning around 180 degrees to the east, to follow its flight until the moment it landed at Lod Airport.

By the time the Shalom Tower was completed there were other fresh landmarks to be seen from it. On Ben Yehuda Street the new El Al headquarters, with an exterior spiral stairway, was opened in 1963 to purvey to contented passengers misleading information about prompt departure times. In the east of the city in the same year the municipality inaugurated, with a basketball contest between Yugoslavia and Israel, its new five thousand-seat sports stadium. Yad Eliahu was imaginatively described as "looking like a mammoth spider with a hundred concrete legs." The spider cost 12 million Israeli pounds.

Two years later Tel Aviv could at last be confident that it had arrived as an international city fit to hold up its head in the company of other international cities; on 16 September 1965 its Hilton Hotel was opened with a gala ball in the very presence of Conrad N. Hilton Junior himself. Twenty storeys high, its balconies jutting outward aggressively, the Hilton had accommodation for 872 guests, as well as a grand ballroom, five halls, two restaurants, three cocktail bars, and the proud reputation of being the first hotel in Israel with running iced water. It cost $23 million to build. At first it lost money, and in 1967 its American and Canadian investors sold out to the Israeli Government—who in their turn, five years later, sold it to four West German Jewish businessmen. For eventually the hotel began to show a profit. By 1970 the Tel Aviv Hilton was recording a remarkable 93 per cent room occupancy, and in March of the following year work began on an extension to include 168 rooms and 27 luxury suites.

This kind of edifice was very different from another building dedicated in November 1965: the Soldiers' House, which provided showers, changing rooms, a hairdresser and barber, a library, a restaurant and an officers' club for servicemen and women passing through the city. But the city was ensuring that functional as well as luxury accommodation was part of its facilities. In 1966 formidable new law-court buildings were opened on Sderot Shaul Hamelech, King Saul Boulevard, which was eventually to become a centre for notable public buildings. The law courts consisted of two structures, one of fifteen storeys, the other with nine, linked by a common entrance courtyard. A battery of elevators, two for the judges, six for the public, six for the prisoners, led to sixty-eight air conditioned court rooms.

Then, on independence day, 15 May 1967, Tel Aviv's new city hall was formally opened. A modern building for the city's municipal administration had been long overdue. This had previously been scattered throughout the municipality in thirty-five different apartments and offices. Under the Mandate Tel Aviv had tried to develop its own services and institutions independently of the colonial government. It had established its own hospitals (which after independence were run jointly with the Government) and its own very good system of education. Its first Mayor, Meir Dizengoff, gave his name both to the museum where independence was declared and to Tel Aviv's Piccadilly Circus. After him, up to the election of 1969, there came five others, of whom Chaim Levanon, during his term of office from 1952 to 1959, presided over major developments in the city's life: the foundation of its university, and the building of the Mann Auditorium, the Ichilov hospital and the Haaretz museum complex in the northern section.

Unusually, for a large urban centre, Tel Aviv had for long been under right-wing political control. In the mid-1950s Golda Meir had failed in a bid to be elected mayor. But Levanon was not as highly regarded as his predecessor, Israel Rokach, who had joined the Cabinet as Minister of the Interior. In 1959 the Mapai list for the thirty-one seats on the city council was headed by Mordechai Namir, himself a former Cabinet Minister as well as an ex-Ambassador to Moscow and Secretary-General of the Histadrut. At last the Left took over in Tel Aviv, and Namir as mayor headed a coalition which, re-elected in 1965 on a programme of cleaning up the city and the sea front, achieved the rehousing of thirty thousand slum dwellers, the building of more museums, and the construction of the new city hall.

Namir was not for long to enjoy the unrivalled view of the Reading D power station which the mayor's room provided. In 1968 he was forced by ill health to retire, and was succeeded by his first deputy, Yehoshua Rabinowitz, who was re-elected in the 1969 election in a coalition combining Labour with the religious and splinter parties. This system of city government depended on paid elected officials—the mayor received 1,800 Israeli pounds a month—backed by a salaried civil service. This was headed, as a relic from British times, by a town clerk. The mayor and his deputies were elected from among the council's majority parties; the deputies were each placed in charge of a department. Revenue came mainly from a property tax but also from an entertainment tax and from government grants for national services: hospitals, traffic development, education, welfare. Tel Aviv's financial situation was always bad. Political or economic reasons could invariably be found for not raising taxes, while demands from the people constantly grew.

However, money had at any rate been found for this new city hall, which had fourteen floors and, at 180 feet high, was the second tallest building in Tel Aviv. Its lines were simple and clean, and its setting was fine. It lay at the climax of a square named Malchei Israel, the Kings of Israel, which was as spacious and dramatic as St. Mark's Piazza in Venice. At the end of the square, paved in decorative zigzags, with its long stone benches, flower beds, lawns, palm trees and fountains, was a wide stairway which led to a broad platform in front of the city hall. Gazing out from this platform, on a Saturday evening, with the first lights coming on and balloon sellers holding bunches of wildly coloured bubbles, it was possible to sniff a placid mood of incipient urban excitement. This excitement was most noisily evoked on summer Saturday nights, when mass dancing, in which hundreds joined, was staged in the square. On other evenings there were film shows, and concerts by the Fire Brigade Orchestra and the Police Band.

After sixty years the city was acquiring a fresh and beguiling character. This was enhanced by the new art museum whose original intended location had been vetoed by two old sycamores. An alternative site had been made available not far from the law courts, and in 1964 the cornerstone was laid. A competition was launched for a design, and the prize went to Yitzchak Yashar and Dan Eitan, whose open-plan conception was aimed at eliminating "museum stress." The central space and entrance, continually in view, were to provide a fixed point of orientation for the visitor as he wandered up the slope which led to the four main galleries, or around the galleries themselves. This museum was to include workshops, offices, a 550-seat auditorium, a lecture hall, an art library, a cafeteria and, essential aid to tranquil viewing of the arts, an air-raid shelter.

The museum cost 14 million Israeli pounds. It was eventually opened on 19 April 1971 by the President of the State. But it owed its existence to Chaim Gamzu, the museum director, an idiosyncratic individualist who lived dangerously by combining this post with an art critic's assignment for a daily newspaper. He made enemies among artists, but his absolute single-mindedness provided them with an enviable showplace for their work.

In the 1970s Tel Aviv also acquired a new coolly elegant Southern Railway Station—equipped, likewise, with air-raid shelter accommodation—in place of the bedraggled siding where travellers arriving from Jerusalem in the early 1960s learned to their dismay that they were now in Israel's largest metropolis But increasingly the emphasis was not just on single buildings but on multi-purpose complexes. The new bus station, replacing the littered slum opposite an equally bedraggled covey of taxi-hire terminals, was planned as a massive "city under one roof" with its own shopping precinct, banks, cinemas and restaurants. At Mograbi Circus, in the old centre of Tel Aviv, where the fairly swish Ben Yehuda Street ran into drab but busy Allenby Street at a hub dominated by a dilapidated picture palace, the new Migdalor commercial centre was rising, combining shops on several levels reached by escalator, and a twenty-three-storey hotel.

On the northern sea-shore, a derelict stretch south of the Hilton was taken over in June 1969 by the Atarim Development Corporation (whose partners included Tel Aviv municipality as well as the Government) to construct a tourist centre planned for completion by the end of 1972 at a cost of 25 million Israeli pounds. A complex of pedestrian piazzas at different levels was to provide access to shops, cafés, clubs and a building which would contain cinemas and a two hundred-room hotel. There were further plans for a series of hotels, a promenade, a six-lane highway and an anchorage basin for small boats and yachts. The plan, explained Yehuda Shaari, Deputy Minister of Tourism, would provide "a recreational area which can compare favourably with any other in the Mediterranean."

Most fanciful of all was the plan for the new Dizengoff Centre. Dizengoff Street was Israel's answer to the Champs Elysées and the Via Veneto. As it ran southwards it became ever more frequented, the pavement cafés fuller and more lively, the shops more tastefully expensive. It contained the Kassit, the café where no

The dream becomes a reality
To Build the Promised Land

David Ben-Gurion

Moshe Sharett

Moshe Dayan

Yigal Allon

Golda Meir

Levi Eshkol

Chaim Weizmann

Pinchas Lavon

Abd el Aziz Zouabi

Menachem Begin

S. Y. Agnon, Nobel prize-winner

Inaugural flight of Aravah aircraft, April 1970

Declaration of Independence, May 14, 1948

Haifa University

Liberty Square, Bar-Ilan University

Arad, 1970

Ashdod port, main loading area

Eilat (Um Rashrash), 1949

Eilat, 1970

Desalination plant, Eilat

Dead Sea Works, Sodom

City Hall and Malchei Israel Square, Tel Aviv

Foreign Ministry at Hakiryah,
Tel Aviv, 1948

Town Hall, Bat Yam

Old Jaffa renovated

Beduin school, Jawarish

Immigrants' reception camp, 1949

Mann auditorium, Tel Aviv

self-respecting Hebrew-speaking Bohemian could afford not to be known, and led to the city's municipal Cameri Theatre. It was interrupted by the Dizengoff Circus, with fountains, ice-cream bars, supermarket and cinemas, and then proceeded more quietly to its appointment with the arts centre at Habimah Square. It was in this less developed section that Arieh Pilz planned his profit-making pleasure dome. Pilz had been the contractor both for the El Al building and the new bus station, and was accustomed to thinking big.

Three tower hotels, from fifteen to thirty-two storeys in height and resembling large springs about to uncoil, were to be the Dizengoff Centre's landmarks. Here was to be 800,000 square feet of shopping and parking space, in a self-contained complex of four levels of curved ramps spanning Dizengoff Street. Even the streets would be air-conditioned. The bridges would contain their own outdoor café areas. The enclosed malls and shops would be illuminated through giant geodesic dome skylights. Cinemas, a convention hall, roof-top gardens, and Israel's first skating rink would be among other features to swallow the 140 million Israeli pounds which the project would cost. Pilz confidently predicted: "In a few years people asking for Dizengoff Circus will be told that it is near Dizengoff Centre."

He even promised "a smoother flow of traffic." This was a matter of increasing concern to Tel Aviv, which was so bothered by traffic clog-ups that it was looking into the possibility of an underground railway. Travel southward had been made easier by the completion in 1970 of the sea-shore road to Jaffa. Access from the north had been less strangulated since the opening, in the same year, of the Bar Yehuda Bridge at a cost of 4,500,000 Israeli pounds. This route would be even more important following the long-awaited start on the "L-plan" residential development in the north-west of the city, where five thousand flats were to be built by 1975. In the centre of the city itself, with buses edging their way along at an average of five miles an hour, an eight-lane expressway along the Ayalon wadi-bed would help unsnarl the traffic and bring Lod airport within seventeen minutes of road travel.

Some parts of Tel Aviv, then, were becoming fitting components of a city of the future. Others were, only too obviously, stubbornly resisting relics of a straitened past. In 1971 the city contained 55 per cent of all of Israel's slum dwellings. Some 28,000 Tel Aviv families were living in sub-standard housing. In the five years up to 1970, only 3,480 families had been rehoused from slum-clearance areas. Moreover, the city's problems were not evenly spread. Tel Aviv was sharply divided between a prosperous north and a seedy south. A V-line, cutting the city at its centre from Bograshov Street to Petach Tikvah Road, formed an internal frontier. The four districts north of the line, mainly residential but including the focus for business and the entertainment and tourist attractions, had low population densities and serene living conditions. The five districts of the centre, south and east included the city centre, large and small workshops, commerce and industry and far more crowded living conditions.

The social divide was also a cultural divide. The most prosperous district of Tel Aviv, a residential area developed in the 1960s, with the lowest population densities in the city, was overwhelmingly of European origin; only 7.4 per cent of its inhabitants came from Africa or Asia. In the most crowded and poorest part of the city, the heavily industrialized eastern section, 31.8 per cent of the population were Afro-Asians. Tel Aviv, in fact, was impregnated with greater social differences than anywhere else in Israel. Like any big city it attracted to it the poorer, more rootless part of the country's population, people coming to look for a livelihood and a future. At the same time, its northern district contained unusually well-to-do persons with professional occupations.

These social contrasts were reflected in the varying income levels of different sections of the population. In 1969 the average annual income of a Tel Aviv family of European or American origin was 11,751 Israeli pounds; for a native-born Israeli family, 11,525; for an Asian or African family, 10,017. But at any rate the gap had been narrowing fast. Only two years before, in 1967, the European-American income had been 11,494 pounds, the Israeli 10,795, the African-Asian 6,709. Moreover, the gap in Tel Aviv was narrower than in the country as a whole. One reason for this was that Tel Aviv standards generally were considerably higher than the national level. In 1969 the average Tel Aviv family income was 11,212 pounds, compared with a national average of 10,500 pounds.

People who lived in Tel Aviv were, indeed, getting more prosperous—and more prosperous than their fellow-Israelis—all the time. The size of their homes—always quite small in Israel if compared with Britain or the USA—showed it. In 1960 49.3 per cent of all new apartments completed in Tel Aviv had only two rooms. Ten years later, in 1970, two-room apartments comprised just 12 per cent of the total. On the other hand, the proportion of apartments with four or more rooms had risen in that same period from 4.9 to 28.9 per cent. The number of private cars in the city had increased from 10,400 in 1960 to 34,514 in 1969, and was 26.3 per cent of the national total in a city whose population was 13.1 per cent of all Israelis. Private cars were owned by 18 per cent of the city's inhabitants, compared with 15 per cent nationally, while telephone ownership, at 46.5 per cent, was half as much again above the national 33.8 per cent. On the other hand, strangely, washing-machine ownership, at 30 per cent, was less than three-quarters the national average. But then, even its most ardent champions had never claimed that Tel Aviv was a notably clean city.

It was, however, an extraordinarily active one. It was the national centre for finance, including the Stock Exchange, commerce, banking, the export and import trade, transport and marketing. It was the home of the political parties, the employers' associations, the Histadrut, the national orchestra, the national opera, all but one of the main theatre companies, all but one of the newspapers. It was the national fashion centre. Three-quarters of all the books issued in Israel were published in Tel Aviv. Although its port had closed down when Ashdod opened, it was still the busiest city in the country. During the daytime its population doubled. At the time of the morning rush-hour—7-8 a.m.—200,000 ve-

hicles, more than half of all there were in the entire
State, moved and parked in its streets. They had 153
sets of traffic lights to stop at—or accidentally to blun-
der through—compared with only seven in 1960.

Two-thirds of all the agricultural produce marketed in
Israel went through Tel Aviv's wholesale fruit and vegetable market, which operated for twenty hours each
week-day. In the year 1965 more than 300,000 tons of
fruit and vegetables were sold there. And that was not
the only market. The Carmel retail market, slam in the
middle of town, creating pedestrian jams right under the
shadow of the Shalom Tower, contained 475 stalls—
300 selling fruit and vegetables, 90 purveying clothes
and haberdashery, all of them supplying sufficient noise
to give the least sensitive ear-drums the hardest time
they could know. In Jaffa the vast warren of a flea market contained genuine antique bargains for those with
discernment to trace them, and stalls full of kitsch for
customers who did not really care.

Tell Aviv was a city which worked hard. Every day a
quarter of all Israelis who earned their living were employed there: 236,400 in 1969. Two out of every five
Israelis who worked in commerce and banking turned
up daily at some office in Tel Aviv. It provided jobs for
36 per cent of workers in industry, crafts and construction, 31.5 per cent of those engaged in public business
and personal services, 20 per cent of employees in commerce and banking. One-quarter of all Israeli working
women worked in Tel Aviv. Of Tel Aviv's labour force,
60 per cent (133,400) came from inside the city, and
40 per cent from outside. Another 19,000 Tel Aviv citizens went outside their home town to work. Employment opportunities in the town were provided in 11,441
factories and workshops, 45.9 per cent of all the plants
in the country. This proportion was placed a little in
perspective by the information that the average of employees per plant was only 6.6. All the time, these establishments gave a tolerable living to those trained to work
in the clothing industry (16.9 per cent of workplaces),
in metal products and machines (16.1 per cent), timber
and furniture (15.5 per cent), shoes and other leather

goods (12 per cent). Two craft and industrial centres
had been set up in Tel Aviv, by the Government and
municipality in Har Zion Boulevard, and by the Rassco
Company in Jaffa. Another was planned near the Hatikvah quarter.

Once the money was earned, Tel Aviv was unstinting
in making available opportunities to spend it. It had
1,015 grocery shops, 1,258 restaurants, cafés and steak
bars (including some of increasing elegance, and even
some where the food was really quite good), 465 kiosks
and 777 hairdressers and beauty parlours. There were
also 85 driving schools—though, in view of the consistently lethal activities on all Tel Aviv thoroughfares,
what went on at these places of instruction was a matter
of continuing mystery.

The city was the national centre for entertainment. In
1970 300,000 music lovers attended concerts there, and
290,000 tickets were sold for theatrical performances.
The attendance at Tel Aviv's 39 cinemas was a whop-
ping 9,097,296. This was three million down on the
peak in 1968—the year television started up in Israel
—but was still twice the national average and ahead of
both other large cities. With 16 per cent of the country's
cinema seats, Tel Aviv movie box offices accounted for
one-quarter of all attendances.

Here too was the national sporting centre. In addition
to Yad Eliahu there were the 22,000-seater Bloomfield
stadium, home of the Histadrut's Tel Aviv Hapoel and
built at the expense of two Canadian brothers named
Bloomfield, and also the Maccabi stadium which, with
15,000 seats, was headquarters of Tel Aviv Maccabi.
There was a one million Israeli pounds youth centre,
financed half by the municipality, half by the Federation
of Jewish Relief Organizations of Great Britain. On the
coast road north, in Ramat Aviv, there was a growing
and impressive museum complex, Haaretz, with a glass
museum, a numismatic museum, a museum of ethnology
and folklore (including the Tel Kassile excavations into
Tel Aviv's own past) and the soft, low dome of the Las-
ky Planetarium. There was even a zoo, established in
1940, always about to move to more spacious pastures,

but meanwhile housing its 797 furred and feathered inmates at a most fashionable address not far from Ben Gurion's Tel Aviv *pied-à-terre*.

If citizens had ample opportunities for playing, they were not denied places where they could pray. There were 682 synagogues, ministered to by 136 rabbis. One of the hotels on Ben Yehuda Street, the Deborah, was of so orthodox a persuasion that it provided on its premises a synagogue for the convenience of pious patrons: for, of course, Tel Aviv with all its attractions was increasingly beset with visitors. In the year 1970–1 one-third of all tourist nights in Israel were spent in Tel Aviv's 2,758 hotel rooms. These nights were spent in varying degrees of comfort, for Tel Aviv could offer a grade two hotel on the most fashionable tourist street where the visitor's rest was disturbed by noxious odours, a grade one hotel near-by where the tourist was slightly incommoded by holes in the floor left by hurriedly departing builders and, slightly up the road, de luxe accommodation perfect in every detail except that an artistically gnawed apple core grinned at the sleepy traveller from the bedside table. Of Tel Aviv's 61 hotels, only 41 were recommended for tourists. All carefully graded by the star system, 32 had no stars at all and just three were awarded five-star rating.

For visitors, however lodged, the city had a racy charm. To wander in the Yemenite quarter—the Kerem Hatemanim—just a footstep from Allenby Street, was to enter a mysterious, dank area of old buildings and winding lanes. Prostitutes lurked hopefully in doorways. Small steaming restaurants offered spiced food intended to be eaten as often as not only with the fingers, while from the wall stared the engrossed photographed faces of the area's beloved Shimshon football team. In this rough-at-the-edges city it was no surprise to learn that only one out of every eight stall-holders in the Carmel Market actually had a permit to trade there, that just 1,100 of the city's 2,500 pedlars troubled to apply for a licence, that 15,000 householders were connected to that most abstruse of all law infringements, illegal sewage. Tel Aviv, as the definitive Jewish urban microcosm, was seized by that gambling mania which had long given even the most downtrodden Jew the wild hope of better times one day Of all the Mifal Hapayis lottery tickets old in Israel one-third—33.6 per cent —were bought in Tel Aviv.

Yet for all that, Tel Aviv was unusual among large cities for the sober good conduct of its inhabitants. In 1968 its crime rate was below the national level, with some 12.7 per cent of the country's transgressors. Juvenile delinquency was even less prevalent; only 11.5 per cent of Israel's young wrongdoers came from Tel Aviv. The city's marriages were extraordinarily stable. The 1969 divorce rate of 1 3 per thousand compared with a national rate of 1 8

Its problems lay in other directions. While Tel Aviv provided services and pastimes suitable for a population containing groups able to afford all manner of personal luxuries, its municipal services were inadequate to meet the needs of the population as a whole. It had remarkably few green spaces. Public gardens, woods, boulevards and parks accounted for only 6.3 per cent of its area. Its fifteen hospitals were appallingly overcrowded. While a Tel Aviv citizen laid low by one of the town's most common ailments—heart diseases, diseases of the genital organs, diseases of the digestive and respiratory systems— was more likely than other Israelis to be driven to the hospital in the family car, when he got there he had far less chance of actually being put to bed. The Ichilov hospital, designed to hold 350 patients at very maximum, was being compelled to treat 500. The number of hospital beds per thousand Tel Aviv inhabitants had risen between 1961 and 1969 from 3.9 to 5. But it still compared poorly with the national average of 7.9.

There was a ready explanation for both Tel Aviv's unusually low juvenile deliquency rate and its difficulty in coping with those afflicted with illnesses associated with advanced adulthood. The city was ageing. In 1948 more than a quarter of its population—26.6 per cent— was 14 years old or below. By 1967 this proportion had fallen to 21.7 per cent. The percentage of over-45s, on the other hand, had risen in the same period from 22.6 to 37.6. And the over-65s had more than doubled, from 4.4 per cent to 10.7. The birth-rate was low; the death-rate was rising; as a result, Tel Aviv's natural increase had fallen from 11.2 per thousand in 1960 to 5.1 in 1969. Fewer recruits for the city's primary schools were coming forward. Between the school years 1961–2 and 1970–1, their pupils fell in number from 60,956 to 41,064.

The people who lived in Tel Aviv remained a varied collection. All but six thousand were Jews, the Arabs being divided 55-44 between Moslems and Christians. As late as 1967 only two in five of the Jews were Israeli-born, with a slightly higher number born in Europe or America, and the remaining 19 per cent coming from Asia or Africa. By far the largest foreign-born contingent, 74,200, were Russians and Poles. Nearly 43,000 more were from Romania and Bulgaria, and 12,116 from Germany and Austria. The main representatives of oriental Jewry were 14,451 Iraqis and 11,251 Turks. But the telling fact, of which the primary school registers were a token, was that these Jewish all-sorts were components of a declining population.

Tel Aviv was a cosmopolis and a metropolis. Although it was individualistic enough not to be a microcosm of all the other major world urban centres, in one characteristic it was fully representative—and at high speed. Other major cities of the world had taken centuries to reach their zenith as areas of mass population, and then found that their centres were less heavily populated than they ought to have been. Tel Aviv managed to complete this process in not much more than half a century. Between independence in 1948 and 1963, the number of its citizens rose at first sharply, and then gradually, from 248,300 to 394,400. But that was the peak. Every year after 1963 the population fell. By 1972 it was down to 362,000. The number of Tel Aviv inhabitants as a proportion of the people of Israel declined from 28.4 per cent in 1948 to 11.5 per cent in 1972. And this, curiously, was in a city which in the same period spread physically to the north, the south and the east, so that its area was nearly tripled.

This did not, however, mean that Tel Aviv was dying, but that—as in other major world cities—its people were growing so prosperous that they had decided they preferred suburban life to city living. Ringed around Tel Aviv, from north to south, were half a dozen suburban or ex-urban areas: Herzlia, Bnei Brak, Ramat Gan, Givatayim, Holon, and Bat Yam. Each had its own character. Herzlia possessed a beach area where the country's most ostentatious hotels opened their doors to tourists whose blinkered view of Israel was confined to sea, sun and room service. Bnei Brak was an enclave of religious orthodoxy, where males, both aged and young, could be observed strolling in costumes and coiffures which Rembrandt himself might have painted. Bat Yam had an architecturally adventurous town hall, with tiles far from an optional extra, which might have been mistaken by a casual visitor for the largest public convenience in the world.

And all were growing at very great speed. In 21 years Ramat Gan had multiplied its population sixfold, to a total of 112,600. None of the others had expanded to over the 100,000 level. But all except Givatayim, whose 44,000 population was a mere five times the 1948 level, had expanded faster. There were seven times as many people in Bnei Brak and Herzlia, nine times as many in Holon, and in Bat Yam—perhaps attracted by the evident facilities—the number of inhabitants had grown from 2,330 to 76,600—a 37-fold increase. The population of greater Tel Aviv as a whole was up from 301,570 to 808,200. Despite the Government's population dispersal policies, the Great Wen that had once been a garden suburb in 1969 housed 27.7 per cent of all Israelis, compared with 34.5 per cent in 1948, when the total population of the new State was very much smaller.

People did not get all soulful about being citizens of Tel Aviv, as they did about Jerusalem. But whereas Jerusalem was a sleepy, surprisingly dreary backwater which was universally accepted as embodying Israel's spiritual aspirations, Tel Aviv was equally undoubtedly Israel's adrenalin. It was not representative of the country because it was over-urbanized, over-sophisticated, and much less socialist politically. But it generated a tension and a somewhat erratic sense of vivacious activity which invigorated the life of Israel.

People loved to go to Jerusalem, but went there out of love not out of necessity. They went to Tel Aviv not out of affection, but because that was where the action was. Nobody needed to know what was going on in Jerusalem because, apart from Parliament, nothing was. Everybody had to know what was going on in Tel Aviv or he did not really know what was going on in his own country.

No one could yet insist that the Israeli who was tired of Tel Aviv was tired of life. Israel was a country where life had many different areas of focus. Nor was Tel Aviv by the 1970s a city which rewarded sightseeing; there was nothing old, and new and attractive buildings had only just begun to go up. But—and this was more than could be said of New York—it was a city with a future. It was getting rid of its old eyesores, its slums and its squalid areas. It was beginning to generate its own excitement. And, most important of all, it was beginning to generate a remarkable charm. To wander in Old Jaffa or in Malchei Israel Square, or to gaze from the top of the Shalom Tower, was to catch in the throat a feeling that this was a place to which one must return.

The garden suburb had been swallowed by megalopolis, Israeli style. But that style was homely as well as sharp, human as well as ambitious. Car drivers quarrelled and blew their horns at each other, but did so in cosy personal antagonism rather than in general irritation. Restaurant proprietors in the very centre of town happily remembered visitors whom they saw no more than a couple of times a year. Tel Aviv had a chance of success because, in the middle of its increasingly fervent efforts to become a great city, it never forgot its small-town heart.

7

Full and Equal

There was an exotic atmosphere of celebration in downtown Haifa on the afternoon of Thursday 14 October 1971. After lying derelict for twenty-three years, ever since 1948, the Istiklal mosque was being reopened; an austere and expensive reconstruction had been carried out at much cost to Moslem community funds. On so festive an occasion many Arab dignitaries were present. They included the Israeli Arab mayor of Nazareth and the mayors of Jenin and Hebron, in the occupied West Bank territory. Sheikh Mohammed Al Ja'abari, itinerant and loquacious Mayor of Hebron, was eloquent in his appeal to the King of Saudi Arabia to permit Israeli Arabs to make the sacred Haj pilgrimage to Mecca—and indeed subsequently received a message telling him that the twenty-three-year ban was at last to be lifted. Also in attendance were representatives of the Jewish majority, headed by the Minister for Religious Affairs. The reconstruction of the mosque had been planned by the architectural office of Silberman and Hoffenberg. After the reopening all guests adjourned for refreshments to a reception at the Zion Hotel.

Nine months earlier, another, grimmer aspect of Arab-Jewish relations in Israel had been highlighted. On 4 January, before a military tribunal at Ramleh, Nasser Mansour, aged twenty-two, and Abdel Karim Mahmud Nasser, one year younger, confessed to charges of possessing three hand grenades, received from a gang of terrorists, and were each sentenced to imprisonment for seven years. Ten days later another military court sent twenty-two-year-old Said Mustafa Abu Barech to jail

157

for thirty years after finding him guilty of planting hand grenades which two months previously had killed two persons and wounded twenty-four in the Tel Aviv bus station. All three were young Arabs who had been born in the independent State of Israel and had known no other homeland.

Which of these violently contrasting examples was the truer reflection of Arab life in Israel, and of the 350,000 Arabs' attitudes towards their Jewish fellow citizens? The semi-literate monthly publication *Free Palestine*, and other propagandists for the cause of what some regarded as terrorism and others as a liberation movement, would be in no doubt. To them the three young convicts were heroes who symbolized the will to freedom which burned among all the Arabs living under the Israeli yoke. The ever-hopeful information services of the Israeli Government constantly sought to persuade outsiders that the ecumenical sweetness and light of the Haifa ceremonial were much more typical of how Arabs felt about being Israelis. They would undoubtedly quote the statement of Suheil Shukri, trustee to the Wakf religious charitable trust in Haifa, that the rededication of the mosque showed the full religious freedom which the Arab citizens of Israel enjoyed.

Neither was a wholly accurate picture. It was true that there was a certain restiveness among some sections of Israel's Arab population. But in the first twenty years of the State, its exceptionally efficient and vigilant security forces had secured the conviction of only 115 Israeli Arabs for aiding saboteurs. That scarcely denoted a seething populace longing for liberty withheld. On the other hand, the undenied freedom of worship available to all Israelis, regardless of religion, was far from an indication that life for all citizens of the State was equal in all other respects. In the State's first quarter-century the Arabs of Israel had achieved increased civil liberties, higher living standards and greater public recognition of their place in society. They were also better off, in both material and intangible respects, than most other Arabs in most other Middle Eastern countries. But such gains as they had attained had been conferred on them by the country's Jewish majority, who decided both pace and timing. And, by almost every measurable criterion, the Arabs were still considerably behind their Jewish fellow citizens.

Right at the beginning they had, in any case, started off at a serious psychological disadvantage. Arabs had vastly outnumbered Jews in Mandatory Palestine. Even in the area which eventually became Israel they had, before the outbreak of hostilities following the United Nations partition resolution, been a comfortable majority. If that partition resolution had been implemented, they would have formed forty per cent of the population in a small Jewish state umbilically linked to an overwhelmingly Arab neighbour. But when the dust cleared over the borders of the new Israel, expanded in battle from the 5,500 square miles conferred by the UN to a much more substantial territory of 8,000 square miles, those Arabs who remained found themselves in a one-in-seven minority.

There had been three-quarters of a million Arabs living in what was now the State of Israel. In Jaffa 70,000 had had their homes. The mixed town of Haifa had contained 52,000. There were 17,000 in Lod, 15,000 in Ramleh, 12,000 in Acre, 10,000 in Safad, 6,000 in Tiberias. But war, fear, propaganda from their own side, all turned prosperous Arab burghers into refugees— some fleeing in fear of their lives, others gulled into believing that a short and temporary absence would be followed by a victorious return and abandoned Jewish property to be had for the picking. A bloody offensive against Jaffa by Begin's Irgun caused the flight of 65,000 Arabs from that historic town. In Haifa the Jews begged the Arabs to remain, but still almost all of them left. At Lod the Moslems broke a surrender agreement they had made with the Jews, and in consequence all except the old and sick were forced across the Jordan. At the village of Dir Yassin an unspeakable massacre of 254 Arab men, women and children, carried out by the Irgun and the Stern Gang on 9 April 1948, and still justified by Begin more than twenty-three years later, was a further incentive to Arabs not to wait and find out how their new Jewish rulers would treat them.

When independence was achieved, only 156,000

Arabs remained to learn for themselves what it was like to be an Israeli. Safad and Tiberias were now completely Jewish towns. Beersheba was deserted. In Acre 7,800 Arabs were left, in Ramleh 2,600, in Lod 2,400. Only in Nazareth did the population stay put, making this sleepy tourist town, with its dubious memorabilia of Jesus, suddenly the biggest Arab habitation in Israel. Galilee, of which Nazareth was a focus, still had a reasonably numerous Arab population. But the centre and south of the country were denuded.

Nor was this exodus weighty only in numbers. It was the kind of Arabs who had gone which left the remainder so lacking in ability to start reshaping their lives. The urban bourgeoisie had gone. And with them had departed political leadership, economic power, intellectual guidance and religious stability; for even the Moslem clergy had run away. Indeed, while half of the Christian Arabs stayed, four out of five of the Moslems had joined the refugees. Left behind were mainly village dwellers who were ninety-five per cent illiterate and whose illiteracy seemed likely to be inherited by their children, since most of the teachers had taken to their heels. This Arab population was to be augmented by some extra thousands who drifted back after the war was over, by others who were subsequently allowed to return under a family reunion scheme, and by an increment of population who came with territory, in the Little Triangle in the centre of the country as well as in the Jerusalem area, which was ceded to Israel under the Rhodes armistice agreements of 1949. But the bewildered rump who had so recently been part of a confident majority now had to pick themselves up and sort themselves out in novel and chastening circumstances.

As far as the new Jewish Government were concerned, it was all going to be all right and there was nothing to worry about. Really, the declaration of independence had made that perfectly clear. What had it said? "We . . . call upon the Arab inhabitants of the State of Israel to preserve the ways of peace and play their part in the development of the State, on the basis of full and equal citizenship and due representation in all its bodies and institutions—provisional and permanent." Had not the Provisional Government which took over after this declaration included a special Minister of Minorities, deliberately assigned to assure the Arabs their rights and to prevent discrimination against them? Were not the Arabs going to be given the vote?

There was, however, a slight problem. Most of these full and equal citizens now promised due representation unfortunately lived in unrepresentative areas. A small proportion—about 20,000—had remained in the mixed towns of Jaffa, Haifa, Acre, Lod and Ramleh. But about half lived in Galilee, where they formed 70 per cent of the population. Some 50,000 were in the Little Triangle area, the very narrow waist which stretched up from Petach Tikvah to Haifa. Another 18,000—all who remained of at least 55,000 before the war—were Beduin roaming the Negev. Well, it would not do for them to roam very much any more; the Negev was a sensitive military area. So far that matter, was Galilee. So, too, was the acute-angled Triangle. In fact it turned out that almost all of these full and equal Arabs were living in closed areas. And this rather limited the way they could live.

It was not the Israelis who could be blamed for introducing the concept of closed areas. These had been invented by the resourceful British, and had been embodied in Section 125 of the Mandate's Defence (Emergency) Regulations, 1945. These permitted a military commander to designate—yes—closed areas, which could be entered or left only on his written authority. So the British, who had handed over to the Arabs of Palestine the apparently impregnable police forts which were sure to give them the victory in any forthcoming hostilities, handed over to the unexpectedly victorious Jews a means by which to control the Arabs. Jaffa, Ramleh and Lod were swiftly, as early as 1948, withdrawn from the sphere of military government. But the other Arab areas remained under it.

And it undeniably made moving about the place difficult. Those who lived inside closed areas could in general travel through those areas without hindrance. But those living outside these areas could not enter them without a permit. Those in them could not move between them or go outside them without a permit. Even inside them, entry into Jewish settlements was not allowed without a permit. Moreover, permit-holders were required to take specified routes, and to be back home by a stated time. And there were frequent roadside inspections to make sure the rules were observed. Permits could be granted for three, six, or even twelve months to Arabs working in a Jewish town. But whether they received a permit was entirely up to the military; and no reason needed to be given if an application was refused. The British had thought of everything.

For the Negev Beduin this system was particularly inhibiting. Tribal chiefs were unrestrained by the pass system. But their followers received permits only in limited numbers and, generally, for short periods. Permits to work outside the reservation were granted only if the written offer of a job was produced, and even then only for a maximum of one month. During the first ten years of the State, this meant that only about one hundred jobs were available outside this particular closed area. In the early 1960s, as many as one thousand Beduin might be allowed out during the citrus picking season. But on the whole the system as operated meant that permanent employment for Beduins outside their closed area was not possible. Nor was this outcome accidental. For, between 1948 and 1958, the government was particularly anxious to ensure job opportunities for Jewish immigrants, and the military government machinery was used as an instrument of this policy. The Ministry of Labour provided helpful guidance to the military, and travel permits for work purposes were not granted without the approval of the labour exchange.

There were barriers, too, in the way of Arabs who had left their homes and now returned with the intention of building a new life. Jews were coming in as well, in very large numbers, and they needed land on which to settle. Now, of course, much land had been abandoned. The Abandoned Areas Ordinance of 1948 even defined it. An "abandoned area" was "any place conquered by or surrendered to armed forces or deserted by all or part of its inhabitants, and which has been declared by order to be an abandoned area." An "abandoned property" was "any property abandoned by its owners in an abandoned area." The problem was that these definitions could be said to cover the majority of Arab villages, where abandonment under the meaning of the ordinance could simply have involved villagers fleeing to shelter in their orchards during shooting. Indeed, there was a *cause célébre* involving six hundred Christian villagers who had done just that.

The population of Kfar Baram, just inside the border with Lebanon, had gone to hide in their orchards and fields when the Israeli army conquered their village. With the war over, they were instructed to take up residence temporarily in the near-by, partly abandoned Moslem village of Jeish. Their exile became more prolonged, and a new Jewish settlement, Kibbutz Baram, took over some of the Kfar Baram lands. In October 1951 the Supreme Court established that the Arab villagers had the right to return to their old homes. But the homes were in a closed area, and they were not allowed back. In September 1953 Kfar Baram was blown up by the army. Some four years later the rest of the villagers' lands were taken over by a new moshav. The dispossessed Arabs were offered compensation—at low 1950 values—and alternative lands. They refused both. From the vantage point of new houses built for them by the Government at Jeish they could watch Jewish settlers farming their own former lands. Their grievance festered long; in 1972 they renewed their campaign to return—and were rebuffed on "security" grounds.

It could be argued that as a conquered people the Arabs of Kfar Baram ought have been grateful for the right to recourse to law, for the offer of any compensation whatever, and for alternative homes provided by the State. All that was perfectly true; except that their government had told them that they were not a conquered people but full and equal citizens. Obviously both Jews and Arabs would take some time to adjust to the new situation and, inevitably, it would be the Arabs who, in the meantime, would be most likely to suffer grievances. There were two views as to how these grievances could best be redressed. One course was to organize and fight the Government. The other was to become part of the governmental system and press the Arab case from within. The first course, obviously, did not necessarily exclude the second, and both were attempted. As the years went by the Arabs discovered that they could make definite, if limited, gains within the ruling coalition. After nearly twenty years they in addition managed to create for themselves their own political party, which made little material headway but did at any rate enable the Arabs to have their own protest movement where they could blow off steam within the system and, indeed, inside the Knesset itself.

The beginning of the long, slow, painful approach to creating this movement took place in November 1948 when rival Jewish and Arab Communist groups united within the Israeli Communist Party, which called for an Arab state in the non-Israeli part of Palestine, the return of refugees, the abolition of military administration and travel restrictions, and equal rights for Israeli Arabs. In the general election of January 1949, 22.2 per cent of all Arab voters supported the Communist Party and helped to elect an Arab Communist to the Knesset. In this election four-fifths of the 33,000 Arabs entitled to a vote actually participated. They included the first Arab women to be given the vote in the whole of the Middle East. But most of the Arabs who participated in this election backed the Government rather than the opposition. Arab lists allied with Mapai attracted 61.3 per cent of the support of their own community, and secured the election of two members to the Knesset. The first outcome of the election was the replacement of the Minister of Minorities by a special adviser for Arab affairs in the office of the Prime Minister himself. This official found himself with a lot of work to do.

It was necessary, to begin with, to re-create the collapsed structure of the minority communities. For there was not only an Arab minority, divided between Moslems and Christians in the ratio of seven to two. There was also another sizeable group, accounting for one-tenth of the non-Jews in Israel. These were the Druses. Throughout the history of the State this small and mysterious sect were to cause the minimum of trouble to the rulers of their country. They had broken away from Islam in the eleventh century. Their tradition had it that they were descendants of Jethro, father-in-law of Moses. Their faith was so arcane that its secrets were unknown even to the majority of those who practised it. Theirs was a religion of the Levant, with the largest group in Syria and others in the Lebanon. In Israel they lived in seventeen mountain villages, nine of their own, eight shared with Arabs, in Western Galilee and on Mount Carmel.

When the Israeli war of independence broke out, the Druse of Palestine had, after an initial hesitation, decided to back the Jews. They therefore backed the winners, and were amply rewarded. Unlike the Arabs they were trusted by the governing majority, and were gradually granted a series of important concessions. Up till 1955 they were permitted to serve voluntarily in the army. But from that year they received the definitive accolade of acceptance: the right to be conscripted. This did not apply to Druse girls, who were carefully sheltered, and whose eventual employment in industry led to a certain amount of controversy. But from now on Druse men were called up for military service. In 1971 a further advance was made in this emancipation under fire, when the Druse were no longer required to serve in special minority units, but could enrol in a number of other units in both the army and navy as well as in the country's two military academies. By then they had distinguished themselves both in the border police (where they were reputed to be particularly tough with Arab terrorist suspects), and ninety of them had been killed in action.

Conscription, then, was one valued token of recognition. Another, and even greater, was bestowed in a law passed by the Knesset in 1956, and proclaimed in April 1957, which for the first time ever gave the Druse the status of a separate religious community. In October 1961 the Druse spiritual leadership was recognized as a Supreme Religious Council. On 25 December 1962 the Druse Ecclesiastical Courts Law was passed, establishing the right of the community to its own courts in all ecclesiastical affairs. On 2 December 1963 the President of the State himself installed the Druse religious judges, and by doing so gave full recognition to this sect's religious autonomy.

Integration continued. In 1967 the Druse were separated from the Arab Departments in the Ministry of Religious Affairs. From now on their dealings with government offices would be through the regular channels available to Jewish citizens, and ahead of them lay novel manifestations of bureaucracy which they had never previously been privileged to encounter. In June 1971 the Histadrut resolved fully to integrate its six thousand Druse members into the labour federation, remove them from the care of the Arab Affairs Department, and award independent status as Labour Councils to the workers' committees in Druse villages. And on 3 October of that year came the ultimate in tributes. Sheikh Jaber Dahish Muadi became the first Druse to hold a government post, when he was appointed Deputy Minister of Communications. Neither he nor anyone else doubted the reason. Said Muadi of his appointment: "It is neither a personal nor a political prize, but a right which the Druse have earned by fulfilling their duty in the country's Defence services." Shmuel Toledano, the Prime Minister's adviser on Arab affairs, confirmed that the houour according to Muadi was "intended to demonstrate to the Druse community and to the whole country the regard and appreciation of the State for its loyalty."

This community, whose numbers by 1971 exceeded 33,000, had earned for itself a tranquil acceptance in a country whose community relations were beset with inevitable suspicion. With a solid agricultural hinterland —farming provided the Druse with forty per cent of their employment—they had also achieved an enviable stability. In Salman Kadmani they had produced their first industrial tycoon, who established his own metal plant near the Druse village of Yarka, and was able to proclaim: "I feel an Israeli citizen 101 per cent."

Stability could not come so quickly to the other minorities. But at any rate early attempts were made to provide it. The first essential was to re-create Moslem religious life in Israel. Most of the clergy had left the country, and religious services had virtually ceased taking place. The newly created Ministry of Religious Affairs launched the reconditioning of the elegant eighteenth-century Al Jazar mosque at Acre. It appointed imams, preachers, muezzins, marriage solemnizers and other functionaries. All judge and court officials having left, the Moslem judiciary had also to be reorganized. This was of especial importance with a nationwide system which assigned all litigation on family matters to religious courts. So four Moslem religious judges—kadis —were appointed to sit in Sharia courts at Nazareth, Acre, Jaffa and in the central region, with a Court of Appeal in Jerusalem. These kadis decided cases in accordance with Moslem religious law. They had absolute and exclusive authority to pass judgment on every aspect of marriage and divorce, including payment of alimony and maintenance, custody of children, legitimization, successions, wills, legacies and administration of property of absent persons.

There were, however, certain State laws under which the kadis had to operate. The Age of Marriage Law, passed on 1 August 1950, made illegal the custom of infant marriage by raising the age of consent to seventeen. The Law of Equal Rights for Women, in 1951, banned polygamy. The Moslem practice of summary divorce, under which the husband could dismiss his wife by the simple formula of repeating "I divorce you" to her three times, was also abolished. These changes, together with the right of the franchise, raised the status of Moslem women higher than it had ever been. But they were still an underprivileged sex, and the continuing source of this inferiority was lack of education.

In 1948 in Palestine only eighteen per cent of Arab girls of school age were actually receiving any schooling. Part of the cause was a traditional feeling that an education was not necessary for females; and this was a notion which would be hard to eradicate. But there was also the fact that educational opportunities as such were limited for Arab children of either sex. Under the Mandate, less than half of Arab children—48 per cent—were going to school. And the ages of attendance spanned only the years from six to twelve. In the first school year of the State, Arab education was minimal. There were 10 Arab kindergartens at which 16 teachers taught 637 infants. There were 45 primary schools, with 170 teachers and 6,766 pupils; 81.4 per cent of these pupils were boys. There was one secondary school, with 14 pupils. There was not a single teacher training college. In the academic year 1951–2, there were just 10 Arab university students.

In 1951 Israel's Arabs took part in a general election whose main issue was Jewish education. By now there were eighty thousand Arab voters, and they managed to increase their community's parliamentary representation. There was a set-back for the Communist Party, which, campaigning for an end to military administration and for complete equality of rights and obligations, including compulsory military service, slipped to 16.3 per cent of Arab support. The lists allied to Mapai, on the other hand, increased their Arab strength to 66.5 per cent, and secured the election of five Knesset members.

These formed part of the parliamentary strength of a coalition government whose main mandate was to pass a Compulsory Education Law, which would benefit Arabs as well as clarify the situation for Jews. But this government provided other benefits too. It introduced complete wage equality for Arabs and Jews in government and public institutions. It provided aid to agriculture, distributing day-old chicks to farmers in a number of villages, granting loans to help with new plantations of olives and bananas, assisting in the installation of olive presses, making grants for ploughing and sowing, providing money for construction of approach roads and for developing springs in the Triangle, and approving 300,000 Israeli pounds as operating capital for Arab tobacco planters, who produced 95 per cent of the country's crop.

Opportunities for Arab self-expression were extended when in October 1954 Arabic broadcasts were extended to an hour a day, with programmes which ranged from news, talks, commentaries and Koran readings, to music, women's and young people's programmes, and greetings from Arab Israelis to relatives abroad. An even greater act of emancipation had taken place the previous year, when Arabs were provided with their own labour exchanges. Up to then, Arabs wishing to find jobs had to do so through the medium of special link men, who had a stranglehold on Arab employment and also depressed take-home wage levels by extracting a cut of the employee's wages as obligatory reward for their efforts. This form of serfdom was made more difficult to practise by the establishment of official institutions where Arabs could find their own jobs. The admission in the same year of Arabs to the affiliated unions of the Histadrut, as well as to its sick fund and mutual aid organizations, also increased their bargaining power.

But it was through education that emancipation would be most assured. Arab education had to be separated from that in Jewish schools because of both language and syllabus differences. But the basic system was to be the same for all communities. Following the passage of the Compulsory Education Law, there was a progressive transfer of Arab school ownership from central government to local authorities. By 1952, eighty Arab local education authorities had been set up, with the responsibility of levying a local rate to pay a twenty-five per cent share of teachers' salaries. Municipal self-government was gradually growing. Nazareth elected its first municipal council in 1954, and in the same year three smaller centres gained their own local councils. More local elections were held in 1955, including a poll for another municipal council at Shefaram. It did not, however, follow that the advance of Arab local self-government would of itself lead uncomplicatedly to progress in increasing educational opportunities.

Arab society was organized in clans, known as *hamulahs*. The heads of these clans accepted the responsibility of delivering the local vote in parliamentary elections to whichever party had offered the best terms for them. This was not corruption but conferment of status in return for positive and observable government help for the village: permits, jobs, licenses, land leases. The *hamulah* heads were generally not keen on the idea of democracy invading their locality. Such an innovation could scarcely increase their influence, and might well diminish it. So they frequently did their best to prevent the establishment of a local council. When one was inevitable, they sought to control it. And if they could not control it, they tried to hamstring it. One way was to have a row about who should be mayor, because such a conflict could bring the whole work of the council to a halt, as occurred at Umm-al-Fahm in 1965, and at Nazareth in 1970. There was, in addition, a generation gap. When a young and personable mayor, Jalal Abu Tuama, gained power in the village of Baka al Gharbieh, and began to proceed with all manner of new-fangled notions—payment of back taxes, paving of roads, extra medical help, university-trained teachers—the traditionalists did not rest until he was unseated.

Where councils did operate, questions of money often caused difficulties. Local taxation was not popular. There was reluctance to accept responsibility for repaying loans or providing a village's share of matching funds. Even when taxation was raised, there was insufficient readiness to spend it. In January 1971 Yosef Burg, Minister of the Interior, complained that, apart from Nazareth, no local authority in a minority area had spent more than two-thirds of its approved budget. Yet the progress of Arab education depended on such expenditure, and secondary education could not progress without it since national compulsory education was confined to primary schools and it was up to the local authorities to provide secondary education. Further, reductions in fees were partly dependent on a contribution from the local authority. Yet secondary education was the key to higher education. What was surprising, therefore, was not that Arab education had fallen behind Jewish education but that it had made such enormous advances.

In the twenty-one years between 1948–9 and 1969–70, the number of Arab kindergartens was multiplied almost eighteenfold, to 177, with 316 teachers—almost twenty times as many as before—and 10,357 pupils, sixteen times more than in the immediate post-independence period. In elementary education progress was proportionately less massive but in absolute terms even more impressive. There were 207 schools, nearly five times as many as in 1948; 2,483 teachers, nearly fifteen times as many; and 65,784 pupils, an almost ten-fold increase. Moreover, within this vastly greater elementary school population, the balance of the sexes was much more even. Whereas in 1948 the boys outnumbered the girls by more than four to one, now they accounted for 56.1 per cent of the names on the registers. And this educational drive brought results. In 1948, 95 per cent of Israeli Arabs were illiterate; by 1971, 95 per cent were literate, at any rate to some extent.

Their school syllabus included Hebrew (from the fourth grade), English (from the sixth grade), Islamic and Arab history, and geography, including that of neighbouring countries. Like Jewish children, they took the *Seker* test. And like Jewish oriental children, their pass mark was specially reduced. Nevertheless, there were still far too few Arab children at secondary schools. By 1969–70, there were eighteen of these, with a total enrolment of 3,820. About a quarter were girls, which was at any rate an improvement on the negligible number in 1948. Including vocational and agricultural schools as well, the number of Arab children receiving some kind of secondary education was higher, at 7,549. Their subjects of study widened to include Arab literature and Jewish history. But their drop-out tendencies were high and their rate of measurable success was low. In 1968–9, only 630 Arab children passed the *Bagrut* matriculation.

This was one of the reasons for the pitiably small number of Arabs studying at Israel's universities. Another was the financial circumstances of the parents of would-be students. The size of Arab families was generally large, and the parents could simply not spare enough money to educate all their children. So although it was perfectly true that sixty times as many Arabs were at university in 1970–1 as in 1951–2, those six hundred were only just over one per cent of the aggregate university population; on a straight proportional basis, there should have been more than six thousand Arab university students. Even of the six hundred, hardly any were girls.

This reluctance to allow girls to receive more education than was insisted on by the state was reflected not only among pupils but among teachers. Whereas among the Jews two out of three teachers were women, among the Arabs the proportion was thirty per cent. Yet at any rate some notable progress had been made in teacher training. A college had been established in Jaffa in 1956, and was transferred to Haifa in 1963. By 1971 it had 372 students. And in September of that year another college was opened in Jaffa, starting with eighty students. Although there were great problems in Israeli society even for those Arabs who received university degrees, those problems could never be solved until there were far more university graduates. This objective could be achieved only by providing sufficient qualified teachers to start off the education of Arab children on the right foot in their very earliest years.

Arab status in Israel was, in fact, indissolubly linked with prospects for material progress. And in this regard the Government and other public agencies were ready to play their part in co-operation with the Arabs themselves. So began the construction of health centres in the villages. One of the most serious health problems was tuberculosis, and in 1955 a new hospital to combat this disease was opened in Nazareth; seven years later there was such a "significant drop" in the incidence of tuberculosis that the Nazareth hospital could be closed down, and treatment relegated to district clinics. Nazareth benefited, too, from the linking of Arab centres with public utility systems. There were mass celebrations there when, at a cost of 300,000 Israeli pounds, the town was at last connected to the water network in May 1955. The following year the village of Taibeh was linked to the electricity grid, and Daliyat al Carmel and Fureidis were connected to the telephone system.

Larger and more comprehensive programmes were necessary, however, if Israel's Arabs were not to become the Jews' poor country cousins. The Cabinet realized this and, in February 1958, adopted a programme of what it called "economic rehabilitation," involving the housing and resettling of twenty thousand Arabs. The cost, in grants and loans, on very easy terms, was to be 10,500,000 Israeli pounds. In the first three years 750 new homes were to be built. But bigger projects were on their way.

Levi Eshkol was one Israeli leader who approached Arab problems particularly imaginatively. Under his auspices, in April 1961, a five-year plan was launched for the development of Arab rural areas. It came into operation the following year, aiming to invest sufficient resources in Arab villages to complete their essential basic services. These services included piped water, links with the power grid, schools, housing projects, and connection of villages with the national highway network. Municipal and health services were to be expanded. Job opportunities were to be improved, and incomes raised in farming, artisanry, industry and commerce. The planned cost was substantial: 55 million Israeli pounds, 31 million from government sources.

In fact, 84 million pounds were spent, 52,500,000 by the government. And the results at the end of the five years were there not only for Israel's Arabs to benefit from, but also for them to show to their relatives from the newly occupied West Bank when making their first cautious forays over the post-Six-Day War "green line" frontier. Water was now piped to nearly all the villages. The irrigated lands of Arab villages had increased from 1,800 acres in 1948 to 8,000—though this was still a very small part of the 190,000 acres under cultivation by Arab farmers. Items of agricultural machinery in use now numbered 500, rather than the five pieces of apparatus of twenty years before. There had been a major expansion of approach roads for sixty-nine villages.

More than half the Arab population was receiving a regular supply of electricity; not one village had had it in 1948. Arab families were living in 3,100 housing units completed under the plan. The number of clinics opened had been fifty-three, the number of mother-and-child stations thirty-four. With results like this from the first plan, another made good sense and was started in 1967. This one was to cost 115 million pounds. Its objective was to complete and reinforce basic services, to expand and strengthen education and health, to increase employment in the villages, and to provide jobs for women.

The expansion of the Arab work-force had already led to a basic change in the constitution of the most significant institution in the State, the Histadrut. Already the Arabs had been admitted to its subordinate trade unions and had won for themselves equality as far as salaries, working conditions, and fringe and social benefits were concerned. They were also allowed to take part in its cultural and sporting activities. They had their own special Arab section, Brith Poalei Israel (Alliance of Israeli Workers). But full membership of the organization had been denied to Arabs. How could it be otherwise, when its full title was the General Federation of Jewish Labour? Now, however, in 1959 the seventy-first Histadrut General Council passed a resolution. "The Council resolves to admit Arab workers and others of minority communities to Histadrut membership on the basis of complete equality of rights and duties, and entrusts the Executive Committee to ready the necessary arrangements for implementing this decision." Recruiting proceeded and, by the time of the 1965 nationwide Histadrut elections, 36,000 Arab members were eligible to vote. Nine out of ten of them did so, expressing a three-to-one preference for the Mapai alignment over the Communists. The following year the Histadrut returned the vote of confidence by changing its name to the General Federation of Labour in Israel.

Admission of Arabs to membership of political parties had not, however, been so easy. The Arabs had been in at the birth of the post-independence Communist Party, and from the start their membership was not in question. But the other political parties, being Zionist in nature, were neither so easy nor so attractive to join. Mapam had steadily championed Arab rights, but was only able to admit Arabs as equal members of the party when Achdut, who had opposed such a move, split away in 1954. This led to an improvement in Arab support for Mapam in the 1955 election, although it was the Mapai allied lists which continued to attract almost two-thirds of Arab support. The *hamulah* heads liked to be on the winning side, and everyone knew that Mapai always won.

Comfortable patronage was not, however, the answer

to minority grievances, and in 1958 an attempt was made to found a protest group, the Arab Front. Renamed the Popular Front, this aroused alarm in the Government, which tried to suppress it by use of the emergency regulations. However, it was in any case a doomed organization. The Communists muscled in, adopting their customary course of attempting to ride on the back of a genuine popular movement. But when President Nasser split with Kassem of Iraq and inconveniently denounced communism, the Popular Front no longer had a chance. As was to be seen in later elections, Nasser had more influence over the Arab Israeli vote than any Israeli Arab, and the Jewish parties shrewdly exploited this situation. The Popular Front was smothered.

The 1959 election was therefore fought between the traditional parties—though with one complication. Mapai thoughtlessly ended its liaison with some of its Arab allies, among whom were two members of the Knesset. These dignitaries indignantly organized their own lists in rivalry to Mapai's own protégés, and drew away sufficient votes to reduce Mapai support to little more than half of the Arab votes. And these were a great many votes, for the registered Arab electorate was now as high as 94,000, and 88.9 per cent were induced to use their franchise. The Communists, recognizing Mapai's difficulties, fought hard for this support, promising an end to military administration and permission for all refugees to return. They had also, in 1956, been handed an extremely telling emotional issue.

During the brief Sinai war of October-November 1956, Arabs had been subject to curfew restrictions. In the southern Arab village of Kfar Kasim, on the border due east of Tel Aviv, this curfew led to tragic misunderstanding. The local police opened fire, and forty-three Arabs were slaughtered in what was an accidental but undoubted massacre. There was a trial. The police commander was sentenced to seventeen years in prison, and his subordinates to seven years. The survivors received financial compensation. But the episode inevitably left psychological bruises, since both during the war and before it Israel's Arabs had shown no disposition to disloyalty and had even formed an army unit of Christian volunteers. Kfar Kasim was a ready-made grievance for the Communist electioneers to exploit in the 1959 campaign.

Curiously, however, they did badly out of it. Although they capitalized on the massacre, and attacked the Sinai campaign for good measure, their support among the Arabs dwindled to only ten per cent. For the first time ever, they were overtaken by Mapam who, whatever else might be said about them, could never be accused of cynicism. In their campaign Mapam continued to urge the end of military administration and also called for employment opportunities for Arab intellectuals. They themselves had done what they could to foster the Arab intellect by initiating the publication of Arab books and periodicals. They were rewarded with one out of every eight Arab votes.

Still an Arab spirit of protest against the system went unrepresented. In 1960 another attempt was made to give it a voice. After considerable litigation Al Ard became the first extremist movement to be legally registered as a company. It was a small group, whose membership probably never exceeded twenty, although its support was certainly much more than that. In any case, it worried the authorities even more than had the Popular Front. At the end of 1964, Al Ard was banned as hostile to the State, which it certainly was. In the 1965 election it made a valiant, if hopeless, attempt to run an Arab Socialist list, but was denied permission and consequently evaporated. By that time, however, a real and much more solidly-based Arab party had made a highly successful appearance.

The 1961 election, forced on Israel by the Lavon Affair, had been for the country's Arabs just another election in which the same old parties competed for its support by emphasizing the same old issues: jobs, land claims, the military administration. Mapai, damaged by a suspect land law, secured little more than half of Arab support. Mapam fought on its pro-Arab record, but lost a few votes on the pro-peace, anti-military administration treadmill. The Communists, however, presenting an uncompromisingly nationalist image, more than doubled their support. They were, indeed, so strong that they were ready to indulge themselves in the Israeli political luxury of splitting. This they at leisure proceeded to do.

The Arab members of the party went on record against what they described as Israeli "imperialism." Then, in preparation for the 1965 election, in August of that year two separate Communist Party national congresses were held. Each concentrated its fire on the other. The split was between Jews and Arabs. One faction was associated with Zionism, the other with Arab nationalism. The Jews fully recognized the rights of Arab Israelis and the struggle for socialism in some Arab countries; but they still wanted to canvass for the support of Jewish Communists, and they were later chauvinistic enough to warn against cutting expenditure on the nation's defence. The Arabs were totally against Israel's Arab policy and attached greater emphasis to the struggles of the Arab peoples towards socialism and liberation. They regarded the Israeli Arabs as an offshoot of both the Palestinian Arabs and of the Arab nation, and equal in national rights to the Jews. Both groups, at odds over almost everything else, were still as one in their addiction to Communist jargon.

The Arab faction broke away from the party to found a new group, called first the Jewish-Arab List and then the New Communist List. But they took the old party's newspaper with them. While the original Communist Party retained scarcely any Arab membership, the New Communists did include a certain proportion of Jews—perhaps as many as thirty per cent. But in the 1965 election they got only 3,344 Jewish votes. This was scarcely surprising. The New Communists made a determined set for Arab votes, aiming at teachers, students and workers, especially Arab villagers whose need to work in the towns gave them a particular feeling of isolation.

The first electoral appearance of this new party was damaging to the established groups. Mapai slipped back a little further to just a fingernail's width more than fifty per cent of Arab support. Mapam had ruled itself out as a party of protest by declaring that it was ready to enter the coalition government. Its attacks on the Government for anti-Arab discrimination were accordingly not en-

tirely accepted, and it received only 9.2 per cent of the
Arab vote. The Jewish Communists did their best to
make the running on the usual issues of military admin-
istration, Arab lands and the return of refugees. But
against the New Communists, who accused them of
"Jewish deviationism," they never had a chance. Even
Cairo Radio had advised the Arab voters to support the
New Communists, and 22.6 per cent of the 130,000 did
so. This was a remarkable showing for a first try. On the
other hand, the support of less than a quarter of Israeli
Arabs for a party which conceded nothing whatever to
Jewish susceptibilities, which was the first ever truly
Arab political party in Israel, and which had been
awarded the endorsement of President Nasser himself,
showed that the bug of stability had infected even that
section of the Israeli population which should have possessed maximun immunity against it.

In any case, this was the last election in which the tor-
mented issue of the military administration was to be
manipulated by any of the parties. For a new Prime
Minister, Levi Eshkol, had found his strength and decided what he wanted to do. Ben Gurion had, against
constant opposition from many Jews, been adamant in
his insistence that controls over movement of Arabs for
security reasons must remain. In face of pressure he had
gradually reduced these controls. The Arab residents of
Tel Aviv, Jaffa, Haifa, Acre, Ramleh and Lod had at
an early stage been freed from military rule. But that
still left nine out of ten Arabs subject to it.

In 1953 certain relaxations were introduced in the
system of issuing movement permits and demarcating
control zones. In 1954 much more sweeping improvements were made. In the north, twenty-nine closed areas
were completely abolished. Within the zones, unimped-
ed travel was permitted. Permits were required now only
for those wishing to travel outside the closed areas. This
greatly reduced delays and shortened the queues. From
August 1955 the validity of temporary permits was extended from two weeks to a month, and what were
known as permanent permits were now good for a year
instead of six months. There were, however, still areas
—notably the border areas of the Little Triangle—

where a curfew was in force. Its duration was cut—in 1957—to five night hours, from 11 p.m. to 4 a.m., giving an extra hour of free movement at each end. At the same time restrictions on access to the northern centres of Afula, Acre and Nazareth were eased, and general entry permits were granted for large areas in the north.

There was an election in 1959 and three months before it, in August, the number of closed areas was drastically reduced, from fifty-four to sixteen. Limitations on non-Jews going to Jewish centres for work and business reasons were removed. Free movement was permitted by day to practically all Jewish centres except divided Jerusalem, perched as it was right on top of the border. Following the election in 1961, there was a further sudden rush of parliamentary activity over the question of military government. Several opposition members of the Knesset introduced bills to abolish the system altogether. These were withdrawn after Ben Gurion had announced a series of relaxations but insisted that it would be unwise to go further. The concessions included making annual permits valid for almost the whole country, with no specified destination or route.

Parliamentary opponents of military government had, however, now tasted blood and were beginning to close in. On 2 February 1963 they forced a debate in the Knesset. And this time it was not simply opposition members. Supporters of the Government too attacked the continuance of restrictions. The assault came from the most loyal benches of the chamber: from Achdut, from the NRP, even from members of Mapai itself. Ben Gurion, fighting a rearguard action, resorted to the most potent weapon in his armoury—the threat of resignation. On this basis he won the slenderest possible victory, by fifty-seven votes to fifty-six. But, like the system of military government itself, Ben Gurion's premiership was in its final phase. When Eshkol succeeded him in that same year he lost little time in preparing liberalization measures. On 21 October he announced them.

Military government as such was not yet abolished. But restrictions on movement in all closed areas was removed, except in the case of Arab villages right on the border, and for individuals regarded as security risks.

General exit permits from the northern and central areas
now became the rule. But Eshkol regarded these mitiga-
tions as neither satisfactory nor final. In January 1966
he announced further relaxations. Except for certain
sparsely inhabited areas on the northern border, Galilee
was to be opened up immediately, with general entry
permits the rule. General exit permits were provided for
the Negev, lifting the burden from the Beduin. And the
Prime Minister promised that the whole apparatus of
military government would be dismantled before the end
of the year. He kept his word. An announcement of the
ending of all restrictions was made on 24 October, and
military administration was definitively abolished on 1
December 1966. The closed areas were "normalized"
and all offices administering the system were shut down.
Israel's Arabs had had to wait more than eighteen years
to be given the same right to move about their country
as other citizens. They could at any rate take comfort
from the knowledge that Jewish parties had fought for
their rights, and a Jewish government had nearly fallen
because of their denial.

To a nomadic people like the Beduin, restrictions on
movement had perhaps been more stifling than to any
other Arabs. The Israeli Government had, however,
from the very beginning of the State done its best to
compensate by taking special measures to help these
tribes, who lived closer than any other Israelis to the
fringes of subsistence. They had been introduced to the
novelties of mass X-rays as part of the Government's
anti-tuberculosis campaign. Pipelines had been laid to
their encampments in the north-east Negev at a cost of
50,000 Israeli pounds. By 1956 drinking water was
being provided for all the tribes in the Negev. A clinic
was built for them in Beersheba. And in the 1960s a
new concept in the approach to Beduin problems was
introduced: "sedentarization," the provision of settled
places of habitation.

It was all very well for a tourist driving swiftly
through the Negev to stare entranced at the Beduin
black tents, and to note with a smile the incongruity of
television aerials attached to the dwelling of the local
sheikh. It was a moment's amusement to tip with a mini-

mal coin a Beduin child who offered to pose pictur-
esquely against an Instamatic depiction of the ruins of
Avdat. But reliable shelter, with satisfactory amenities
and good prospects for their families, were as important
to these dark-complexioned slum dwellers of the desert
as they were to an immigrant from New York or Moscow. A start was made not in the Negev, but in Galilee,
where twenty-five tribes—more than a third of the Beduin—lived. By 1965 the first Galilee Beduin village,
Bosmat Tivon, was ready, and three more were planned.
Not only houses were to be built, but schools, public
buildings, a clinic and a mosque. The same pattern was
to be applied in the Negev, where the first two sites—
Shuval and Ksifa, near Beersheba—were assigned. The
locations were chosen to suit existing encampments as
well as tribal structure.

That structure was, however, having to adapt itself to
a changing world. Not only were Beduin living habits
changing. So was the way they earned their living. Cultivation of wheat and barley, keeping of such livestock as
sheep, goats and camels, were, with the slowly won consent of the sheikhs, gradually undergoing a transition to
industry and services. Education, too, was coming to
the Beduin. Under the Mandate, the sixty thousand then
living in the Negev had had to make do with seven
schools. During Israel's war of independence, many Beduin, marginally involved in the fighting, had left Israel.
Now, in the early 1970s, with their numbers down to
twenty-five thousand, 2,500 of their children were being
taught in sixteen schools. Their education was far from
perfect. Only seven of the 103 teachers were qualified,
and northern Arab teachers refused to go among them,
regarding such postings as "exile." But successes were
being chalked up. On 7 January 1971 Yunis Abu Ra-
beiyeh celebrated his achievement as the first Beduin
ever to complete medical studies in Israel, having graduated from the Hadassah Medical School. He was one of
ten children. His eldest brother was an electrical contractor in Beersheba. One of his younger brothers was
studying law at the Hebrew University.

Israel's Beduin, more than thirty thousand of them,
were coming in out of the heat. On 17 June 1971 the in-

auguration ceremony was held for their latest permanent settlement, Bir el-Maksur, in western Galilee. The village contained 150 villa-type homes, all with running water, and paid for by the Beduin themselves. The occasion was marked by euphuistic encomiums. The local Mukhtar pledged on behalf of his tribe, many of whom served in the army and border police: "There is no sacrifice we will not make for the State," adding, more practically: "We are farmers and shepherds, soldiers, and now that we are not illiterate any more many of us have outside jobs, too, and we all make good money." The guest of honour at the ceremony, the officer commanding Central Command, was no less fulsome and no less down to earth. "You go with us shoulder to shoulder into danger and fire . . . . As you share our fate in war, so shall you share it in peace, and we shall see to it that you share the same amenities as Jewish citizens."

On a heady summer day, addressed to a proud, euphoric and somewhat idiosyncratic audience, these remarks rang true. But how, after twenty years and more of Israeli independence, did the progress of the country's 350,000 Arabs measure up to such large and undoubtedly honestly intended promises? In many ways the Government had been beneficent. Whether it was distributing compensation to Arab tobacco farmers faced with losses caused by blue mould, or providing special school broadcasts for Arab children, or supplying running water in every house in Nazareth, the Government undeniably meant well.

It could cite example after example to prove how Arabs were prospering as citizens of the Israeli State. To begin with, Arabs were part of that State, represented in its Parliament. After the initial elections Arab representation in the Knesset had never fallen below seven members and had sometimes risen as high as eight. Local self-government had spread to nearly fifty Arab towns and villages, with others included in regional councils. These centres were easier to reach: eighty had been provided with approach roads, and only seventeen of the smallest still lacked such access. The community had its own, very ample, radio and television programmes, including even the latest Middle Eastern pop songs, recorded off transmissions from neighbouring countries. They were an increasingly healthy community. There were seventy-five mother-and-child care centres in Arab and Druse localities, and the Histadrut's Kupat Holim had established forty-three medical centres for them.

The results could not fail to impress. By 1970, nine out of ten Arab births took place in hospital, compared with one out of twenty in 1950. More Arab babies were surviving. Between 1955 and 1970 the infant death-rate fell from 62.5 per thousand to 41.8, and although this was still twice the more slowly falling Jewish rate, it was less than half of that in Egypt and lower than in any other Arab Middle Eastern country. The death-rate had fallen from 8.8 per thousand to 6.6 between 1951 and 1970, while the Jewish rate had actually risen and, at 7.3, had overtaken the Arabs. Accordingly, in 1969 the Arab natural increase rate per thousand was 39, with the Jews panting hard behind at 16.9. Israeli Arabs were increasing faster than almost any other group in the world. Moreover, they could expect to live for 70 years, while a Jordanian's life expectancy was 52.6 years and an Egyptian's 51.6.

So more Israeli Arabs were being born, more were staying alive, and they were living progressively longer. What could they expect from life itself? It was here that the outlook was less promising. Despite all the efforts of the Government, Arabs were still living far less well than Jews. In 1968–9, the average income of an Arab family was 601.2 Israeli pounds a month, while the national average stood at 1,005.8. But the situation was even worse than these comparative incomes implied. For the average family nationally numbered 3.7, while the average Arab family was six. So, when it came to material goods, the Arabs were well behind in the race for affluence. In 1970 only 11.8 per cent had a washing machine, compared with 42.8 per cent nationally. Refrigerator ownership was 26.8 per cent, compared with 88.9 per cent in the country as a whole. Less than two-thirds of Arab families—60.7 per cent—had a gas range, as against a national figure of 85.8 per cent. They were even behind in ownership of the most widely available consumer toy: 75.6 per cent had radios, the national percentage being 89.9. As for television, the most recent entry in economists' sedulously compiled lists of luxury consumer durables, by 1970 half the families in Israel owned a set, but only 14.3 per cent of the Arabs.

The gap was wide; but no one would deny that it had been wider in 1948. The problem, however, was that Israel's Arabs, while insufficiently emancipated economically, had since the foundation of the State acquired higher expectations. By the early 1970s well over half of them had been born into Israel as Israeli citizens, and it was by Israeli standards that they judged themselves. Those members of the working class whose education did not extend beyond primary level were the most contented. Their living standards and working conditions were far higher than those of other Arabs in other countries. It was true that Israeli Arabs who wanted good wages in factories had to travel from their villages into the towns, as forty thousand did, to work for Jewish employers. But at any rate their full membership of the Histadrut ensured that they received the same trade union protection as Jewish workers. By 1971, 60 per cent of the Arab and Druse labour force belonged to the Histadrut: 36,000 out of a total of 60,000. Histadrut activities reached into 90 of the 115 Arab and Druse localities in Israel, and even involved 1,200 Beduin. Including wives and children, nearly half the Arab population of Israel was covered by the Histadrut and its welfare services and agencies.

Those Arabs who aspired to something higher than well-paid factory work did not, however, bask in unthinking placidity. For their occupational opportunities were more restricted than those either of Israeli Jews or Arabs in neighbouring countries. The white collar jobs of the Mandatory civil service and the British army had gone. And now most Arabs who had received higher education found that they had been educated above the range of jobs available to them. They could teach, of course. But if they wanted a clerical job they found that there was not much scope among their own community. To get such a job in the Jewish sector depended largely on personal connections, and lack of such connections stringently limited choice. It was the same in other fields. An Arab knew that he could not, say, become a fighter pilot, with the singular social prestige that brought; he was a security risk. Jobs in government service were limited for the same reason. If he was a student, he could not feel that the path to a lectureship was open to him. All too often the Arab with a post-primary education, who did not himself wish to remain part of the educational system, faced the bitter choice between manual work and unemployment.

The Israeli Government was, of course, aware of these difficulties and, being genuinely anxious to remove them, was ready to make gestures. Recognizing that the proportion of Arabs in government offices was too low, it decided to provide civil service jobs for 150 Arabs even though their paper qualifications did not make them eligible. But even so, these Arabs were not accepting what was naturally their right, but receiving largesse. A writer in the newspaper *Maariv* admitted: "Nor is the day close at hand when an Arab will serve as Director-General of a Ministry, or as manager of a major Israel public company." It was the same in politics. Arabs found their way into Parliament, it was true. But they did so mainly through deals with the Jewish politicians, rather than on the strength of their own qualities. They generally concentrated on specific Arab topics rather than participated as equals in national political controversies. And with the State's quarter-century milepost approaching, no Arab had yet sat in an Israeli Cabinet.

Indeed, it was only in 1971 that Arabs were appointed to junior ministerial office. And this happened not because two members of the minority communities were outstandingly eligible for government posts, but as the consequence of a municipal squabble in Nazareth. Its population now risen to 33,000, the town had gone to the polls in municipal elections and—complete Israelis in this characteristic if in nothing else—the voters had produced deadlock. The position was almost inextricably entangled because political differences were snarled up with personal rivalries. Two of Nazareth's leading politicians were distant cousins and deadly rivals. Seif ed-Din Zouabi, Labour Party ally, Deputy Knesset Speaker, and ex-mayor of Nazareth was faced by Abd el

Aziz Zouabi, Mapam parliamentarian and would-be
Minister. But Abd el Aziz was younger than Seif ed-
Din, as well as member of a less important component of
the coalition. So Seif ed-Din had to be accommodated
first. Seif ed-Din's Nazareth opponents were determined
to stop him becoming mayor again, so the only way out
seemed to be to make him a Minister too—and first.

Unfortunately, Seif ed-Din had said he would not accept such a post if Abd el Aziz got one. The result was
immobility. The situation was only sorted out when in-
tervention at the highest level secured the Nazareth
mayoralty for Seif ed-Din. Accordingly, the way was
now clear for Abd el Aziz; and on 17 May 1971 he
made Israeli history by becoming the first Arab to hold
government office when the Cabinet confirmed his appointment as Deputy Minister of Health. But this was
not the end of the acrimony and confusion. Both Zoua-
bis were Moslems, and the Druse and Christian communities now felt slighted. Their respective susceptibilities were smoothed in October when Sheikh Jaber
Muadi was appointed Deputy Minister of Communications, and when a Christian member of the Knesset, Elias
Nakhleh, was appointed to the Deputy Speakership
which Seif ed-Din Zouabi had vacated after returning to
the mayor's office in Nazareth. This was not the politics
of merit so much as the politics of the smoke-filled room
and the pork barrel. Nevertheless, this episode in manipulation had with one exception involved every leading
Arab politician in Israel. Seif ed-Din Zouabi, born in
1913, had sat in five of the first seven Knessets. Abd el
Aziz, thirteen years younger, had entered Parliament
only in the sixth Knesset but, during a prolonged love-
hate relationship with Mapam, had been director of the
party's Arab publishing house and editor of its Arab
weekly, as well as, inevitably if briefly, mayor of Nazareth. The Arab with the longest continuous record of
parliamentary service was Tawfik Tawbi, a Communist
who, like many of his fellow-Arab members of the only
party which had throughout permitted Arab membership, was a Greek Orthodox Christian. He was probably
the single Arab member of the Knesset who genuinely
represented his community's feelings.

For those Arabs who were now in the Government were open to the charge of being Uncle Toms. Although Arabs had made progress in many fields since 1948, their position in society had congealed. They were stuck geographically, living in the same places as they had inhabited more than two decades before. The Christians, who still formed about a quarter of the Arab population, were mainly urban. The Moslems were two-thirds rural, and dominated the Triangle area. As a proportion of the population in Galilee the Arabs had, it was true, fallen only to fifty per cent. But this was because Jews had been brought into such new towns as Upper Nazareth and Carmiel as part of a deliberate policy of diluting Arab areas: scarcely a token of communal trust.

The Arabs were permitted to have many Arabic newspapers, and these were subjected to no greater censorship than any others in the country; Arabic poetry and fiction tended to be critical of the State, and no harm was done. The editors or reporters or proprietors of those newspapers with the largest circulations were, however, likely to be Jewish, although the Communist paper was completely Arab run. The Arabs were allotted sixteen hours a day of radio programmes and an hour a day on television, but it was Jews who decided the allotment.

The Arabs were not controlled by the Jews, but they were supervised. The two sectors, completely separate before 1948, were now integrated economically and in terms of employment. But they were far from integrated socially. It was not that there was major friction. When, as happened in Jaffa in 1969, for example, Arab pedlars were set upon by Jewish louts, a Jewish passer-by was ready to come to their aid, and the magistrate inflicted punitive sentences. Well-meaning attempts at finding amicable meeting-points were made. The Haifa municipality set up a mixed Arab-Jewish community centre, managed by young Arabs, and with one thousand members. At the Hebrew University a Jewish-Arab student circle was formed. But these were exceptional enterprises. David Zekaria, who became Director of the Labour Party's Arab Department in 1970, ruefully admitted that "usually—despite everyone's best intentions—Arab-Jewish gatherings draw only about ten per cent

Jews and real dialogue is rare." Social contact between
school pupils or students, let alone among adults, was
minimal. In more than twenty years there had been only
about six hundred marriages between Arabs and Jews;
generally, as in the marriage of Abd el Aziz Zouabi, it
was the bride who was Jewish. Generally, any social
contact was made on Jewish terms. It had to be since,
while it was a necessity of life for Arabs to speak Hebrew, Jews could get along without knowing a word of
Arabic. By 1971, sixty thousand Arabs aged between
sixteen and twenty spoke fluent Hebrew, and had studied such Jewish works of literature as Bialik's *Slaughter
Town*, dealing with a pogrom in Russia. But that same
year only 21,665 out of 483,000 Jewish schoolchildren
were learning Arabic. Of Israel's Prime Ministers, the
only one who could speak his country's second legal language was Moshe Sharett.

The Arabs complained that the Israelis did not trust
them. They cited their exemption from conscription to
the armed forces, and their exclusion from Knesset
standing committee deliberations on defence and foreign
affairs. But they were honest enough to confess that in
some ways the mistrust was merited. A young Arab,
questioned about where his loyalties lay, would admit
that he thought of himself not simply as an Israeli but as
an Arab Israeli. He would be frank in agreeing that he
was sorrier to hear of the death in battle of an Arab
from another country than about the killing of a Jew
from his own. He insisted on his willingness to serve in
the Israeli armed forces—but not in the front line,
where he might kill another Arab.

The Jews, for their part, would claim that the problems of their country's Arabs were similar to those of
oriental Jews; that the gap existed because the two communities were jogging along the course from different
starting points, and that a couple of decades had not
been long enough for the Arabs to catch up. They pointed out that Arabs were often held back by their own traditional restrictiveness rather than by any wish of the
Jews to suppress their aspirations.

In the end, the future place of the Arabs in Israel depended on two developments. The first was a definitive

settlement between Israel and her Arab neighbours, so that simultaneously, Jewish mistrust of a possible enemy in their midst, and the tug on the Arabs of conflicting loyalties, might at last disappear. The second requirement was the emergence of a new generation of Arab leaders, ready to take their place in the country's political life not as the agents, the cat's-paws or the clients of the Jewish politicians, but as their confident equals. Jalal Abu Tuama, ousted by the *hamulah* system as mayor of Baka al Gharbieh at the age of twenty-three, knew that such emancipation involved a fight—a fight against his own parents, against the preconceptions of his Arab friends, and against the clan system as much as against the Jewish party system which had allocated a fixed place in Israeli politics to Arabs. Two of his sisters had, in the face of parental reluctance, attained secondary education. He himself had been appointed director of a new section at the Histadrut dealing with problems of young Arab workers. He planned to return to politics and to fight elections. But he saw that new Arabs had to set themselves new objectives:

"The State of Israel did not just come about by accident; it was planned. We have to work out plans to employ university-trained Arabs in the villages. If you give them jobs in Tel Aviv, you do not solve the problem. The young Arab will never really be happy in Tel Aviv, and his village will remain backward. If we brought industry to the villages and also employed educated Arabs in fields like public administration, we could solve the problems of the individual and of the village. They will not live in the village if they cannot find cultural and social life there. But there will never be real cultural and social life if we, the young educated people, do not create it. We have to take the initiative, but the Government must help."

The Israeli Government had to do all it could—more than it had—to ensure that the Arabs of its country achieved full equality. But the Government could not do it all. The young Arabs, too, had to decide whether they wanted to sit back and enjoy their grievances or set out to eradicate them.

8

A Great Wind Blew

Twenty-five years after the end of the Second World War, in which so many of them had been killed so methodically, there were some fourteen million Jews living in 117 countries, including, at the latest count, thirty in the principality of Liechtenstein. At the outbreak of the war, when the world's Jewish population had been 16,600,000, three per cent of that population was living in Palestine. In 1948, six per cent of the world's much smaller residue of Jewish survivors found themselves citizens of the new State of Israel. By 1969 Israel accounted for eighteen per cent of world Jewry.

But these two decades and more had not witnessed a simple process of more Jews being born and more of these moving from their birthplace to go and live in an Israel which, by the power of the law, had its gates open ready to receive them. Matters had been less uncomplicated than that. The post-1945 period had certainly brought about a strong, direct tidal flow of Jews from every continent heading for home in Israel. It had also seen sub-currents taking migrant Jews from one exile to another, rejecting Israel as a home while accepting it more than ever before as a mythic homeland. The most convulsive movements of wandering Jews which the world had known for nearly two thousand years had produced not only a new pattern of world Jewish population, but also a totally new relationship between the Jews scattered through the Diaspora and the holy land to which they had ever turned to pray.

Some of these 117 communities had been relatively little touched by the migratory movements. Others had actually been augmented. Many had been drastically reduced. And a number of the oldest and largest had been almost eliminated.

In Curaçao eight hundred members of the most venerable Jewish community in the western hemisphere whiled away their time in the Caribbean sunlight, worshipping at an eighteenth-century synagogue and burying their dead in a seventeenth-century cemetery. The thirty of Liechtenstein had no synagogue at all, nor any Jewish school, and conducted their religious services amid what amenities were provided by the tiny tax haven's capital of Vaduz. Immediately to the west twenty thousand Swiss Jews lived comfortable, tidy lives in such neat centres as Zürich, Geneva, Basel and Lausanne, provided with schools, libraries and newspapers, but legally prohibited from providing their own meat by the traditional method of ritual slaughter. Half a world away in distance, centuries in time, the twenty-five thousand Falashas of Ethiopia, whose Judaic history went back at least two thousand years, lived a primitive village life at subsistence level and practised a stern form of pre-Talmudic religion. Another exotic community, certainly one thousand years old and perhaps much more, centred around Bombay in India: the Bene Israel, still numbering fifteen thousand after ten thousand had left for Israel, and celebrating their Judaism devoutly yet in a manner which was nevertheless strongly influenced by the colourful Moslem and Hindu traditions around them.

Augmented by refugees from Europe and Africa, the Jewish centres of Latin America with one exception survived strong, occasionally deeply troubled, but prosperous and loyal to Zion. There were thirty-five thousand Jews in Chile, mostly living in Santiago; ten thousand in Colombia, three-quarters of them in Bogota; more than thirty thousand in Mexico, mostly in Mexico City, but also including 120 Indians claiming Jewish origin; fifty thousand in Uruguay, with one of their number to speak for them in Parliament and two Yiddish daily newspapers in which to read of his activities; more than ten thousand in Venezuela, whose separate Ashkenazi and

Sephardic organizations each had impeccably Spanish titles.

The two largest Jewish communities in the Americas south of the United States were in Brazil and Argentina. The Brazilians had increased to 160,000, following waves of immigration from Europe before the Second World War, and from both Europe and Egypt up to 1962. Centred mainly around Rio de Janeiro and São Paulo, Brazil's Jews had won for themselves a lively place in the country's life. They had supplied it with Ministers of Foreign Affairs and of Finance, as well as members of both the Parliament and state legislatures. But internally the community was in poor shape. Its central representative body, the Jewish Confederation of Brazil, failed adequately to co-ordinate the many Jewish institutions. And the appearance of these institutions was sometimes more imposing than the reality. The boast that there were six thousand pupils in eight Jewish schools in Rio could not fail to impress; but only ninety minutes of their weekly curriculum was devoted to Jewish studies. The 250 families in Recife made up the longest-established Jewish community in Latin America. Despite their offer of a monumental salary they were, however, unable to attract anyone to perform the necessary ritual duties of cantor-slaughterer-circumciser-Hebrew teacher. Among the country's Jews generally, intermarriage was widespread and increasing.

There were more than twice as many Jews in Argentina as in Brazil. In fact, totalling 475,000; this was the fifth largest Jewish community in the world, comprising 140 local communities and dating back some 110 years. The Jews of Argentina were mainly Ashkenazim of Eastern European, German and Hungarian origin. But there were also 55,000 Sephardis who originated in Arab countries and others whose natural language was Argentina's own Spanish. The community was mainly concentrated in the capital of Buenos Aires, where its 350,000-plus adherents accounted for one-tenth of the total population. Twenty thousand of their children were being educated at forty-two Hebrew day schools. Their parents enthusiastically participated in the activities of variegated organizations, covering so-

cial, cultural and professional groups as well as catering
for women and young people. They prayed together at
two hundred synagogues, mainly of Orthodox affiliation
and tended by seventeen rabbis. They could relax at
home reading a lively Jewish press, including two Yiddish dailies, or watching a weekly sponsored television
programme. If they wished to take their entertainment
away from home, they could choose between presenta-
tions at two Yiddish theatres.

Yet venturing out of doors was not always a safe project for an Argentinian Jew. This was a country where a
large, busy and prosperous Jewish population—mainly
of middle-class status and continually improving their
material position—lived in the shadow of recurring and
ugly anti-Semitic outbreaks. When in 1960 Israeli agents
in Argentina seized the Nazi war criminal Adolf Eichmann, who had pseudonymously found refuge in the
country, an extremist organization named Tacuara retaliated by harassing and even attacking Jews, and was not
clamped down upon by the authorities for two years.
Again, there was no urgent government action to curb
another anti-Semitic campaign in 1969–70, involving
twenty bombing incidents in Jewish schools, synagogues,
newspapers and other institutions. Some Jews, particularly in the smaller communities, responded by opting
out of the community by intermarriage. Others stayed
ardently Jewish but opted out of the country instead. In
1969 there were 1,300 emigrants to Israel, and in 1970
the outward flow increased to two thousand.

This was, however, a small proportion of a large community. In one Latin American country, on the other
hand, a massive exodus of Jews had taken place. Before
the Castro regime came to power in 1959, fourteen
thousand Jews lived in Cuba. In Havana there were
twelve thousand, amply supplied with synagogues, a day
school, rabbis and cantors. The revolutionary government treated them well, readily permitting Zionist activities and even paying the salary of their ritual slaughter-
er. Nevertheless, the new economic atmosphere in the
country did not suit most of them, and they made steadily off, mainly to near-by Miami in the United States,
but to South America and Israel as well. By 1970 there

were less than two thousand remaining, but these were likely to form a permanent remnant; for after May of that year no further emigration applications were being accepted. The Jewish population of Havana, now down to 1,400, continued doggedly to worship at their five synagogues, though able to supply a regular quorum at only one of them.

If Cuba was the one exception to a relatively stable pattern of Jewish life in Central and South America, the only country of the old British Commonwealth where Jews did not live in placidity as well as prosperity was the one Commonwealth member to have been extruded from that organization. Yet the Jews of the Republic of South Africa were so outstandingly well-to-do that, in Harry Oppenheimer, they provided their country with its very richest millionaire. Their plush repose was, however, marred by a niggling fear—the fear that they might be next in line for subjection to the apartheid which Harry Oppenheimer so outspokenly opposed.

Other Jews fought South Africa's racial policies even more courageously than Oppenheimer. They were the core of the anti-apartheid Progressive Party. They sat in Parliament, like Helen Suzman. Like Rabbi Louis Rabinowitz, they lined up with other religious leaders in opposing discrimination. It was Jewish lawyers who led the defence in the four-year treason trial in the 1950s. With the apparatus of a police state ready to crack down upon them, these were people of courage. But in a Jewish population of more than 100,000—3.7 per cent of South Africa's whites—they were only a minority.

It was not surprising that some should try by silent complaisance to ward off a threatening future. For they had a very agreeable present to defend. Not only did South Africa's Jews enjoy all the special comforts reserved for whites. Of Lithuanian origin, they had built up for themselves their own rich and busy Jewish life. Mainly concentrated in Johannesburg—where more than half of them lived—and in Cape Town, and with a communal leadership in which lawyers were especially prominent, this overwhelmingly urban Jewish society met and mated in 345 organizations, prayed in many Orthodox but also in fourteen Reform synagogues, educated more than six thousand of their children in fifteen day schools, and eagerly read their four weekly newspapers. They took part in the republic's politics, and were represented in local government, the Senate, and the House of Representatives. Three Jewish judges sat in the Supreme Court. Distinguished former South African Jews were among Israel's leading diplomatic representatives, having supplied the State with two Ambassadors to London as well as a Foreign Minister, Abba Eban.

But it was in that very relationship with their co-religionists in Israel that the Jews of South Africa were at their most vulnerable. On the one hand, their Zionist feelings were exceedingly strong, and were expressed in outstandingly generous fund-raising. On the other hand, Israel would keep on doing things which South African Jews found very unsettling; for, from time to time, international events compelled Israel to stand up and be counted. On such occasions the South African Jewish Board of Deputies would instinctively recall that their country's most famous bird was the ostrich. Accordingly, their posture tended generally to be rather undignified.

Israel herself believed she had no choice. Shimon Peres, when Minister of Communications, stated the dilemma and how his country faced it. "World Jewry is an Israeli national interest. But when we have to choose between a local Jewish interest and a basic moral problem we give up the local Jewish interest. Such was the case on apartheid. If it weren't for the racist issue I would continue to abstain on UN votes and thus assist local Jewry." But the racist issue existed, and in 1961 Israel voted to censure South Africa at the United Nations. The South African Government retaliated by for a time banning the export of charitable funds to Israel. The Board of Deputies and the Zionist Federation whimpered that Israel should have abstained in the vote.

Ten years later they reacted in a similar way to a similar test. In the spring of 1971 the Israeli Government responded to an appeal by U Thant, Secretary-General of the United Nations, by deciding to contribute 10,000 Israeli pounds to the Organization of African Unity. Once again, the South African Government froze all funds for Israel. Once again the Board of Deputies and the Zionist Federation gathered up their skirts and dissociated themselves from what Israel had done. Some Jews went further. One, cancelling his contributions to the Israel Appeal and the Jewish Day Schools, declared in the *Rand Daily Mail:* "The real protector of the Jewish community in South Africa, strangely enough, is none other than our beloved Prime Minister, Mr. B. J. Vorster, God bless him." All these protestations were pointless, for the OAU rejected the Israeli contribution. By September the ban on funds to Israel had been lifted, and the Finance Minister, Dr. Nicolaas Diederichs, had absolved Israel of the charge of assisting terrorism.

Sometimes the soft-spined loyalty to South Africa of her Jews became quite demeaning. When in 1971 the son of a Scottish immigrant hypothesized that, just as South Africans of British origin would not wish to fight in a war against England, so South African Jews would be unwilling to be involved in a conflict against Israel, Lionel Hodes, General Secretary of the Zionist Federation, drew himself up to his full height. "South African Jews," he insisted, "have always regarded themselves as loyal citizens of South Africa. Past history has shown that South African Jewry rose to the occasion and volunteered during the last war." That, of course, was not the point at all. But it was better to miss the point than to risk causing offence in a country where almost every Jew was comfortably off but no Jew could feel completely comfortable.

In the countries which remained part of the old Commonwealth, however, being radical was no risk, and Jews were more firmly established than they had ever been. The community in New Zealand was small, numbering fewer than five thousand. But they had won more than their share of high national office, from the Premiership to the post of Chief Justice. In Australia there had always been a greater number of Jews, and their total was steadily increasing. The twenty-three thousand living there in 1933 had, as a result of immigration which continued into the post-Second World War period, increased to more than seventy thousand. In this new country the Jews had supplied the first native-born

Governor-General, the uncompromisingly named Sir Isaac Isaacs, as well as Sir John Monash, one of its most famous generals. They were active in national politics, particularly in the Labour Party, and in addition had their own complexly organized communal life.

Australian Jews were mainly Ashkenazim, and nine-tenths of them lived in the two large cities of Sydney and Melbourne. But Jewish life in these two centres was very different. The 28,500 in Sydney tended towards assimilation. In Melbourne, however, the thirty-four thousand Jews were very Jewish indeed. Most of them were of European origin, and they were generally acquainted with the Yiddish language. One in four spoke Yiddish at home. Melbourne's Jewish education was especially well provided for including, in Mount Scopus College, the largest Jewish private school in the world. But these parents were not satisfied to educate their children in general Jewish studies. Seven per cent were actually receiving a full Yiddish education. In the heat of the southern hemisphere, the lore of the Russian *shtetl* was being kept alive.

In Canada, too, the Jewish population was overwhelmingly Orthodox. And it was much larger than in Australia. Augmented by more than sixty thousand post-1945 immigrants, the Jews of Canada numbered 280,000. They lived in Ottawa, Vancouver and Winnipeg, but predominantly in Toronto—some ninety thousand of them—and especially in Montreal, whose 110,000 Jews were disproportionately influential in the city. They had their own Jewish public library. Although Canadian Jews formed less than two per cent of the country's inhabitants, more than a quarter of the students at McGill University, Montreal, were Jewish. At Montreal's Expo 1967, the designer of Habitat, an ingenious new format for community housing, was an expatriate Israeli named Moshe Safdie.

Although there was a problem of intermarriage, with one Canadian Jew in every five marrying out of the faith, education was ensuring a continuing supply of devout infants. Between half and two-thirds of the children in the large cities attended Jewish schools, and in the smaller centres the proportion was even higher. To ensure that the process continued undisturbed, there were three teachers' training schools. And there to welcome the children when they came of age were 206 Hebrew congregations.

Yet the Jews of Canada were not turned inward. With writers like Saul Bellow and Mordecai Richler they provided novels for their fellow-Canadians to read. They helped to govern them, too, in the provincial legislatures and the Federal Parliament: the first Jewish Senator was appointed in 1955. They assisted in the country's administration, by providing public servants as elevated as the Governor of the Bank of Canada. They even had distinguished Jews to spare for Israel and, in Dov Joseph, had supplied that country with one of its most eminent Ministers of Justice.

Jews from Britain, curiously, had made little impact in Israel. Not very many had gone there; in the first twenty years of the Israeli state, there were only eighteen thousand immigrants from England (still generally retaining British passports), although the annual flow had increased to over 1,300 after the Six-Day War. But of course Britain was a very good country for Jews to live in. After an absence of 366 years, following the expulsion of 1290, they had enjoyed more than three hundred years of continuous and increasingly entrenched settlement. The Board of Deputies of British Jews, whose four hundred members were elected by synagogues and other associations, had celebrated its bicentenary in 1960. The *Jewish Chronicle,* the oldest Jewish newspaper in the world, had been founded in 1841 and 130 years later waxed fatter and fatter, its occasional property supplements slightly embarrassing readers who felt that Jews ought not to be so ostentatiously affluent.

The unabashed participation of Britain's 450,000 Jews in their country's life took not only themselves but sometimes also their fellow citizens by surprise. When in 1971 the BBC drew up a list of articulate members of the intelligentsia who might be suitable for a new radio Brains Trust programme, it discovered to its embarrassment that, of the thirty-five names which had been collected, every single one was Jewish. Jews like Harold Pinter, Arnold Wesker, Bernard Kops, Frank Marcus,

Peter Shaffer, were among the best-known playwrights. The Grade family dominated popular entertainment; Sir Isaac Wolfson combined retailing with philanthropy to an extent rivalled only by the Sieffs of Marks and Spencer; the name Clore symbolized property deals. In every election dozens of Jews were elected to Parliament—in 1970 there were forty—and no Cabinet was complete without its Jewish representative, whether John Diamond or Harold Lever in a Labour government, or Sir Keith Joseph in a Conservative administration.

Yet all this was the icing on a happily humdrum cake. Jewish life in Britain was in the main based firmly on the home and the synagogue. What was remarkable was not that many marriages—between a fifth and a third —were made out of the faith but that, in a country which made assimilation so easy, the proportion was so low. The main communities were in London (280,000), Manchester (38,000), Leeds (15,000) and Glasgow (more than 13,000). Other substantial centres were Liverpool, Brighton, Birmingham and Cardiff. Here were to be found synagogues—more than two hundred in London alone—butchers' shops, delicatessens and restaurants, including Bloom's of Whitechapel, the most famous kosher restaurant in Europe, whose portions of salt beef were sizeable enough to match its reputation.

The proportion of children in Britain provided with a Jewish schooling was probably higher than anywhere in the world except Israel. Of those aged between five and seventeen, it was reckoned that fifty-four per cent received some form of Jewish education: ten thousand in Jewish day schools, twenty-five thousand on Sundays or on some other part-time basis. In November 1971 the Chief Rabbi, Dr. Immanuel Jakobovits, launched a £6,500,000 education programme for primary and secondary schools in London and the provinces, and aimed at covering the next ten to fifteen years. Its motivation was "the primacy of education in securing the survival and regeneration of Anglo-Jewry." Meanwhile, Anglo-Jewry was ensuring that Israeli Jewry survived. Millions of pounds were collected every year: £12,430,000 was raised during the year of the Six-Day War, and the appeal on the eve of the Day of Atonement in 1970 brought in £400,000. The contribution was not only in money but in people. Athough emigration to Israel remained at a low figure, those who went were young, forty-seven per cent of them aged between nineteen and twenty-nine. Nine Zionist youth movements, whose nine thousand members were all linked with political parties in Israel, existed to maintain the flow. And a seventeen thousand-member Federation of Women Zionists urged them tearfully on.

British Jews were lucky. Their relatives and friends may have suffered cruelly during the Hitler war; but they themselves had remained untouched. On the Continent of Europe, only a stride away across the Channel, there had however been changes—brought about by mass murder and mass population movements—which had drastically altered the Jewish demographic map. Before the Second World War, in Europe west of the Soviet frontier, there were major Jewish communities in Romania (800,000), Hungary (725,000), Germany (525,000), Czechoslovakia (360,000), France (300,000), Austria (181,000), Holland (140,000), Greece (77,000), Yugoslavia (75,000), Belgium (more than 65,000), Bulgaria (45,000), Italy (45,000). Poland, with 3,250,000 Jews, forming ten per cent of the country's population, was one of the major Jewish centres of the world. By the early 1970s, Nazi extermination, Communist persecution and the magnetic attraction of Israel had reduced the Jews of Poland to only nine thousand. Yet this pitiful remnant was still the third largest Jewish community of Eastern Europe.

Some of the Communist satellite countries treated their Jews well. Bulgaria at the end of the war had freely allowed them to leave for Israel, and only six thousand remained behind. East Germany was regarded as the very best place for Jews in Communist Europe. There were only 1,300 left, and most of these were elderly. Nevertheless the State had built new synagogues at public expense in Erfurt, Dresden and Magdeburg, and government representatives made a point of attending Jewish memorial services. Hans Seigewasser, Secretary of State for Church Affairs, pleaded: "We hope that among our Jewish fellow citizens the conviction will grow that the Socialist German Democratic Republic is the true political homeland for all of them." To prove it, three Jews were placed on the Politburo. Like other Communist regimes, the East Germans distinguished between anti-Semitism, which they professed to abhor, and anti-Zionism, of which they were guttural exponents. Nevertheless, their "Jewish fellow citizens" in 1967 felt sufficiently secure to reject a government suggestion that they hold an anti-Zionist protest demonstration.

In Hungary, too, there was this careful separation of Judaism and Zionism. In 1949 the Communists had liquidated the Zionist movement, and imprisoned many of its leaders on charges of encouraging and organizing illegal emigration. In that same year, however, three thousand Jews were permitted to leave for Israel. Another ten thousand were allowed to go there in 1956–7, under a family reunion scheme. This was brought to an end in September 1957. But if the Jews who remained in Hungary were in effect prisoners, at least they were reasonably popular prisoners. Indeed, one cause of anti-Semitic tendencies in the country had been that until 1953 the dictator of Hungary, and head of its Communist Party, was a Jew named Matyas Rakosi who tended to have other Jews as his associates. By 1970, almost a quarter of the members of the Central Committee were Jews, as were two out of thirteen Politburo members. Hungary had shown itself ready to give positions of power to members of a small minority.

For, of almost three-quarters of a million Jews in 1941, 400,000 had been put to death by the Nazis. By 1971 only 80,000 remained, most of them in Budapest. Their communal life was controlled by the Central Board of Hungarian Jews, under the supervision of a state authority for religious affairs. It was, especially by the standards of Communist Europe, quite a colourful communal life. In Budapest alone there were thirty synagogues. The Jews had their own secondary education system, as well as a yeshivah and a rabbinical seminary. The Central Board published a fortnightly, *New Life*, and maintained a museum. The State played its part. It subsidized the payment of ecclesiastical and lay officials, and the maintenance of schools, a hospital, an orphanage, and social welfare services including old age homes. There was even a monthly radio broadcast of Jewish religious services.

Comparable government support existed in Romania as well. Here only half the pre-war number of 800,000 Jews had remained at the end of the war in May 1945. Large numbers had been in territories ceded to Hungary and the USSR. There was a mass emigration to Israel, totalling more than 200,000. Still, 100,000 were left, and found themselves in the only Eastern European country which was ready to maintain good relations with the State of Israel at the time of the Six-Day War. In Romanian life, Jews found it possible to reach key positions, most notoriously the Foreign Ministry appointment of the redoubtable Anna Pauker. They were, in addition, allowed great freedom to live their own lives as Jews.

Indeed, the bi-monthly publication *Revista Cultului Mozaic*, issued by the Federation of Jewish Communities, contained the only Hebrew page available in all Eastern Europe. The Jews here were recognized as an ethnic minority, with their Chief Rabbi sitting in Parliament to represent them. Anti-Semitism was a punishable crime. The Jewish population, nearly half of it living in Bucharest, had two hundred synagogues from which to choose. It could refresh its mind with entertainments at a State-financed Yiddish theatre, or with books either borrowed from the Jewish library or published in Yiddish by the State Publishing House. *In the Light of the Torah*, the first book on Judaism to appear in Romania since the Second World War, was issued in 1971 as the work of the Chief Rabbi himself.

In Yugoslavia, too, the small residue of Jews— 60,000 had been killed by the Nazis, more than 7,000 had gone to Israel, some 6,500 survived—were not prevented from reaching key political positions, and were permitted to organize in their own Federation of Jewish Communities. But in Poland and Czechoslovakia existence had been more traumatic. Of that vast pre-war Polish community, 2,900,000 Jews had been the victims of Hitler's final solution. But, for those who were left, trouble was not at an end. For a period it seemed that less anguished times had arrived. In the first two years of the State of Israel, 84,260 Polish Jews were allowed to go there. Emigration was subsequently limited but, when it resumed in 1956, another 35,000 departed, again mainly to Israel.

Meanwhile, Jews in the country were accepted into its political life, and were provided with such showpieces as a Yiddish State Theatre in Warsaw, a Jewish Historical Institute and a Yiddish newspaper. But, after the student riots of 1968, an anti-Semitic campaign was launched, under the familiar anti-Zionist disguise. Jews were purged from government and party posts, from the armed forces, the universities and the mass media. This was the cue for further emigration, which the Government positively assisted by providing special facilities for Zionists to leave for Israel. But life for those who remained was one of dismal harassment. The announcement in June 1969 of a 1 September deadline for emigration applications led to a further frantic rush, and to the twelve thousand who had already left were added a further five thousand. Many drifted to Denmark. The few thousands who stayed were mostly old and ill. A wonderfully strong and vivacious nine hundred-year-old Jewish community had been blown away on the wind.

If the fate of the Jews of Poland was tragic, that of their neighbours in Czechoslovakia was even more bitter. More than a quarter of a million had died at the hands of the Nazis, and it seemed that Czechoslovakia had taken their slaughter to heart. She helped to supply the infant State of Israel with badly needed arms and, in the first two years of her independence, twenty thousand Czech Jews were allowed to go there. But in 1954 emigration was abruptly stopped. Yet during this time it had become hell to be a Jew in Czechoslovakia.

In 1951, under the impetus of an anti-Jewish campaign in Russia, most Jews in high places in the Czech Communist Party and the State structure were removed from office and imprisoned. Then, on 24 November 1951, Vice-Premier Rudolf Slansky was arrested on a charge of conspiracy. With thirteen others—and eleven of the fourteen were, according to the indictment, "of Jewish origin"—he was exhibited in a show trial. Slan-

sky himself confessed to having engaged a doctor to kill
President Klement Gottwald. Eleven of the defendants,
including Slansky, were executed, and at another trial
not long afterwards five defendants, three of them Jews,
received very long sentences. The press accompanied
these proceedings with virulent anti-Semitic comments.

Subsequently, and gradually, Jews were reinstated in
influential positions. But it would have been better for
them to be left in obscurity. For, during the "Prague
Spring" of Alexander Dubcek in 1968, several Jewish
politicians, journalists, writers and artists were actively
involved in his liberalization movement. They shared his
disgrace and, after the Russians took over in August
1968, were even accused of being part of an international Jewish conspiracy. Another ten thousand were im-
pelled to get out of the country. Of this thousand-year-
old community, no more than ten thousand now
remained. They were old, predominantly over fifty, and
their confidence was gone. It was perfectly safe for the
State to make generous gestures to them: to give financial support to the Jewish Museum in Prague, to finance
the salaries of their rabbis, and to allow them to have
kosher meat. After all, even animals at the zoo were fed
the food they liked.

The two main Jewish communities of southern Europe had fared very differently. Just eight thousand of
Italy's Jews had been killed by the Nazis, for Mussolini's
variegated vices did not include fixated anti-Semitism.
The Jews of Italy were later augmented by some 2,500
co-religionists who arrived from Libya after the Six-Day
War. The population hovered around the thirty-five
thousand mark, with nearly half in Rome. If Rudolf
Slansky darkly symbolized Czech Jewry to the world,
Italian Jews were more cheerfully represented by the
typewriter king, Arrigo Olivetti. In Greece, however, a
much stronger community had suffered a much more
doom-laden fate. Salonika had been the principal Jewish
city of the eastern Mediterranean. It was thought to
have been settled as early as the fourth century B.C., and
St. Paul was said to have preached at a synagogue there.
By the outbreak of war in 1941, 56,000 Jews out of a

national total of 77,000 were still living in Salonika, and worshipping at sixty synagogues.

The Germans soon put a stop to that. Out of every eight Greek Jews, seven were murdered. Of the five thousand who remained, three thousand clustered around Athens. Only 1,300 stayed in Salonika, and just two of their synagogues remained open. The Athenian Jews were predominantly middle class—wealthy tradesmen, industrialists, bankers and lawyers—and were able to maintain their own day school in a plush suburb. Their Central Board of Jewish Communities, which coordinated communal activities, was, like all similar organizations, appointed by the colonels' junta. But, after everything they had been through, the Greek Jews could put up with that.

In Austria, Jews were not only at the receiving end of the laws; they also made them. Even though he was a non-observant Jew, Dr. Bruno Kreisky, the socialist Chancellor who in 1971 made Austrian history by winning the republic's first over-all parliamentary majority, was still Jewish enough to attract anti-Semitic jokes from the forty-five per cent of Austrians who admitted to harbouring anti-Jewish prejudices. But there were not many other Jews to act as focus for such sentiments. One-third of Austria's Jews had been murdered, and of the eleven thousand who remained in 1971—9,180 in Vienna—many were refugees from Poland and Hungary.

In West Germany, too, a high proportion of the thirty thousand Jews—indeed, more than half—had come from Eastern Europe. Of the pre-war population, 200,000 had been disposed of by Germany's own most famous Chancellor. Now the survivors, mainly middle-aged and elderly, cowered at such anti-Semitic manifestations as swastika daubings and desecration of Jewish cemeteries. Some of the more fastidious cringed also at the ostentatious manner in which the state demonstrated its magnanimous readiness to be forgiven, as at the ceremonial observation in 1971 of the 1,300th anniversary of West Berlin's Jewish community. In West Berlin six thousand Jews were present to witness the celebrations.

Hovering over them, as witnesses from the past, were the 150,000 Jews who had once lived in the now divided city. There was at least the solace that the reparations paid in their name had helped the State of Israel to survive.

Some of the German Jews had moved over to Holland, where they helped a little to fill the massive gap caused by the massacre of 100,000 Dutch Jews. Of the thirty thousand who by the early 1970s lived in the country, about eleven thousand were in Amsterdam, where they helped to maintain a Portuguese synagogue which was in itself a handsome architectural monument, a Jewish museum, and the house where young Anne Frank had hidden with her family. But the Jews of Holland were a frail group. Their death-rate was fourteen per thousand, while their birth-rate, at nine per thousand, was less than half the national level. The intermarriage rate was high. And it was estimated that only 280 men regularly attended Sabbath morning services.

Belgian Jewry, like that in Australia, was divided between two very different cities. Out of the forty thousand who remained following the murder by the Nazis of twenty-six thousand, and after cross-currents of emigration and immigration, some twenty thousand lived in Brussels and another twelve thousand in Antwerp. Brussels was the headquarters of the Chief Rabbi, who was paid by the state. But the city contained no Jewish quarter, and few of its children received a Jewish education. In Antwerp, on the other hand, there was a very rich Jewish life, based on the prosperity of the diamond industry. Here there were five day schools, a yeshivah and, for the fraternally minded, a B'nai B'rith lodge.

But while most European Jewish communities had experienced their vicissitudes, some of the very harshest nature, none had received the revivifying transfusion of population which totally transformed Jewish life in France. From being in Jewish terms no more than a middle-ranking state before the war, it had by the 1970s become by far the largest Jewish community on the European continent west of Russia; for Jews, indeed, it was now the fourth most important country in the world. Up to 1939 the 300,000 French Jews had been divided into two groups: those whose families had lived in France for many years, and others, often Yiddish speaking, who had come from Eastern Europe between the wars. The Germans killed 110,000. But the survivors were augmented by 80,000 Jews who came from Central and Eastern Europe. This, however, was far from the end of the influx. Jews had long played a prominent part in French political life, contributing Prime Ministers such as Léon Blum, René Mayer and Michel Debré (who, though himself non-observant, was the grandson of a Chief Rabbi). Another of these, without consciously planning it, was to be responsible for political changes which doubled the Jewish population in France.

It was Pierre Mendès-France who, by giving internal autonomy to Tunisia in 1954, provided the impetus to Jewish emigration from North Africa. Between 1954 and 1970 hundreds of thousands of Jews moved across the Mediterranean. They travelled from Tunisia, Algeria and Morocco. But 250,000 of them, instead of going eastwards to Israel, went north to France. Partly it was because they were French speaking. In the case of 130,000 Algerian Jews, they had the added incentive of all the privileges of French citizenship. In France these North Africans found to their dismay that their co-religionists already established on the mainland were apathetic towards their Jewish identity; many were even assimilationist. It was for the Sephardi newcomers to redress the balance. And this they very readily did.

They transformed the composition of the Jewish community. The Ashkenazim were businessmen, teachers and members of the liberal professions. The North Africans were artisans and small shopkeepers. The Ashkenazim contributed militants to the New Left, including even anti-Zionist partisans. The Sephardim were ardently Zionist. It was they who numerically came to dominate the community and took over its leadership. And, as traditionalists who set great store by family life, they ensured the preservation of Jewish customs and the Jewish spirit in France.

Now there were 550,000 Jews in the country. There were 300,000 in Paris, 70,000 in Marseilles, considerable numbers also in Nice, Toulouse and Strasbourg. The 128 Jewish communities of 1957 had increased to 300 in 1970. They continued their contribution to French national life, with several sitting in the National Assembly and others bagging Nobel prizes in physics, physiology and medicine. But they maintained their Jewish existence as well, with social and cultural organizations, an educational system, and three Yiddish daily newspapers. Moreover, their differing origins did not divide them. By the early 1970s, forty-three per cent of the North African Jews were marrying Ashkenazim.

Support for Israel was stronger than ever before. When the Six-Day War broke out, $2 million was collected in half that period. President de Gaulle did not like any of this. He denounced the Jews as "an élite people, sure of itself and dominating." If the Jews were dominating, de Gaulle himself presently had cause to regret it. Many political commentators took the view that the Jewish vote, coupled with Jewish influence, was decisive in the referendum which in 1969 drove him into his final exile.

That so many North African Jews should have opted to live in France was a decided snub to Israel. But the Israelis, while sad at the loss of a single Jew who could have helped to settle spaces which only a people with an idiosyncratic notion of emptiness could have regarded as vacant, did not have time to mope too much. For in the ten years after independence they were fully extended in settling hundreds of thousands of other Jews—many, indeed, from North Africa—who had come not only from the disaster areas of Europe but also from the remotest recesses of the Moslem world.

For a strange and infinitely moving process had begun. The Jews of the Orient, many of whom had never heard of Zionism, were making the trek, sometimes long, sometimes slow, and sometimes exceedingly painful, back to the reborn holy land. When their journeyings were finished, only three Moslem countries retained any substantial Jewish population. Many of the most ancient centres of the Hebrew exile were left almost completely devoid of Jews.

It started in the Yemen. Here, at the very tip of

southern Arabia, lived a devout, simple and exceptionally pious community of Jews who had survived centuries of repression and underprivilege. When the message came to them that the State of Israel was in being—and they received the tidings through the prosaic medium of the radio—they began to set out to Aden as the base for the journey up the Red Sea. In a harsh and barbarous country many of them endured great privation and some of them died. But they struggled on, in increasing numbers. The Israelis, with the help of other Jews, decided to set up camps near Aden to receive the Yemeni migrants, and to organize an airlift—"Operation Magic Carpet"—to ferry them to Israel. This fulfilled the dream of the Yemenis that they would one day return to the land of David "on the wings of eagles."

These people were so small, so thin, so light, that dozens could be loaded on to each aircraft. The first cargo of Yemenis left Aden on 15 December 1948. In more than four hundred flights between then and September 1950, at a cost of over $4 million, some 48,000 were carried, together with belongings whose weight averaged out at less than twelve pounds. The ingathering of these pious Jews, noted especially for their equable temperaments and fine filigree workmanship, left only five hundred behind. The Jews of Aden itself, numbering more than four thousand, also made their way to Israel.

They came from the south; and, in even greater numbers, from the east. Of the five thousand Jews of Afghanistan, five hundred remained. There had been Jews in Mesopotamia ever since the Babylonian exile of the sixth century B.C. Now, in 1950, they were told by the Iraqi Government that they could leave for Israel, provided they were gone in a year and left their property behind. Another airlift was mounted, variously described as "Operation Ali Baba" and "Operation Ezra and Nehemiah." By the end of 1951, 121,512 out of 130,000 Iraqi Jews were in Israel. They left just in time, for anti-Jewish repression became the policy.

For a time, under the regime of General Abdul Kairm Kassem, from 1958 to 1963, there was an improvement. But it did not last. Jewish existence in Iraq reached a new nadir on 27 January 1969, when eleven alleged spies were publicly hanged. Nine were Jews and, so that there might be no mistake about it, their bodies were labelled accordingly. Ever since 1951 Jews had been managing to get out of Iraq. By the 1970s a small number, perhaps as many as 2,500, remained, mainly in Baghdad, some in Basra. They still had their synagogues and Jewish schools. But their predicament was summed up by Martin Ennals, Secretary-General of Amnesty International, who visited Baghdad in 1970 and reported that Iraqi Jews "live in fear and suffer extreme economic pressure."

The situation of the Jews of Syria was, if anything, worse. Even before the Israeli state was founded, Syrian Jews had begun entering Palestine, with others settling in Lebanon. After 1948, movement into Israel itself was banned, but some thousands still managed to get there. A number, however, remained behind of their own free will. They discovered that they had opted for life in a permanent prison punishment block. These small shop-owners or craftsmen, with their homes principally in Damascus and Aleppo, were barred from many occupations, including the liberal professions, and were permitted to perform manual labour only for other Jews.

They were, moreover, compelled to carry special identity cards—marked in red with the word "Jew"—and, subject to a curfew, were confined to their ghetto and not allowed to move more than two miles from their homes. In a Knesset debate on 1 November 1971, Abba Eban lamented: "The terrible truth is that 4,500 Jews are living as hostages in Syria." And he alleged that interrogations of Jews were "accompanied by indescribably cruel torture." His charges were corroborated by the testimony of a Jewish girl who had escaped from Syria and who painted a grim picture of those still there, living "in constant fear of governmental measures against them."

For those Jews who remained in Egypt and Libya, existence was almost as harsh. But very few had remained. In 1948 there had been 75,000 living in the land out of which Moses had led the exodus. That exodus was repeated, and mainly to the same destination, after riots, arrests and confiscations of property had marked Israeli independence. Following the Suez war of 1956, many Jews were expelled from Egypt, and their property appropriated. At the time of the Six-Day War, eleven years later, there were hundreds of arrests and expulsions. By mid-1971, only a few hundred Jews were left in the country, mainly in Cairo and Alexandria.

An even more exiguous remnant stayed in Libya. Of the thirty-five thousand Jews who were in the country at the time of Israeli independence, thirty-two thousand had settled in Israel by the end of 1951. Less than four thousand had stayed put in Tripoli and Benghazi, where the 1967 war brought vengeful attacks upon them. Most of their property was destroyed, and twenty of them were killed. As many as possible got out, mainly to Italy, leaving behind less than a hundred Libyan Jews who were stripped of what they owned and prevented from leaving the country.

More than half a million Jews had been living in the three French North African territories of Tunisia, Algeria and Morocco. The Jews of Tunisia had lived comfortably and, up to the country's independence in 1956, emigration—mainly to Israel and France—had been undramatic. The 100,000 Jews who became citizens of the newly emancipated republic were able to play a full part in its life, including membership of its Parliament and even of its Cabinet. In 1961, however, new nationalist policies were adopted, coloured by a strong anti-Jewish tinge. In the years leading up to the Six-Day War there was renewed emigration, and anti-Jewish riots sparked off by the war itself added a new impetus. Although all of the main communities survived, including that on the lotus-eating island of Djerba, Jewish settlement in Tunisia was reduced to little more than ten thousand.

Along the coast, in Algeria, the 1962 independence agreements were the signal for a mass evacuation which reduced a historic two thousand-years-old settlement of Sephardim to a rearguard of 1,500. Most of them opted for the maintenance allowances and housing offered in France to "repatriated" citizens. Others went to Israel, to Spain and to Argentina. Next door, Morocco still harboured the largest Jewish population in North Africa —and indeed in any Arab country—mainly in Casa-

blanca. But these fifty thousand were also a small minority of the Jews who had been living in Morocco after
the war. Even before Moroccan independence in 1956
some sixty thousand had left for Israel. More continued
to go, with tensions created by the Six-Day War adding
force to the urge to move out. The census of July 1970
showed there had been a reduction in ten years from
159,806 to 31,119. It was a mixed population, with
some Moroccan Jews regarding themselves as second-
class citizens while others—judges, lawyers, civil servants—were still part of the ruling élite. Jewish communal and religious life was well organized, and the
synagogues continued to be full.

There were two Moslem countries where the Jewish
population was even higher than in Morocco. And, since
neither of these was an Arab state, Israel was even able
to maintain trading and diplomatic relations with them.
In one of them, Turkey, this contact led to tragedy; for,
in May 1971, Ephraim Elrom, the Israeli Consul-Gen-
eral in Istanbul, was kidnapped and murdered by an organization named the Turkish People's Liberation
Army. Nevertheless, by then an army-backed regime
had come to power and aroused greater confidence
among Turkish Jews, demonstrating its good intentions
by closing down an anti-Semitic newspaper. Before that,
manifestations of extremism from both the Left and the
Right, with threats of violence against individuals and
business firms, had led to a wave of emigration to Israel.

This had not been the first such outbreak nor the first
such departure. There had been eighty thousand Jews, in
Turkey at the time of Israeli independence, and by 1971
half had left. Most of those who remained—a faded and
self-effacing group—lived in Istanbul, with a further
substantial community in Izmir. These had their own religious and educational systems, and their own press.
But no national representation of Jews was permitted,
nor were contacts allowed with Jewish organizations
abroad. This was not a sign of anti-Semitic discrimination; Turkish citizens, whatever their religion, were
banned from maintaining relations with organizations
centred outside the country.

In Iran, however, the ancient Jewish community was

organized into Central Committees in each city, affiliated to the Teheran Central Committee, which in its turn was a member of the World Jewish Congress. Moreover, the Jews were allotted autonomy in matters relating to marriage, divorce, death and inheritance. They had a hereditary rabbinate. And, recognized by law as a religious minority, they were entitled to one representative in the Majlis, the lower House of Parliament.

However, this was the only parliamentary representation that they were permitted. Nor were they even allowed to vote for anyone else. It was not surprising that this rather limited ration of Iranian democracy led the Jews of the major community of Teheran and the minor centres of Shiraz, Isfahan, Abadan and Hamadan to turn their steps westwards to Israel. In the State's first twenty years, fifty-three thousand Iranian Jews made their way there. And there continued a steady, substantial draining away from the sixty-five thousand or more who remained.

It was a new Israel to which these immigrants came: new not simply because it was an independent Jewish state, nor even because mass immigration had faced it with unanticipated problems of absorption. The arrival for the first time in modern history of hundreds of thousands of oriental Jews was changing the nature of the country. Ben Gurion, speaking of mass immigration, had told the Knesset on 26 April 1949: "It was for this that the State was established, and it is by virtue of this alone that it will stand." A Knesset law had affirmed, in 1952, that "the mission of gathering in the exiles is the central task of the State of Israel." By the time that law was enacted, those Jews who had been Israelis when Ben Gurion made his 1949 statement had learned exactly what their Prime Minister's unforeseeing enthusiasm meant for the country which they had built up as pioneers.

Between 1882 and 1948, nine out of every ten immigrants to Palestine had come from Europe, more than half of them from Russia and Poland. They had been the core of Israel's formation and development, planting in it not only trees and crops but also their secularist ideas of Zionism, socialism and personal simplicity. Now the nation which they had called into existence was taken over by newcomers of an entirely different kind. The new Israelis came often as refugees, either from a Europe which had cruelly punished them or from Moslem lands where Jews lived on stringent terms laid down by the host government. They came, generally, not as individuals or in self-organized groups, but as whole communities wishing to maintain the occupations, habits, devotion to religion and patterns of life they had always known. Rather than attempt to create a new situation in a new land, they sought to adapt to conditions they found awaiting them. Often they settled in family, neighbourhood or local groups. And they came in floods.

Between independence day and the end of 1950, more Jews entered Israel than had come in the whole thirty-year period of the British Mandate. By the end of 1951, the number of post-independence Israelis already outnumbered those who had been in the country to take part in the celebrations on the evening of 14 May 1948. They brought with them something that Palestine's Jews had not recently experienced: a class structure. An established élite was supplemented by a rabble from refugee and displaced persons' camps, and from the ghettos of a dozen oriental cities. The original citizens lived in neat collective or co-operative settlements, or in city apartments. Those who now crowded into Israel were huddled in camps taken over from the British army— where one immigrant group was ready to accuse camp officials of showing favouritism in matters of diet to groups from other countries—and into abandoned Arab dwellings. They were resettled by a bureaucracy, rather than absorbed by those among whom they had come to live. Socially and economically they became a lower stratum. And thus a unified community was turned into a pluralistic society. A quarter of a century later the problems created for Israel by this flood-tide of wistful humanity were still a major national preoccupation.

But meanwhile they had to be found homes and jobs and to be fed. It was also necessary to provide them with a juridical right to remain. This was established by the Law of Return which, rushed through the Knesset in July 1950, entitled every Jew in the world to settle in Israel unless he was guilty of offences against the Jewish people or liable to endanger public security. In May 1971 an amendment to the Citizenship Law by the Knesset widened the welcome of Israel's outspread arms; now Israeli citizenship could be granted while an applicant was still abroad. But, just as in the 1970s citizenship did not necessarily carry with it the right to enter Israel, so in the 1950s entitlement to return did not entail entitlement to comfort. Four years after the State was founded, nearly a quarter of a million immigrants were still living in tents, in huts made of canvas, tin or wood, and in hostels. But during this period major progress had been made in settling newcomers in 330 new villages, where they could simultaneously find employment and grow food to feed themselves and others. And amid all the stress of this initial phase, an extraordinary miracle was accomplished. Of the 696,407 immigrants who arrived between 15 May 1948 and 1 April 1952, 677,750 were absorbed into the Israeli economy.

Not even a country as voracious for immigrants as Israel could continue to swallow them at this rate. A pause for breath was essential, and in 1951 it was decided that for a while uninhibited immigration must give way to a principle of selectivity. Any Jewish communities who were in urgent need of rescue would, of course, be brought in at whatever cost. Jews who were able to make their own way to the country would also be automatically admitted. But otherwise immigration organized by the Jewish Agency would be limited to young or skilled immigrants, and to those bringing in substantial sums of capital.

The Jewish Agency, which was the executive body of the World Zionist Organization, had been set up under the League of Nations Mandate to co-operate in developing the Jewish national home. The World Zionist Organization itself had been established in Basel in 1897 to attain that national home. But the achievement of 1948 did not mean the end of the WZO. Indeed, its status within Israel was carefully defined by the World Zionist Organization-Jewish Agency for Palestine (Status) Law in 1952. This laid down that the Jewish Agency was to be responsible for immigration into Israel, for settlement and for absorption. Thus the Jews of the Diaspora, who dominated the WZO, accepted a shared responsibility with the Government of Israel for settling immigrants. With head offices in Jerusalem and New York, they raised money, acquired and reclaimed land, planned, financed and administered the development of new settlements, and gave help to established villages.

These responsibilities were subdivided in 1968 when, because of the special needs of the increasing proportion of immigrants who came from Western countries, a Ministry of Absorption was set up as a Department of the Israeli Government. But the Jewish Agency was still in charge of classifying prospective immigrants in their countries of origin and helping to arrange transport for them and to ship their belongings, and in Israel of running the absorption centres, sponsoring the Ulpanim (language schools) and assisting with immigrants' problems. Even so, many in the WZO were dissatisfied with this institutional framework; and in 1971 at a special assembly which opened in Jerusalem on 21 June, the organization was split into two. The Jewish Agency, which expanded to include representatives of large Jewish fund-raising organizations around the world, was to operate within Israel, dealing with immigration—including youth immigration—and absorption, housing, settlement, education, health and welfare. The WZO, based abroad, dealt with Jewish education, youth and student affairs, information, community organization, and the encouragement of immigration.

At the beginning of the State, as the exiles poured in, no one had had time for such sophisticated machinery. On 20 November 1949 Israel acquired its millionth citizen. Just over a year later, on 29 November 1950, the five hundred thousandth immigrant since the founding of the State was welcomed. In 1952, following the implementation of the policy of restriction, the number of newcomers fell dramatically. During the two years from May 1950 to May 1952, there had been 304,457 fresh arrivals. In the following 27 months the total was only 30,057. The next couple of years, up to October 1956, brought 89,052 more, in a phase where the emphasis was on cultivation of desert lands and settlement in development areas. Up to 1960 a further 148,466 arrived, including many technicians and professional men. Between 1960 and 1964, the annual average was more than 50,000: the one millionth immigrant arrived on 30 July 1961; but subsequently a decline set in. Then, however, in 1967 came the Six-Day War. And this whirlwind victory created not only a new mood of strength in Israel, but also a new harmony between the Jews of Israel and those of the Diaspora.

Israel itself had been changing. In the freshly independent state of 1948, four out of five of its citizens were of European origin; and an even higher proportion of that year's immigrants came from Europe. But by 1950, immigrants from Africa and Asia had become as numerous as the Europeans; in 1951, almost three-quarters came from the oriental countries. The trend continued for some time. In 1956, for example, four out of five of the 55,100 immigrants came from North Africa. Eventually three-quarters of all oriental Jews were to make their homes in Israel. They brought with them their own customs, their own allegiances, and even their own diseases, such as trachoma and ringworm of the scalp. But as they came, placing increasing social burdens on their fellow Israelis, too many Jews settled in other countries seemed to be losing interest in what, in the early years of the State, they had eagerly regarded as their very own land.

Ben Gurion could thunder, as he did in 1952, that "the Zionist movement, the Jewish people and the State of Israel now constitute one cohesive unity impossible to break." He could insist that the new State was "a buttress for the position of respect which the Jews now enjoy among their neighbours." But an alienation was taking place. Since many of the native-born *sabras* were non-believers, religion could not serve as a link. And, looking at their fellow Jews in other countries, their tendency was somewhat scornfully to ask: "What are they doing over there? If this is their country, why do they not come here to build it?"

Zalman Aranne grew so worried that, as Minister of Education in 1959, he introduced special "Jewish consciousness" syllabuses into non-religious Israeli schools.

"We are creating two peoples, not one," he lamented; and insisted that *sabra* children should be taught about the Jews' struggle for national survival, their faithfulness to their nation and their religion in the face of persecution, the solidarity of their communities in the Diaspora, and their contribution to world civilization. But the young Israelis failed sufficiently to be impressed.

The Eichmann trial, which opened in 1961, changed their attitude. It dragged their horrified attention back to the holocaust and helped to explain, to a generation which knew how to fight, how six million of their fellows had been led to the slaughter. Even more, it helped them to understand why it had been necessary for their State to come into being. And it made them utterly determined that there should never be another holocaust again. When the crisis of May 1967 crept leadenly upon them, they knew exactly what they would be fighting for if they had to fight. And they learned something else. "The Six-Day War changed things in Israel in a way that was almost tangible," recalled Edward Ginsberg, Chairman of the United Jewish Appeal in the United States. "Until then the Israelis had not understood the Diaspora, had never wanted to understand it. When all the allies and supporters of Israel disappeared one by one, they realized that they had only one friend on whom they could rely, the Jews."

Those Jews of the Diaspora, for their part, arrived at a similar understanding. They had listened rather irritably to Ben Gurion lecturing them on how the State of Israel had "straightened the back of every Jew wherever he lived." Now, abruptly, watching events unfold on television, it dawned upon them that at any moment the national home which they had taken for granted might cease to exist. And they did not like the idea at all. Money poured into Israel. So did volunteers. From forty countries, 7,500 of them came to work in kibbutzim and moshavim, and in civilian auxiliary squads. Many were to stay for good when the brief war had ended. This two-way realization, by the Jews of Israel and of the Diaspora, of how much they needed each other, was summed up by Prime Minister Levi Eshkol. "May and June of 1967 showed that, beneath the ashes of a seeming separation, there were still burning the embers of a single people, and a great wind blew the ashes away and rekindled a fierce new flame of Jewish reintegration."

Nor did the flame die down with the end of the war. Jewish businessmen came to Jerusalem in 1968 to take part in an economic conference aimed at building up the nation's industry. The businessmen, having completed their deliberations and laid practical plans, went away again. Other Jews, however, came for good. The sag in immigration was at an end. Between the end of the Six-Day War and December 1970, 125,000 newcomers arrived. More than two-thirds were from Europe and the West; one out of five was from North America. And, as in the pre-independence arrivals, these were predominantly people who brought with them skills and university degrees. No fewer than forty-one per cent were members of the liberal professions or otherwise trained academically. Moreover, they carried with them ideals as well.

Those twenty-four thousand North Americans did not come for a better standard of living; they were voluntarily surrendering the comforts of the world's most affluent society. Certainly they did not spurn the incentives which were available to immigrants: priority in housing; tax reliefs; facilities for running a car much more cheaply than longer-established Israelis; a three-year exemption from customs duties; and free tuition, a living allowance and priority hostel accommodation for students. Some of them came under the temporary residence scheme, which allowed them to keep foreign bank accounts and exempted them from military service. But it was likely that many of them would have come without baits such as these. When in the Beit Hachayal hall in Tel Aviv, Golda Meir addressed a mass meeting of American immigrants, she found, from their sharp complaints against bureaucratic unefficiency, that they had already become proper Israelis. But in the practical determination that communicated itself from the auditorium to the platform there glowed a pioneering idealism that Israel had not for a long time experienced on that scale.

It made a foreign Jew who was not intending to settle feel small.

By the 1970s most of the world's Jews lived in ten great communities, each numbering 100,000 or more. In Europe there were France, Britain and Romania; in the Americas, they included Argentina, Canada and Brazil; at the tip of a continent from which most of the Jews had fled remained the care-worn bastion of South Africa. The three largest communities of all were in the United States, in the Soviet Union and in Israel itself.

Jewish immigration to North America had begun in 1654. In the twentieth century the USA had become the chief country of Jewish immigration. Even after the creation of the State of Israel it succeeded, during certain periods, in attracting almost as many Jews as did Israel itself. They went on coming, from Cuba, from Hungary, from North Africa. By 1971 there were 5,870,000 of them, more than in any other country on earth. In New York there were at least 2,400,000—almost as many as in the whole of Israel. In Los Angeles there were more than half a million, in Philadelphia and Chicago over a quarter of a million, in Boston, Miami, Baltimore, Essex County, New Jersey and Washington DC, 100,000 and more. They were not only numerous; they were influential. The magazine *Newsweek* said of them, on 1 March 1971: "Jews exert more power in US society today than ever before."

And it was true that they served in the union's Cabinet and on its Supreme Court. In the White House itself, Walter Rostow and Henry Kissinger had the ear of successive Presidents. Although they formed only three per cent of the population of the United States, they provided ten per cent of its college teachers; there were more Jewish teachers in New York than in Israel. They provided leading musicians like Leonard Bernstein, Isaac Stern, Yehudi Menuhin. They helped in other ways to fashion their country's culture—indeed, some said that they imposed their own culture on the country —through films, whose now moribund studio structure they had once totally dominated, and through the writings of such best-sellers as Philip Roth and Norman Mailer.

Materially they were much better off than their fellow Americans. Two-thirds of the way through the century four out of five Jews of college age were studying in college: twice the national level. Seventeen per cent were actually college graduates, compared with seven per cent in the country as a whole. More than half of them—fifty-seven per cent—lived quite plushily on an annual average family income of over $7,000, compared with thirty-five per cent of all United States families in the same bracket. Jews who held professional and semi-professional posts accounted for twice the national average. There were more than twice as many Jewish businessmen and executives than was justified by the proportion of Jews among the white population. Only twenty-two per cent earned their income from manual work, as against fifty-seven per cent nationally. Yet they were not content.

They turned their attention away from their relative affluence to the 800,000 among them who were living below the poverty level of a $3,743 income. They were conscious that America's Jews were ageing—their median age was six years higher than the national average, and a consequence of their lower birth-rate was that one American Jew in every ten was aged over sixty-five—and that old age often brought poverty. For them it was a badge of shame that eight thousand elderly Jews in Los Angeles were receiving public assistance. Moreover, pausing to note with due satisfaction the evidence of their influence and the regard in which they were so often held, they pointed even more vehemently at the evidence of discrimination against them.

A Gallup Poll among Jews found 34 per cent who believed that anti-Semitism had increased in the past few years. A 1964 survey of white collar and executive levels in Ford's, General Motors and Chrysler in Detroit showed that only 328 out of 51,000 were Jews. A 1966 tally of the 50 leading commercial banks demonstrated only eight Jews among 632 top officers, and just 32 out of 3,438 in middle management. The B'nai B'rith Anti-Defamation League in 1971 accused 38 gas and electricity companies in the big American cities of employing a mere 15 Jews in their leading executive positions.

A check among 1,152 city and country clubs in 1966 found that 665 discriminated against Jews. When in 1970 the British Prime Minister attended a Pilgrims' reception in New York, he discovered to his horror that it was taking place in a club which did not admit Jews.

This feeling of not being entirely wanted by the host society caused some Jews to emigrate to Israel; more than twice as many left between 1967 and 1971 as in all the previous twenty years. And it brought many of the remainder closer together. The Jews of the United States, though overwhelmingly middle class, continued consistently to vote liberal. One aspect of their liberalism was an alliance with Negroes against racialism. Now they found that too often this alliance had been transformed into hostility, as black militants turned against them and Black Power threatened them. A strike of New York teachers in 1968 became a Jewish-Negro confrontation, and the Jewish voters of the city only relented at the last moment in their determination to oust John Lindsay as Mayor of New York because of his support for their Negro adversaries. A Jewish Defence League was formed to protect Jewish merchants and their families in the predominantly black areas of Brooklyn, and degenerated into an extremist organization, led by a bigoted rabbi, which took to harassing Soviet diplomats.

Some Jews had little Jewish consciousness; the number opposing intermarriage fell by half in only six years. But forty-three per cent considered themselves religious, and hundreds of thousands were active in Jewish organizations. There were 650,000 registered Zionists, 394,000 in the B'nai B'rith fraternal and service organization, 30,000 in Hadassah, the women's Zionist organization. Half the Jewish children in the United States were receiving some form of Jewish education. Higher education was provided in such celebrated establishments as Hebrew Union College, Yeshiva University, and Dropsie College. Two Yiddish dailies had a circulation of over 100,000.

The Jewish organizations were not affiliated to any central body, such as the British Board of Deputies. To some extent they were divided among class lines, the

American Jewish Committee, with its monthly journal *Commentary,* representing the upper middle-class establishment, and the American Jewish Congress drawing in the lower echelons. But they all had in common a passionate support for Israel. In the first twenty years of the State, $1,500 million had been contributed through the United Jewish Appeal. The American Joint Distribution Committee, which mainly obtained its funds through the UJA, spent millions of dollars on rescue, relief and rehabilition services for hundreds of thousands of Jews in dozens of countries, including Israel itself. Pinchas Sapir, Israel's Minister of Finance, confessed in September 1971 that "without the UJA and Bonds we would long since have been prostrate." And the *Jerusalem Post* paid a tribute all the more meaningful because it came from a newspaper in a country which almost worshipped its air force: "Today's active American Jews take a double pride in their work and in Israel itself. They know that their fund-raising techniques and capacities can be compared for determination and success only with the Israel air force pilots, and that they are entitled to a feeling of brotherhood in Israel's battle even if their share of the fight is waged out in hotel lobbies and restaurants."

At almost that very same time the battle for the future of the Russian Jews was being waged within the walls of the Kremlin itself. For on 26 January 1971 a portent occurred. Thirty Jews from Vilna, in the Soviet Socialist Republic of Lithuania, marched into the Central Committee building in the Kremlin. They demanded to see the Police Minister about visas to allow them to leave for Israel. When they were sent about their business they staged a sit-in, eating sandwiches the while. Presently a low-ranking official hurried out to hear their complaints. He promised the Jews from Vilna that their applications would by reviewed; and eventually every one of them received an exit visa. Nothing quite like it had ever happened before.

Ever since the October revolution of 1917 the Soviet Communists had been trying different ways of dealing with their Jews. Emollient treatment had alternated with persecution and even murder. But still the problem refused to go away. There had been hopes right at the start that there would be no Jewish problem at all; after all, many of the leading revolutionaries were Jews, as was Yakov Sverdlov, the first President of the Soviet state. Under the constitution anti-Semitism was outlawed as a criminal offence and Jews were accepted as one of the Soviet nationalities; but in return the Jews were expected to abandon any tendencies to separatism. Zionism was prohibited. In an avowedly anti-religious state, religious and Hebrew education were frowned upon, literary societies and newspapers were not permitted, a campaign was launched against the Jewish festivals and the Sabbath, and Jews were allowed neither a central organization nor any meaningful contacts with their counterparts abroad. Jewish elementary and higher schools were closed in 1922, and synagogues became the only legal Jewish institutions. On the other hand, under the internal passport system created in 1932, Jews aged sixteen and over were enabled to declare their Jewish nationality. The Yiddish language was accepted as a fundamental component of that nationality.

So the Jews were given a special place in the structure of the Soviet Union. And, in 1927, a further attempt was made to satisfy any yearnings they might have for their own recognized territory to accompany their recognized nationality. A land—the vulnerable, strategic and only sparsely populated Birobidzhan—in the USSR's Far East was offered to them. In 1934 it was formally proclaimed a Jewish autonomous region. But regrettably the Jews did not want it. At no time did they make up more than twenty-three per cent of the region's population. After a further unsuccessful attempt to popularize the region was made after the war, all Jewish institutions were closed down in November 1948. By the 1970s, only fifteen thousand Jews were numbered among Birobidzhan's 170,000 population. Washing his hands of the project, Prime Minister Nikita Khrushchev snorted that it had failed because Jews were incapable of doing collective work and did not like agriculture. This statement was studied with respectful attention in Israel's kibbutzim.

In 1947 the Soviet Union had voted at the United

Nations for the establishment of a Jewish state in Palestine, and in 1948 she bestowed *de jure* recognition on Israel within two days of its proclamation. But the Israelis, while grateful, were not grateful enough. They exhibited no incipient tendency to become a Soviet satellite. Moreover, they seemed quite shameless about stirring up the Russian Jews. Golda Meir, Israel's first Ambassador in Moscow, had aroused a commotion when on 16 October 1948 tens of thousands of Russian Jews turned up to greet her at the synagogue where she was attending the New Year service. This and similar demonstrations brought a reaction. Emigration to Israel was banned. Between 15 May 1948 and the end of 1951, only five Jews were allowed out.

That, however, was not all. An "anti-cosmopolitan" campaign was launched in 1948. The last two Yiddish schools were closed down, as were the last Yiddish newspaper, the last two Yiddish theatres and the only Yiddish publishing house. And then began the most tragic years for Jews in Russia since the revolution. Almost all their leading writers, poets and actors were arrested including, in 1949, Peretz Markish, the only Yiddish writer to have received a Lenin Award. On 12 August 1952 more than twenty were executed at Lubianka prison. Nor was this the end of the frenzy. For next came the "doctor's plot," denounced by *Pravda* in January 1953. It was a demented story. Nine leading doctors, six of them Jews, were accused of being Zionist spies, in league with American and British agents, and assigned to poison all the Soviet civil and military leaders. It was alleged that they had killed Andrei Zhdanov, party chief in Leningrad. The madness spread, and hundreds of doctors were tried and executed on trumped-up charges. Only Stalin's death brought the purge to an end. Moscow Radio announced on 4 April 1953 that the charges had been false; survivors were released. Among its other consequences, this episode caused the USSR briefly to break off diplomatic relations with Israel, following the planting of bombs in the Soviet Embassy in Tel Aviv.

The succeeding years saw a return to comparative calm. In 1955 those Jews who had been arrested in the

1948 campaign, and who still survived, were freed. The victims of 1952 were "rehabilitated." The following year, despite a brief lapse in diplomatic relations with Israel following the Suez war, the first Hebrew prayerbook since 1917 was published, and a yeshivah seminary was permitted to open in Moscow. In 1957 an Israeli delegation was allowed in to attend an International Youth Festival. In 1959 the first Yiddish books for eleven years were published, and 1961 saw the founding of a new Yiddish-language magazine, *Sovietish Heimland* —non-political, of course—first as a bi-monthly and then in 1965 as a monthly periodical. Meanwhile, however, a new anti-Jewish offensive had been launched.

This was the anti-black-market campaign of the early 1960s, in which about forty of one hundred miscreants sentenced to death for economic crimes were Jews. It was probable that there were many other trials, not involving Jews; but those in which Jews had been indicted were especially singled out for publicity. During this period there was in addition a petty crack-down on the baking of the Passover matzo unleavened bread—denounced as "the counter-revolutionary bread"—and in 1963 three Moscow Jews were imprisoned for illegal matzo-baking; the ban was eventually lifted. It was left to foreign Communists to denounce the publication in October 1963 of a spitefully anti-Semitic tract, containing vicious cartoons and linking Jews with hypocrisy, bribery, greed and usury. Entitled *Judaism Without Embellishment,* this elegant work by one Trofim Kichko was issued by the Ukrainian Academy of Sciences, was denounced in April 1964 by the Ideological Commission of the party's Central Committee, and was presently withdrawn as a "stupid mistake."

The schizophrenic Soviet attitude to Jewry was tellingly illustrated during 1965. On the one hand, on 5 September, Prime Minister Alexei Kosygin and *Pravda,* in an editorial, denounced anti-Semitism. But the following month Russia demanded at the United Nations that Zionism should be classified as a racial crime. The Six-Day War of 1967 led to a greater emphasis on anti-Zionism. Once again diplomatic relations with Israel were severed. But this same war led to the greatest Jewish revival the USSR had known. One Russian Jew who later emigrated to Israel stated that the war "shook us into a realization that we belonged to a proud, free and defiant people." Forced assimilation had succeeded culturally. But, said Michael Zand, a Soviet academic who after many tribulations was allowed to leave for Israel in 1971, "they failed to assimilate us spiritually." Jewish consciousness had survived and was galvanized both by Israel's fight and by Soviet support for the Jews' enemies. It was the Six-Day War that turned the Russian Jewish movement into a mass movement.

A semi-legal network of Hebrew schools sprang up. Jews began openly to assert their wish to emigrate to Israel by sending petitions to Soviet leaders and taking part in public demonstrations, and also by posting letters abroad to international bodies. In April 1970 the first issue of *Exodus*, an illegal journal, began to circulate. At first these stirrings were met by repression, and only a few Jews were allowed to leave for Israel. But the rumblings continued, and a show trial was felt to be the answer. In December 1970 two Jewish defendants were sentenced to death in Leningrad for trying to hijack a Soviet aircraft in an attempt to get to Israel. A storm of international protest forced the sentences to be commuted to fifteen years in a prison camp. But an even more unwelcome surprise for the Russian authorities than the reaction abroad was the effect on Soviet Jews. Instead of being suitably cowed, they let loose a flood of applications to emigrate to Israel. At first the number of exit permits was minimally restricted. Then the gate was opened considerably wider. In 1971 a quarter of all immigrants to Israel came from the Soviet Union.

The turning-point had arrived in March 1971, when the total allowed to leave topped one thousand, compared with only 130 the month before. Prime Minister Kosygin revealed more of the truth than ever before when, during a visit to Canada in October 1971, he admitted that in the first eight months of the year more than four thousand Jews had gone from Russia to Israel; this compared with 4,667 in the previous twenty-two years. He pointed out that the USSR was reluctant to lose young people who had received an expensive education, and did not wish to supply Israel with young men trained as soldiers. Kosygin might have gone on to confess that his government was correspondingly ready to rid itself of Jewish activists, and to let Israel take on the burden of unskilled and unproductive Jews. "We are opening doors and will go on opening them," he claimed. By the end of 1971, the year's total of Russian Jews arriving in Israel touched the thirteen thousand mark. The following year, however, a penal exit tax was suddenly imposed.

Deploying the most notorious cliché in current usage, Kosygin had boasted: "There is no anti-Semitism in Russia. In fact, many of my best friends are Jews." But the atmosphere in philo-Semitic Russia was chillingly evoked by Yevgeny Yevtushenko, author of "Babiy Yar," a poem which was regarded in 1961 as courageously pro-Jewish, when he unburdened himself to a group of Jewish youth leaders whom he encountered in Santiago, Chile. "I am not an anti-Semite," he dutifully declared. "But the Jews leaving the Soviet Union are shitting on our country. And these Jews are shit."

Those who met with his approval by staying behind were part of a declining community. It was not known exactly how many Jews there were in the USSR; a government guess was three million. But the number willing to admit their Judaism had fallen, between the 1959 and 1970 censuses, from 2,268,000 to 2,151,000. More than one-third were in the Russian republic. Those claiming Yiddish as their mother tongue were down from 410,000 to 395,000. For the first time in two hundred years avowed Jews formed less than one per cent of Russia's population. Partly this might have been due to a wish to hide their Jewish identity, partly because of assimilation. But natural decrease was also a factor; children, who by the 1970s would themselves have been producing children of their own, had been killed by the Nazis.

The survivors lived in a country where Jews rose naturally to the surface unless deliberately suppressed. David and Igor Oistrakh, the internationally famous violinists, were a Jewish father and son. In ballet the Jews were represented by Maya Plissetskaya, in chess by

Mikhail Botvinnik, in literature by Isaak Babel and Ilya Ehrenburg (whose death in 1967 deprived his government of a valued anti-Zionist propagandist), in the cinema by Mikhail Romm, Mark Donskoi and Sergei Yutkevich, as well as by perhaps the greatest director in the entire history of the cinema, Sergei Eisenstein.

The Government's own statistics showed that in 1966 14.7 per cent of the country's doctors, 8.5 per cent of its writers and journalists, 10.4 per cent of its judges and lawyers, 7.7 per cent of its actors, musicians and artists were Jews. Students formed 3.15 per cent of the Jewish population, compared with 1.82 per cent in the USSR as a whole. The Academy of Sciences had 57 Jewish members. In the 1968 list of Soviet State Prizes awarded for science, art and technology, 32 of the 185 winners were Jews.

That was the information that the official propaganda machine was delighted to make available. Less emphasis was attached to the tidings that after the April 1971 elections to the Central Committee of the Communist Party, there was only one Jew, Benyamin Dymshitz, on a committee numbering 241. Nor was the pathos of Jewish religious life made widely known: the impediments to religious circumcision, the difficulties placed in the way of ritual slaughter of cattle. There were massive Jewish populations in Moscow—thought to be the second Jewish city in the world, after New York—as well as in Leningrad, Kiev and Odessa. Yet for all of these Jews there were no more than forty rabbis, and, as estimated in 1966, sixty-two synagogues. One-third of these synagogues were in oriental areas, especially Georgia, where only one-tenth of the Jews lived. If the Jews were managing to survive as a separate entity, the reason was that given by Eliezer Podriachik, a writer and scholar who was allowed to leave for Israel in 1971: "The existence of the State of Israel is the most important factor in uniting the Jewish people in Soviet Russia."

The Russian Jews looked to Israel. Israel looked to Russia for more Jews. Although the special privileges granted to new arrivals from the USSR aroused friction among native-born Israelis who found difficulty in raising the money for an apartment, still they could not have enough of them. A carefully contrived coincidence occurred at Lod Airport on 11 January 1971, when Natan Peled, the Minister of Absorption, welcomed the immigrant whose arrival brought the population of Israel up to a precise three million. His name: Natan Tserulnikov. His original home: Leningrad.

Comrade Tserulnikov, with his wife and daughter, arrived in an Israel where the number of Jews had risen to 2,610,000, and where the proportion of native-born *sabras* had increased from 35.5 per cent in 1948 to 45 per cent in 1969. It was an Israel which shared many of the trends of the Diaspora. Natural increase had fallen sharply, and was even declining among the previously highly fertile oriental Jews, just as the Jewish fertility ratio was falling far below the national level in Canada, Australia, New Zealand, the Netherlands, Switzerland, West Germany, Austria and Italy. The improvement in Israeli educational levels was matched by the above-average Jewish educational achievements in the USA, the Netherlands, Austria, the USSR and Romania; and the unsettlingly low proportion of manual workers in Israel paralleled the tendency among Jews in other lands to pursue white collar occupations. Jews the world over were city dwellers: 89 per cent in Israel, 95 per cent in the USSR, 96 per cent in the USA.

And the Jews of the world were increasingly realizing how much more they had in common. Jewish unity was not just a matter of the immigrants and money flowing into Israel, or the emissaries and teachers sent abroad by the Jewish Agency. It was a matter of ever stronger feeling and ever warmer sentiment. It was exemplified by the action of the pupils of the Reali School in Haifa, who in 1970 sent letters urging intercession for Soviet Jews to every diplomatic representative in Israel. It was voiced by Chaim Topol, the young Israeli actor who became a world celebrity for his role in the Jewish musical, *Fiddler on the Roof.* "We in Israel," he said, "are divided from Yiddish culture by the holocaust. We were ashamed for a long time of that background . . . Youth in Israel is now going back to Yiddish culture. Plays are being performed in Yiddish by *sabra* actors, and the young are going to see them."

The Jews of the Diaspora, and the culture they had created, were coming to mean more than ever before to the tough young Israelis. And Israel was providing a new cohesive power for Jewish communities in other countries which might otherwise have fragmented. A survey in the London suburb of Edgware showed that while only thirteen per cent of the Jews attended synagogue regularly, fifty per cent made regular financial contributions to Israel. Jews who were losing interest in their religion were staying Jewish because of their interest in Israel. It was Ben Gurion, not for the first time, who summed up the state of affairs. "The future of Israel depends on world Jewry. And the future of world Jewry depends on the survival of Israel."

9

The Muses Learn Hebrew

A bitter controversy troubled the State of Israel in the last days of 1970. Thousands, it was said, had gone on strike. The newspapers were full of the dispute. The strike was among the thirty-five thousand subscribers to the Israel Philharmonic Orchestra, who had handed back tickets and left seats in the Mann Auditorium empty in protest at the inclusion of a particular work in the orchestra's repertoire. The opus in question, denounced as unacceptably adventurous, was the violin concerto of Arnold Schoenberg, born in 1874 and already dead for nineteen years. The IPO managers, put to flight by consumer rejection, withdrew Schoenberg and substituted Mendelssohn. Furthermore, "to give the public a little rest," they then took out of their planned future programme a new work by the Israeli composer Mordechai Seter. Heaving a little sigh, the Chairman of the Musicians' Committee confessed that IPO subscribers regarded even Bartok and Stravinsky as avant-garde.

This imbroglio epitomized Israeli cultural attitudes. On the one hand, in this tiny country, here was an orchestra of the first rank sustained by a massive subscription list. Here too were subscribers who felt they were so much a part of their orchestra's life that they took it upon themselves to dictate what it should play. Here was a country so aesthetically oriented that an affair of this kind provided eagerly perused newspaper copy. Yet, in a battle between conservatism and a timid flicker of musical adventure, it was conservatism that had won hands down.

The Israelis were voracious consumers of culture.

Only *protektzia* could wangle a seat for any of the two hundred concerts the IPO gave each year. Israel had the highest theatre audience per head of population in the world, 2,500,000 seats being sold every year, and 15 per cent of the population seeing a play every month. It was third in the world for the number of book titles published per head, and 47 per cent of its people read at least one book a month. Its 271 cinemas were visited every week by 40 per cent or more of the potential audience. Yet in what they chose to hear and see this massive public did far too little to foster indigenous artists.

In the first thirty-six seasons of its existence the IPO, founded by Bronislaw Huberman in 1936, had been dominated by the symphonic works of Beethoven, Brahms, Mozart, Mahler and Haydn. Only about one play in ten performed in the Israeli theatre was the work of an Israeli dramatist. In 1970 locally produced films accounted for one pound in every twenty taken at the box office. It was true that the new state harboured only one really accomplished playwright and only one outstandingly gifted film director. But occasional incursions by others proved that the talent was there to be nurtured if only the public would demand a showcase for it, instead of preferring to wallow in the comfortably familiar.

And the talent was unusual. It could draw on backgrounds and experiences rare among artists in other parts of the world. Two of Israel's most eminent painters, Arie Aroch and Reuven Rubin, had been diplomats, and another, Fima, was a construction engineer. Among poets and writers, Uri Tzvi Greenberg and S. Yizhar had been members of Parliament, Avraham Huss was a lecturer in meteorology, Avner Trainin a lecturer in chemistry, Omer Hillel a landscape architect, and David Rokeah an electrical engineer. War and suffering were deeply imprinted on these practitioners of the arts. Avigdor Arikha (painter) and Dan Paggis (poet) had been imprisoned in concentration camps. Shamai Haber (sculptor) and Abba Kovner (poet) had fought with the partisans in Poland and Lithuania. Menachem Shemi (painter of landscapes) had lost two sons killed in action with Israel's defence forces; the father of Gila

Almagor, the country's most glamorous film star, had been murdered by an Arab; Tuvia Rivner (poet) had been with his wife when she was killed in a bus ambush. Ram Da-oz (composer) was blinded in the war of independence; Hannah Maron, one of the *grandes dames* of the Israeli theatre, had lost a leg in a terrorist attack on an El Al aircraft at Munich.

These experiences, inevitably, were reflected, if sometimes only indirectly, in their work. And in every sphere of art except the cinema—which was too young—there had been the same progression: the immigrant to the new land comparing it with the exile left behind; the novice settler exploring his domain, drinking in its sights and sounds; the pioneer making the land his, describing his experience in minute detail but sometimes in grandiose tones; the native taking his homeland for granted, criticizing it, and looking for something that had somehow got lost. In art, literature, music, film, remote biblical sources postled with the deeply bruising experiences of the holocaust and the struggle for national independence.

Palestine's first Jewish painters were certainly dazzled by what they found. As, during the first three decades of the twentieth century, they arrived from Hungary, Romania, Lithuania, Russia, they were startled by the dazzling colours and the piercing light, and enchanted by the fairytale landscapes and exotic genre scenes confronting them in Arab coffee shops. They saw eastern Mediterranean visions through the eyes of their European styles, and made the pilgrimage back to Europe to keep up with what was happening. The pictures they painted, heavily influenced by Rouault, Dufy, Matisse, Cézanne, Rousseau, were amazingly pretty.

They drank in what they saw. Then they began to flavour it with their own ideals. Yeheskiel Streichman (particularly influenced by Braque) studied in Paris and Florence, but was much more the product of his kibbutznik days. Any Mapam veteran would have approved of his socialist realist utterances: "The physical fact of Israel is the very source of my inspiration." And: "I feel that I am an integral part in the rebuilding of Israel—not unlike a construction worker."

The founding of the State gave some artists the notion that a national style should be attempted, and several of them hived off for a time from the very militant Artists' Association, founded in 1923, to form a New Horizons Group, which held its first exhibition at the Tel Aviv Museum in November 1948. They went on holding exhibitions, but as a movement with recognizable identity of its own they were a failure. It was left to a few individual artists to break away from the conformist norm.

Chief of these was Mordechai Ardon, variously regarded as one of the country's most influential teachers, its artistic doyen and even its Augustus John. He had been born with the name of Bronstein in Poland in 1896, was a disciple of Paul Klee at the Bauhaus, and came to Jerusalem in 1933. He drew on all the conventional religious and biblical sources, and painted the Negev desert and the Jerusalem hills. But he saw them, mysteriously, in his own way, using marvellous colours which he ground himself. He began as a realist and went on to abstractionism, but everything he painted was unmistakably his. His own reverence for Rembrandt at first seemed incongruous with the huge molecular constructions he was presently to produce. But their majesty and self-sufficiency made the comparison less strange. His "Missa Dura," painted between 1958 and 1960, and based on the European holocaust, was a dazzling explosion of shapes, colours, forms and scrolls.

Equally individualistic, perhaps even wayward, was Yossl Bergner, born in Poland nearly a quarter of a century later than Ardon. A stay in Australia added a remoteness to his view, and a visit to Europe in 1959 brought about a major change in his work. An abstract realist, Bergner presented people and objects in strange and fascinating forms. His attitude to colour changed as his approach to painting altered. At first he concentrated on monotones, generally greys, black and white; then he began to replace natural colours with abstract colour values. His humour and menace were given play in his illustrations of Kafka and his stage sets (for Nissim Aloni's *The Gypsies of Jaffa* in 1971, for example), which were often judged far more artistically distinguished than the plays themselves. A surrealist approach began to affect his work, in which angels and clowns appeared as recurring motifs. There was a doom-laden grotesquerie about some of his pictures, as in "Destination X," painted in 1969, which showed the personal possessions of the Jews over the ages moving in a neat and orderly file towards some unknown objective.

Samuel Bak, one of Israel's younger artists, born in 1933, was also a surrealist. His choice of subject matter was given an extra dimension by his style, which was one of the most immaculate Renaissance perfection. Yaakov Agam—five years older than Bak—chose material linked more with technology. The *sabra* son of an Orthodox rabbi, he was a kinetic artist who executed his coloured geometric forms with machine tools, wood, aluminium and cans of paint. His aim was to produce "a foreseeable infinity of plastic situations flowing out of one another, whose successive apparitions and disappearances provide every-renewed revelations." This was rather a high-flown way in which to describe the large-scale and expensive visual toys he produced on corrugated and revolving surfaces. But no one could escape being intrigued by them, and one of his larger puzzles provided an enticing bait into the new Tel Aviv museum, where visitors walked slowly to and fro in front of it, testing the fresh patterns available from each viewpoint.

Anna Ticho could not easily be deposited inside one artistic card index rather than another. As did Leah Goldberg in poetry, she brought a precise and somehow dainty feminine approach to her illustrations of the Israeli scene. Her pictures were lyrical, but for a long time included the detailed naturalism of trees, plants and rocks drawn with a neatness which would have told any Israeli that she was a *Yeke* who came from Vienna. Jerusalem became her subject, which she drew over and over again in charcoal until the city and its surrounding hills seemed to belong to her. As she grew older—she had been born in 1900—her later works evolved into fantasy with the appearance of reality. The style throughout remained totally personal.

Ardon, Bergner, Agam, Ticho were artists who did

not fall into the general pattern of painters. But most Israeli pictorial art, immensely pleasing though much of it was, might well have rolled off a conveyor belt. The setting up of artists' colonies in Safad, in the derelict Arab village of Ein Harod on the top of Mount Carmel, in Jaffa, and eventually in Jerusalem, could have had an effect. But mostly it seemed simply to be something in the air. Artists of the most variegated backgrounds and tendencies succumbed to the spell.

Joseph Zaritsky, five years older than Ardon, was regarded by many as at least as influential a teacher. His Kiev art training was followed by study in Paris. Superb water-colours of cities and landscapes in the 1930s were followed later by his leadership of the Israeli abstract movement, with great patches of colour arresting the gaze of the spectator. Israel Paldi was born in Russia in 1892 and, arriving in Palestine in 1907, was another of the country's earliest art pioneers. He progressed from depicting lovable creatures in charming colours to abstract works which resembled Rorschach test specimens. Reuven Rubin, born in Romania the following year, encompassed in his baroque conception of the Israeli scene snapshot views of Arabs in Jaffa, a huge and almost supernatural depiction of Jerusalem, and a series of twelve lithographs on the life of King David. A painting of olive groves in Jerusalem could perhaps best be chosen to typify his work, because his love of olive trees made them a Rubin motif as readily identifiable as his signature. The olive, he mused, was very much like the Jewish people, adapting itself to every situation and outliving every other tree.

Marcel Janco, founder of Ein Harod, where he provided workshops, an exhibition hall, jewellery and ceramics, as well as a café, had an entirely different pedigree. Although born in Bucharest in 1895, he had not come to Palestine until very late (1941), having first won a place in international art as a founder of the nihilist Dada movement in Zürich. He was a focus for young artists at the Oranim kibbutz seminar and a founder of New Horizons. He began as a semi-representationalist, then went abstract, using colour brilliantly, and in independent Israel became an expressionist realist. His larky, colourful figures, his elongated animal shapes, could have nestled familiarly under Rubin's olive trees.

Menachem Shemi had only ten more years to live when Janco came to the country. He left behind after his death landscapes of Safad which glistened with seductive colour, and would have loved to paint the park which was eventually dedicated to him in Haifa. Arieh Lubin's background was far different from that of all his contemporaries, since he was born in 1897—a year after Shemi—in the United States. Yet his pictures and landscapes slotted in neatly next to theirs, and his view of Safad was as wondrous as that of Shemi; or indeed as that of Mordechai Levanon. Levanon, a Hungarian, began with beguiling descriptive landscape. He painted Jerusalem dozens of times. But it was to Safad that he retired in the 1960s, and where he lived to the end of his life in 1968. Having already moved on to cubism in the mid-1940s, he spent his self-imposed isolation in the mountain city painting canvases which became ever larger; and his subjects progressed from the city itself to the recurring Israeli obsession with the holocaust.

Of all these older artists, Moshe Castel was the only one who was a native Israeli. He had been born in Jerusalem, in 1909, a member of a family which had arrived in the holy land five centuries before as refugees from medieval Spain. He studied in Italy, the United States and Paris, and divided his time between the French capital—and Safad. He did not have to discover the Orient; it came naturally to him. He captured its colour in illustrating the folk rituals of the Sephardic communities. Even when he went abstract he remained an instinctive Palestinian, deploying the exoticism of Aramaic calligraphy. The charming attenuated figures he painted might have been relatives of Janco's.

And they would have sat down happily next to the animals of Naftali Bezem. Bezem was born in Germany fifteen years later than Castel, and was a student of Ardon's. His pictures were sad and symbolic. His motifs included the lion, the Torah scroll, the fish, the boat, the wheel and the ladder. The mute and slaughtered fish for him symbolized the Jewish people, the weeping lion of

Judah the surviving mourner. Bezem's animals were certainly grotesque and grave. But, whether he intended them to be or not, they were also lovable. Origins differed; so, too, did styles and intentions. But the line stretched unmistakably through from Zaritsky through Shalom of Safad—a religiously orthodox recluse and everybody's favourite primitivist pet—to David Shariv, born in 1936, whose frieze-like "Noah's Ark" of 1971 was yet another specimen of the bewitching evocation of mythical atmosphere which had become the dominant feature of modern Israeli painting.

Sculpture, on the other hand, had had far less chance to evolve. Semi-theocratic Israel, which took with literal seriousness the biblical injunction against graven images, was not the ideal setting for a Henry Moore (though one of his works reclined outside the new Tel Aviv museum) or a Barbara Hepworth. Public monuments were infrequently commissioned, and a really ambitious artist who wished to create three-dimensional work lived in hope of being asked to design a gate.

Such sculptors as there were began conventionally enough with figurative realism. But artistic adventure beckoned them on to abstraction, which in any case was a neat solution for the graven image problem. The founder of contemporary Israeli sculpture was Yitzhak Danziger, born in Berlin in 1916, who after study at the Slade in London became a teacher in three-dimensional design at the Haifa Technion. Danziger immersed himself in the values of ancient Near East sculpture, and wanted his products to safeguard "the channels uniting us with the soil." He began working in stone, but then moved on to clay, plaster, welded iron and bronze, and he abandoned figuration. Danziger was responsible for some of the most striking of such public monuments as Israel possessed, including at Holon the Yad Labanim monument in iron to the nation's fallen soldiers.

David Palombo lived a short but productive life before dying in a horrific road accident at the age of forty-six on Mount Zion in his native Jerusalem. The old Arab house which had been his home was turned into a museum which was a memorial to him. Palombo worked in almost anything that came to hand: wood, stone, welded metal, glass, mosaic. Most visitors to Jerusalem saw examples of his output, since he designed both the entrance gates to the new Knesset and the gates to the Yad Vashem building. Yad Vashem was the unbearably moving memorial to the millions killed in the holocaust, and Palombo's gates provided a strident symbol of imprisonment. They represented the gates of the concentration camps or even the death chambers themselves, and their metal resembled charred wood, evoking thoughts both of fire and also of struggling human limbs. Shraga Weill's gates were very different. They were designed by this colourful painter of the story of Joseph and the Song of Songs for the Hilton Hotel in Tel Aviv and the President's controversial new residence in Jerusalem.

Such bland propositions were not for Yigael Tumarkin, the hell-raiser of the Israeli artistic scene. A painter, décor designer (he worked for Bertolt Brecht and did sets for Euripides' *Medea)* and sculptor, he had been born in Germany in 1933 and arrived two years later to begin causing trouble in Palestine. He caused plenty. "Israel is a country in the process of rebuilding and in which I am at home," he challenged—as he challenged alleged art dictators such as Chaim Gamzu of the Tel Aviv museum. Tumarkin's work was often literally based on destruction. Odd pieces of metal adhered to tarry canvases. He turned the Sinai debris from the Six-Day War into sculpture. "Lion's Den," which he presented to a unit in the army's Central Command, was fashioned entirely from scrap parts off weapons and armaments and could be regarded either as a roaring lion or as the yawning mouth of a cannon.

Israel had not so far produced a genius of the visual arts. But it fostered a number of painters of talent, charm and even profundity; and these painters faced no competition from counterparts overseas. When Chaim Gamzu did dare to smuggle in foreign masterworks to show in his galleries he was liable to be upbraided by the touchy Tumarkin—whose own work he then defensively put on display. As for that third of the population —ranging from government officials to kibbutzniks— who wished to line their walls with originals, their pockets could at most run to local products. So Israeli art had a relatively clear run at home. In the same way, the path was open for Hebrew literature.

It was not that Israelis did not wish to read classics and contemporary works written by foreigners; they did, and they were amply provided for, both with the originals and in translation. But no nation could be content with reading only about other countries: certainly not Israelis, notorious for their obsession with their own land. Moreover, people who spoke in Hebrew liked to read in Hebrew, and preferably works by people who wrote in Hebrew. As was evidenced by the inclusion in every Israeli newspaper of a Friday literary supplement, there was a large public for modern Israeli literature; and it was generously supplied.

The basic vocabulary of Hebrew was in use two thousand years before Christ. There had been no continuous Hebrew literature in the Jewish exile; it flowered only sporadically. Until a century before the founding of the modern Israeli state there was hardly any Hebrew lay prose. As this revived, its practitioners faced problems which did not afflict their contemporaries in other countries. A new vocabulary had to be created to deal with modern sentiments and modern implements. There was the question of how pure the language should be kept. If it incorporated the argot of spoken Hebrew, would it be polluted? If it did not, would it not seem stilted? Every writer had to solve this problem for himself each time he came to put words together. But, unlike a writer in English or French, he had to think about it; he could not compose thoughtlessly or automatically.

The earliest of the modern Hebrew writers in Palestine, some of whom survived to become citizens of the Israeli state, saw the holy land as their escape from exile and looked at it through the eyes of exile. Yitzhak Lamdan, who in 1920 came to Palestine from Russia at the age of thirty-one, wrote Hebrew poems about sleds passing over snow-covered steppes. His greatest work, "Massada," was a description of the road from the Diaspora to Israel. Uri Tzvi Greenberg arrived four years later, and saw the new land as salvation from bitter experiences in his native Galicia. His poetry, laden with invective and lamentation, was epitomized by its titles:

"We were not likened to dogs among the Gentiles"; "To the mound of corpses in the snow." He was fiercely political, an extreme nationalist, and his work was not always attractive. But what he wrote was powerful, and undeniably more effective than some of the windy declamations of his contemporaries.

Natan Alterman came from Poland at almost exactly the same time as Greenberg. But his approach was entirely different. He wrote lyrical verse, topical verse—as well as a topical satirical newspaper column—and even children's verse. He could summon up an image in a phrase, and an entire dreamily happy world was evoked in his poem "A winter evening," by his relish of the "glamour" of "a barber's shop lit after six." His urban folk poetry elicited the happiness out of humdrum things and brought a response from everyone who had experienced them. After his death in 1970, Moshe Dayan said of him: "Alterman not only expressed our feelings, he fashioned them. He was the voice and we the echoes."

Many regarded him as the first *sabra* poet. But it was versifiers like S. Shalom and Avraham Shlonsky who dealt with the more conventionally accepted *sabra* themes. Shalom, whose real name was Shalom Shapira, was a little over lyrical for some tastes, but could vividly evoke the tension of darkness in a poem such as "They who sow at night." Shlonsky, like Greenberg and Shalom the product of a Chassidic rabbinical family, brought a more colloquial style to the poems in which he celebrated the return from the rootless Diaspora to the real soil of Israel. His physical love of the land could almost be touched or tasted in poems like "Jezrael" and "Toil," in which the minute sensations and impressions of physical work were described.

The link from these writers to the Zionists of the "Palmach generation" was direct. Not all of the Palmach poets were born in Israel; but those who were not had come there as small children. An exception, T. Carmi, had not settled permanently in Palestine until he was in his twenties, but had been brought up in a Hebrew-speaking religious household in New York. For these writers Hebrew was their natural language, and their work emerged naturally from the country itself.

Much of the material produced by the Palmach men was autobiographical, deriving from experiences at school, in the youth movement, in the kibbutz, in the underground or in the army: all institutions where the individual was seen as part of the collective. Perhaps the most conventional and the one whose work was the quickest to become dated, but undoubtedly extremely influential, was Moshe Shamir. He was the author of the novel *He Walked through the Fields* which, combining kibbutz life with the war of independence, most surely captured the new nation's mood and, adapted eventually for every possible artistic medium, would certainly have been performed on ice if Israel had had any. After this first novel Shamir showed his ability to anticipate another vogue by going on to pioneer the modern Jewish historical novel with *The King of Flesh and Blood,* whose subject was the Hasmonean king Alexander Jannaeus. After the Six-Day War he was to become a chauvinistic advocate of a Greater Israel.

S. Yizhar was more adventurous and produced better work, tortured by conscience about the Arabs, and dealing with the conflict between *sabras* and settlers. His style was unusual, even tortuous, and his matter was outspoken. In a novel, *Days of Ziklag,* which some critics hailed unreservedly as great, he examined an episode in the war of independence—a week on a hilltop on the Egyptian front—from the perspective of later years. The writing of Yehuda Amichai, too, was given impetus by the independence war. "Simply, when you see a dead buddy, and you carry him to a field hospital, and the doctor asks you: 'Why did you bring him, he's dead?' —a poem is born." Nor surprisingly, Amichai's poems had a bitter taste. It could hardly be otherwise with a poet who declared: "Each poem is a lullaby. It recalls all the bad things in the world." Deploying subjects which drew on Jewish prayers and legends and on the Bible, he mingled poetry with prose, and literary language with the vernacular. He could push it too far. A critic reproved him for "the tendency to publish too much and to indiscriminately," and his 1971 novel *Hotel in the Wilderness,* dealing with Israeli expatriates in New York, was dismissed as "entirely trash."

By contrast Aharon Megged was gentle and wry, and Carmi simple and pellucid. The way was being prepared for Hebrew writing which did not have to draw directly on contemporary experience for subject-matter, but instead used it as incidental material for the depiction of emotional states. Personal situations were no longer used to symbolize the settling of a new land or the predicament in that land; instead they were drawn upon for the discovery of truths about human beings. By being less specifically Israeli this work told more about Israelis as individuals.

Some of this writing was trying to the patience, but some was decidedly successful. Amos Oz was a novelist and short story writer who employed irony, pathos and symbolism. The jackal was a recurrent symbol in his work, representing a threatening enemy. The animal provided the title for his first collection of stories, *Lands of the Jackal,* and appeared also in his novels, one of which—*My Michael,* the story of the wife of a dull geologist in Jerusalem—was a runaway best-seller. Oz was an advocate of Israeli-Arab reconciliation, and his contemporary, A. B. Yehoshua (referred to familiarly by fellow Israelis as "Aleph Bet"), equally had an uneasy conscience over Israel's treatment of its Arab minority. His short story *Facing the Forests,* in which a fire warden burns down a forest which had been grown over a razed Arab village, was imbued with a guilty discomfort. Yehoshua, born in Jerusalem in 1939 and subsequently a teacher at Haifa University, was a master of the immaculate short story. He was equally accomplished in the specifically gruesome—the slow realization of a protagonist's madness—and in clouding over an everyday situation with sultry menace.

These were mainstream writers. Others could not be grouped with those poets or novelists who were their contemporaries, but had something specific and unique to contribute. Leah Goldberg was a translator of Shakespeare, as Alterman was; she was a literary critic like Shlonsky; she came from Eastern Europe as did both these two and Lamdan, Shalom and Greenberg as well. Yet she was unique. Unlike any of these others she was not influenced by holy Jewish literature. Her models were Italian, French, German and Russian, and her ardent Zionism did not distort her poetry. It was very feminine verse that she wrote, which caught the emotions quietly and noted small objects with precise adjectives: a "grey stone," an "orange bird," "the wise-eyed creature," "pale skies." She brought to Hebrew literature the rare quality of self-controlled dignity.

This was entirely absent from the work of Ka-Tzetnik 135633, a former concentration camp inmate who wrote under the pseudonym of his camp number. His novels *House of Dolls* and *House of Love* drew hysterically on his own appalling experiences, and sold millions throughout the world. *House of Love* preached Arab-Jewish reconciliation. His poetry, however, was searingly unforgiving and horrifyingly effective. In "The Clock Overhead" he provided a terrifying picture of Auschwitz inmates, made ready for the march to the bath-house, prepared with petrified resignation to be gassed and then, as threatening vapour hovered from the sprinkler-pores, suddenly realizing that what was coming out was simply hot water. The poem encapsulated an abominable moment of time.

There were Hebrew writers to cater for every literary predilection: Naham Arieli, who described the collision between faith and secular culture, Aharon Amir, who frighteningly evoked personal desolation, Yariv Ben-Aharon, author of a novel based on his experiences in the Sinai campaign, Omer Hillel, a poet of optimism and emancipation. There was Chaim Hazaz, regarded as a literary doyen, whose range covered the Russian revolution and the Jews of the Yemen, whose output included a novel about the terrorists who assassinated the British emissary, Lord Moyne, but whose style could strike some observers as obscure, unattractive and even gross. One writer, however, dominated Israeli literature for decades up to his death on 17 February 1970, and in 1966 won for his country the garland of the Nobel Prize for literature.

Some of the writings of Samuel Yosef Agnon were sharp and amusing; some of them were wise and far-seeing; some so moving as to bring tears. He was compared with Kafka but, when told of this, confessed that

he had never read him. In any case Agnon was entirely
original. He spanned all Israeli writing, from stories of
the old home in Europe to symbolism as accomplished
as Yehoshua's. He drew on his knowledge of the Bible
and Rashi's commentary on it, and on the Mishna and
the Talmud, to write folk tales, Chassidic tales, legends,
parables, and surrealist stories. Born in 1888, Agnon arrived in Palestine at the age of twenty, but did not settle
permanently until 1925. His literary lifespan encompassed the whole subject range of modern Hebrew writing, from tales of Galician villages, to a novel about the
second great immigration wave to Palestine, to a novel
about the generation of the holocaust, right through to
the summing up of his life in *A Guest for the Night,* in
1968. He wrote about faith and change; he could be
harsh, and he could induce in the reader a great placidity
and contentment. He had his critics, and his style was
sometimes deliberately quaint. But he was very special
indeed, and a compelling witness on behalf of Israel and
Jewry. For nowhere except Jewish Israel could have
produced him.

Even without an Agnon, Israel had more than enough
novelists to be astringently reviewed in the literary supplements; more than enough poets—of varying compre-
hensibility—to be included in the anthologies which
Carmi and others were endlessly compiling. In the theatre it was different. Modern playhouses had been constructed and were increasingly equipped with ingenious
technological contrivances. There were large and enthusiastic audiences to fill them. Lacking, however, were
sufficient Israeli playwrights of quality, and a supply of
trained as well as talented actors.

The State that was born in 1948 possessed three main
theatrical companies: two long-established; one lately
launched. The first, the longest lasting and the best
known, had been founded in, of all places, Soviet Russia. Habimah (The Stage) had been started as a Hebrew
theatre studio in Moscow in 1918 by a former Hebrew
teacher, Nahum Zemach, under the friendly eye of the
greatest figure of the Russian theatre, Konstantin Stanis-
lavsky. Hannah Rovina, who took part in the first performance on 18 October 1918, was still gallantly offer-

ing herself to a reverent public when the new Jerusalem theatre was inaugurated on 17 October 1971. Along the way Habimah acquired two melodramas which in the beginning formed the core of its repertoire but eventually served to congeal it. These were *The Dybbuk,* a play about supernatural possession in a primitive *shtetl* community, which received the first of more than a thousand performances in 1922; and *The Golem,* a legend of the Frankenstein variety (only this time with a presumably circumcised monster), which from its première in 1925 continually recruited fresh addicts to the occult.

The Golem was the first play performed by Habimah when it visited Palestine in 1928. After a prolonged stay the company went on tour again, but returned to Tel Aviv for good in the spring of 1931. Over the years its virtues came to be taken for granted, but its shortcomings were asphyxiating it. Habimah was run on a co-operative basis, with equal salaries even for actors who were not currently working or had retired. This meant that pay was low, and compelled actors to take outside work in order to make ends meet. It was also not an ideal way in which to run a lively company. Habimah, in fact, got less and less lively as its repertoire became increasingly stilted and its acting style monotonously stylized. With insufficient training, its performers fell far below international standards.

Habimah acquired a new 1,100-seat theatre in 1948, and in 1958, on its own fortieth anniversary and the Israeli state's tenth, it was recognized as the National Theatre. But it went through a series of internal crises, involving public disenchantment, internal bickering and financial emergency, from which last it was saved only by government subvention. The old guard gave way to fresher ideas, and foreign directors—including most notably Harold Clurman and Lee Strasberg from New York, and Tyrone Guthrie and Peter Coe from London —were brought in to release the company from its stylized straitjacket. The old collective system of management was abandoned and eventually replaced by a representative board. The repertoire was spring-cleaned, to include such novelties as *Irma La Douce* and the musical *Oliver!*. Israeli plays found their way into the programme. An additional more intimate theatre was opened in 1962. But although Habimah remained an Israeli institution, it was no longer the outstanding theatre company in the country.

Its competitor was not, however, the Ohel (Tent) theatre of Tel Aviv. And yet Ohel had been founded as a theatrical collective, sponsored by the Histadrut, long before Habimah ever arrived in Palestine. Its first performance, an adaptation of Yiddish stories, took place in May 1926. This was a socialist and nationalist theatre, founded by Moshe Halevy, a member of Habimah in Russia, and based on the same formalized approach to acting. Its plays were ideologically respectable: Upton Sinclair, Brecht, Maxim Gorky, Bernard Shaw. As a home in which to stage them, it acquired in 1940 the first permanent theatre ever built in the country. But Ohel could not capture the nation's imagination. Its participants—actors and directors—were ageing. So was its audience. Its popularity declined. In 1958 it was dealt a body blow, when the Secretary-General of the Histadrut (an obstreperous personage named Pinchas Lavon) denounced it as meaningless and expensive, and severed the Histadrut-Ohel link.

The financial subsidy involved had not been large. Nevertheless, the implications of its withdrawal inflicted on Ohel an injury from which it never recovered. Having got rid of Halevy, it staggered on for some years, tinkering with its management, desperately experimenting with its repertoire. In 1961 it was astonished to find itself with a success on its hands—the comedy *The Marriage Contract,* by the Hungarian-born humorist Ephraim Kishon. It went on to stage a popular run of plays by young foreign writers, and capped them with a drama about the 1967 battle for Jerusalem. But these were the last twitches of a mortally sick body, and in 1969 Ohel's tent was quietly folded away. A young and lively company had in any case arrived to supplant it. The Cameri (Chamber) theatre staged its first performance in October 1945. The play was Goldoni's *The Servant of Two Masters,* and it was an enormous success. The Cameri was founded as a reaction against the conservatism of Habimah, and the man who generated its vivacity was Yosef Millo, a director of panache and some temperament. He looked for modern plays, lighter plays, and even Israeli plays. And it was with an Israeli play that Cameri really established itself.

This, it went without saying, was a dramatization of Shamir's *He Walked through the Fields,* in whose adaption Millo himself had a hand. It received the first theatrical première in independent Israel on 31 May 1948, and its theme caught the national mood. For a Tel Aviv theatre audience it was an almost shocking change to listen to stage characters speaking the same vernacular in which they themselves excitedly discussed the play during the interval.

Other Israeli plays were added: Yigal Mossinsohn's *Casablan,* whose principal character was a brooding Moroccan immigrant living in a Jaffa slum; Leah Goldberg's *The Lady of the Mansion,* an ironic and sad story dealing with Jews looking for homeless children and lost manuscripts in Bohemia; Nathan Shahan's *They Will Arrive Tomorrow,* the most successful of all the War of Independence plays.

The Cameri nourished stars, most notably Hannah Maron. It launched into Shakespeare. In 1961 it acquired its own new modern theatre, in the heart of Tel Aviv. It branched out into a children's theatre. It experimented, with enormous *réclame,* in musical comedy, and provided its audience in 1965 with the first all-Israeli musical. Even though it was so simple as to be almost anaemic, *The King and the Cobbler,* a fairy tale about King Solomon with lyrics by Alterman, won huge affection. The Cameri even provided a scandal when, after the Six-Day War, it staged a satirical revue, *Queen of the Bath-tub,* which, with its cynicism about Israeli invincibility and its irreverent allegory about Abraham's sacrifice of Isaac (in which God on this occasion did not intervene), caused such a public outcry that it had to be closed down.

All, of course, could not go smoothly. Millo clashed with his colleagues and flounced out in 1958, never to return. But Cameri prospered without him. After experiencing varying species of management, including a committee of actors, it settled down under the firm hand of an administrator, Yeshaya Weinberg. It was staging nearly seven hundred performances a year, and covering nearly two-thirds of its budget by ticket sales, when in 1970 it was proclaimed Tel Aviv's municipal theatre.

For a long time the trouble had been that all the theatres, municipal or not, were based in Tel Aviv. But Haifa was not going to put up with that. On 29 January 1961 its city council passed a resolution setting up the Haifa Municipal Theatre. The theatre was provided with a modern, 854-seat playhouse with an electronically equipped stage. Attendance was to be on a subscription basis, and finance provided by the municipality. The theatre was to be under the supervision of a public board, headed by the mayor, with an administrative director and an artistic director. The artistic director would be the only head of a theatre in Israel with full authority and an assured budget. Signed on for the job was Yosef Millo.

He started on 12 September 1961 with a splash, starring Chaim Topol, Israel's most popular comedian, in Shakespeare's *The Taming of the Shrew*. But Topol did not stay long. Nor did other actors in the company which Millo tried to build up with the lure of pay higher than that offered by Tel Aviv theatres. In fact, Haifa became known as the "theatre without actors," making such impression as it could with exceptionally beautiful visual productions. Millo did what he could to foster native Israeli drama, staging a revival of *He Walked through the Fields* (which he later also directed as a film starring Moshe Dayan's actor son Assaf) and experimenting—unsuccessfully—with another play by Shamir, based on the biblical story of Ruth. Of course Millo could not for long maintain an equable regime. His spendthrift ways aroused irritation, as did his penchant for accepting outside theatre and film directing assignments. His period as artistic director (and occasional actor) had been lively and inventive. But, although he had been taken on for ten years, his clashes with the municipal authorities brought about his departure in 1967.

In any case, the Israeli theatre was changing. Star actors were turning freelance, imposing themselves even on the repertory groups, and expecting, by Israeli standards, very high salaries. These inevitably were most easily forthcoming from a new breed in theatrical management, the commercial impresario. The first of them was Giora Godik, an immigrant from Russia whose initial essay in entertainment, in the mid-1950s, was as an importer of top-of-the-bill transatlantic talent: Marlene Dietrich, Harry Belafonte, Frank Sinatra. Then in 1961, with the assistance of American choreographer Jerome Robbins, Godik brought over an American cast in *West Side Story*.

He next decided that it was time for Israel to see a Broadway musical in Hebrew and, a thick-skinned enthusiast with the instincts of a gambler, decided to go for broke with *My Fair Lady*. There were grave fears that such an innovation might have a deleterious effect on Israeli cultural life; what was undeniable was that it was a massive success. Other American musicals followed, including *The King and I, How to Succeed in Business Without Really Trying,* and *Fiddler on the Roof.* Godik matched Cameri's *The King and the Cobbler* with his own Israeli musical, *Casablan,* based on the Cameri's own play but naturally rewritten with a happy ending. It was his greatest achievement at the box office (the only measure of Godik's productions, whose highest artistic ambitions were to make large sums of money), running for eighteen months.

But Godik's touch was fading. Operating with crude optimism from a stuffy little office off Dizengoff Circus, and communicating a gusto for the theatre which was not matched with an equivalent instinct for it, he now, after producing fourteen musicals, began to feel the combined effects of the national economic recession and the introduction, in 1968, of Israeli television. He had branched out into non-musical foreign plays. But the West End thriller *Sleuth* flopped as disastrously as the Burt Bacharach musical *Promises, Promises.* When in 1971 Godik took all theatrical strings into his own hands by personally directing the Broadway comedy *Father's Day,* it was denounced as "an unqualified disaster." Not long after, leaving vast debts behind, he mysteriously disappeared from Israel.

Godik had faced competition from an impresario with

more fastidious predilections. Yaakov Agmon, who as administrative manager of Cameri had saved that company from collapse during a period of difficulty, in 1966 staged the first production of his Bimot (Stages) company. Agmon was a committed socialist whose real ambition was to run a newspaper, and whose interests extended far beyond the theatre. He had his own radio programmes; he could mount celebrations of special events, for the Histadrut, for Interflora, and for the tenth anniversary of the State; he was a bidder for concessions to stage fairs and exhibitions; and he became a film producer too, with the psychological war drama *Siege,* starring his wife, Gila Almagor.

Agmon's approach to the theatre was ideological. He would not stage a production in whose message he did not personally believe. He tried to portray facets of Israeli life, and most of his productions were based on Jewish material. When a new venture was ready for rehearsal, he always took it for the first week to the kibbutz Haogen, where he listened attentively to the ideas of the kibbutz members.

His approach, not only political but chic, was typified by his office, overlooking Tel Aviv city hall, which was equipped with ostentatiously non-utilitarian furniture and dominated by the set from one of his productions. He commissioned original Israeli plays, such as A. B. Yehoshua's *A Night in May,* which set the tangled emotions of a Jerusalem family against the background of national tension following the 1967 closing of the Straits of Tiran. He staged controversial foreign plays, like the American homosexual weepie *The Boys in the Band.* But his reputation was mainly based on his loving—and commercially shrewd—explorations of the Jewish past. An evening of Chassidic folklore, performed by a young cast in jeans, won him two prizes, grossed millions of pounds, and sold fifty thousand long-playing records. He staged a Yiddish production with Hebrew commentary, introduced many Israelis to Sephardic culture with his *Spanish Garden,* looked back nostalgically on the world of the pioneers in *Little Old Tel Aviv,* and unearthed unsuspected archives of bawdy eroticism in *Ribald*

Scrolls, a culling from the love poetry and stories of medieval Sephardic rabbis.

Only two of his early productions were commercial flops: an original play about Napoleon, and a documentary about the Rosenbergs, whom the Americans had executed as spies. He did not weigh himself down with the burden of a permanent company, financed his productions from the contributions of investors, and received a minute annual subsidy from the Government —"Just to say hello." Agmon stated his credo bluntly: "We are anti-kitsch and anti-nostalgia. Above all we avoid sentimentality like the plague."

Israeli theatrical life was stimulating. Small new companies, with names like Do-Re-Mi, the Green Onion, Li-La-Lo, and the Corner, were constantly being born. Entrepreneurs like the film director Menachem Golan, the comedians Chaim Topol and Uri Zohar, the musician Frank Pelleg, the actor Oded Kotler—and the political party Mapam—all had a try at creating something miniature but memorable. They staged satirical revues, operetta, and avant-garde drama. But few had staying power. There were special touring companies to perform plays in immigrant settlements. In 1966 the Ministry of Education, which was also the Ministry of Culture, organized an Art for the People scheme, aimed at bringing plays on a regular basis and at reduced prices to all parts of the country. The national companies themselves toured to the remotest regions. The Israelis had an insatiable appetite for theatre. And that in fact was one of the problems.

There was so much theatre that actors had little difficulty in getting parts. There was an absence of selection through competition, and little incentive—as well as few facilities—for training. Israel produced few top quality actors. Easy audience reactions were aroused by the broadest effects and simple clowning around. There was no real tradition of acting, little discipline, insufficient lightness and agility. The public made too few demands on the performers. There were not enough leading actors of real quality.

And such as there were generally made their reputations in foreign plays. After her mutilation by terrorists, Hannah Maron scored a come-back in Euripides' *Medea*. Misha Asherov won the King David prize for his role in *Who's Afraid of Virginia Woolf?*. For the Israeli theatre's mass audience was also its curse. By its very nature a public drawn from all strata was both conservative and puritan. It did not call out for originality, and it received little enough of it.

Natan Alterman, who wrote both humorous and dramatic work for the Cameri, and Yehuda Amichai, who explored the Bible for his *Nineveh and the Prophet Jonah,* both made the attempt but were not very successful. Other literary practitioners, like Leah Goldberg, Megged, Shamir and Yehoshua, also undertook theatrical ventures and scored limited success. The only Israeli playwright who actually made enough money out of the theatre to live on was Nissim Aloni. Uri Zohar, the film director, described Aloni as Israel's only real theatrical talent.

He had been born in Bulgaria in 1926, was a play editor at Habimah, studied direction in Paris, and for a brief period in the 1960s had his own little-theatre company. His plays were always events. They had intriguing titles: *The Emperor's Clothes, The Revolution and the Chicken, The American Princess, The Bride and the Butterfly Hunter.* His work was satirical and even grotesque, as with *Aunt Liza,* whose plot, dealing with multiple murders, was the occasion for dourly witty comment on local and human problems. Aloni specialized in allegory, employed situations remote in time and place, and even in totally mythical countries, in order to comment on matters relevant to current Israeli life.

His plays were snapped up by Habimah, Cameri and Bimot. They were technically ingenious, blending music with action, involving cabaret scenes, employing a radio announcer as a one-man chorus, making use of loudspeakers. A rebel against nationalism, religion and militarism, Aloni was obsessed with royalty, which constantly recurred in his work. As a man he was aloof and pessimistic, continuing to persevere in the theatre but despairing of it, wishing the public would ask more of him instead of simply visiting his plays as a ritual.

The condition of the Israeli theatre in the 1970s was epitomized by the opening of the grandiose and expensive Sherover Theatre, which in October 1971 was inaugurated as the first ever purpose-built playhouse in the city of Jerusalem. It was fashioned of concrete and stone, decorated with sculpture, carpeted in crimson and upholstered in yellow. It had the biggest and most modern stage in the Middle East, with mechanisms for shifting scenery which contained six hundred electrical circuits, all push-button and pre-set. The height of the proscenium was adjustable; the acoustics could be tuned. It cost 11 million Israeli pounds, and the President of the State was there to attend the opening.

There was, however, no play for him to see, nor a resident company to perform in any play. Teddy Kollek, the mayor of Jerusalem, had dismissed the idea of a permanent company as "a system proven antiquated here and abroad"; that put Britain's Royal Shakespeare Company in its place. So for the inauguration a collection of national and international celebrities presented poetry readings, monologues, dialogues and a pageant. What precisely the future of the building was to be, as a home for the performing arts, remained unclear. But sooner or later someone in Jerusalem would remember the plaintive query of a Haifa councillor concerning the entertainments to be seen in that city's lavish playhouse: "Why did the theatre not succeed in presenting Jewish plays, when this is being done throughout the world?"

Jerusalem had a theatre but no company of players. By contrast it had an orchestra, sponsored by Israel radio, which, since there was no satisfactory concert hall in the capital, broadcast weekly from the YMCA. Tel Aviv had both a luxurious concert hall and an orchestra to go with it, the Israel Philharmonic. The country had also produced outstanding musical soloists, who achieved world reputations: Daniel Barenboim, pianist, Mindru Katz, pianist, Yitzchak Perlman, violinist, Pnina Salzman, pianist, Pinchas Zuckermann, violinist, as well as conductors like Moshe Atzmon and Gary Bertini. There was a musical audience whose aesthetic appetite rivalled that of the mass theatre-going public. But it was similarly reluctant to dip its toes into the cold but possibly bracing water of modern Israeli music.

The Schoenberg affair had illustrated the cosy but militant conservatism of the nation's music lovers. Even those too young to have been present at the Israel Philharmonic Orchestra's opening concert under Toscanini were strangely reluctant to give a hearing to any music composed in their country since Toscanini's death. Of course when foreign musicians such as Yehudi Menuhin performed works specially written for them by the Israeli composers Paul Ben-Haim and Mordechai Seter, Israelis were ready to preen themselves vicariously and to listen briefly.

But when, attracted by the lure of the country, Menuhin or Casals or Stravinsky or Walter came to perform there, something a little more familiar was hopefully anticipated. Israel provided as much music as any rational person could reasonably want, in the two hundred concerts a year of the IPO, in the appearances of the Israel Chamber Ensemble, in the annual musical festival staged principally in the restored Roman theatre at Caesarea, and in the Passover festival held at the Sea of Galilee kibbutz of Ein Gev. There were radio concerts and gramophone records. But the audience for modern Israeli music was estimated at only ten thousand, and a recording of an Israeli composition was doing sensationally well if it sold three thousand.

That was why the IPO—satisfying its ageing audience —stuck doggedly to the eighteenth- and nineteenth-century classics, and why it had for so long been left to the broadcasting orchestra, which did not depend on ticket sales, to provide a showcase for Israeli works. Yet there was a composers' association with more than a hundred members, of whom about forty were regularly and actively at work. And if none of them had so far produced a masterpiece, some of their output was impressive and some at any rate highly tuneful. Israeli music had evolved through two phases. It began with the composers who arrived in Palestine from Central and Eastern Europe in the late 1920s and the 1930s. These were looking for a spiritual identification with the country and seeking to link themselves with its evolution. They were searching for musical roots. They tried to absorb into their rhythms both the authentic elements of oriental music and the modulations of Hebrew speech. They sought to trap the Mediterranean colour in their orchestration in the same way that the painters had attempted to pin it down with their brushes. Their music was part inspiration, part quotation.

Chief among them was Paul Ben-Haim, who was born in Munich as Paul Frankenburger in 1897, graduated from the Academy of Music there, and was persuaded by a composer who was the brother of Herzl's secretary to devote his gifts to Jewry. He composed works for orchestra, chamber ensembles, solo instruments and choirs, and absorbed within the framework of his Central European modernism a study of oriental folk songs. His aim was to capture the oriental flow of his new environment within the Western musical tradition, and he explained: "I am of the West by birth and education, but I stem from the East and live in the East." Ben-Haim was a somewhat vain craftsman who could write a sonata for solo violin for Menuhin, and a Jew who could draw on the Dead Sea Scrolls for his "Hymn of the Desert" for soloists, choir and orchestra. His symphonic work in the concertante manner, "The Sweet Psalmist of Israel," was commissioned by Koussevitzky and won Ben-Haim the 1957 State Prize.

Alexander Uria Boskovitch, who arrived in Palestine from Transylvania at the age of thirty-one, in 1938, had studied under Paul Dukas, was attracted by Middle Eastern music, and claimed to be a member of the "Eastern Mediterranean School." He drew charmingly on this background in his "Semitic Suite," which, if conventional, was engagingly colourful. Boskovitch, however, abandoned conventionality after the war when, having deliberately given up composing in order to reflect on his musical role, he changed his style completely, synthesizing dodecaphony with oriental Jewish elements. He did not, however, go as far as Joseph Tal, who became Israel's foremost electronic composer, even to the extent of composing an electronic opera, *Tower of Ba-*

bel. Yet this Polish-born musician had begun conventionally enough with a training in Germany, and acquired proficiency as a pianist and harpist.

Tal's techniques may have been Western European, but his music had a specific Hebrew character. This intermingling produced Tal's *Ashmedai*, the first full-length Israeli opera, which had a basis in Hebraic legend and yet was commissioned and first performed by the Hamburg State Opera in November 1971. Tal was one of a number of composers who had arrived in Israel as men young enough to look at the country from inside rather than outside. These included also Oedoen Partos, who came from Hungary in his early thirties, and Mordechai Seter, a Russian who arrived in 1926, twelve years before Partos, at the age of ten. Partos had studied under Zoltan Kodaly, and was himself to become a professor at Tel Aviv University. He was an accomplished instrumentalist who composed concertos both for violin, of which Menuhin gave the first performance, and for viola. His music had an oriental approach, even drawing on Arab traits. Seter, like Boskovitch, studied under Dukas and in choral works drew upon his insight into the spiritual sources of Judaism. His settings of the psalms were inspired by Gregorian Chant. A pious work called "Midnight Vigil" ensured wakefulness at any hour by being over-declamatory in the accustomed Israeli way. The critic Benjamin Bar-Am described Seter's Fantasia for Symphony Orchestra—dropped from the IPO season following the Schoenberg furore—as containing "nothing to offend the most tradition-minded listener."

The music of the youngest composers grew naturally out of the country, and it was claimed that their natural acquaintance with Hebrew as an unforced first language gave their music a distinct identity. Ben-Zion Orgad came to live in Palestine from Germany at the age of seven, in 1933. He studied with Ben-Haim and Tal, and in the United States under Aaron Copland. He was brought up with the Bible as a living book, and developed his musical language from its rhythms. Orgad was capable of organizing the most complex combinations of voice and orchestra, and, in a work such as his "Mizmorim" (Psalms) he could achieve moving effects. He was one of the country's most successful composers and, in a good year, could earn from his music enough money to live on for three months.

Zvi Avni, too, studied under Copland and Ben-Haim, and his compositions ranged from chamber works to electronic music. Noam Sherif, unusual among composers in having been born in Israel, extended his field to cover music for theatre and films, as well as for the symphony orchestras he had himself learned to conduct as a pupil of Igor Markevitch. These and others were no longer searching for Israeli music, but were just composing music as Israelis. It took a musician born in Russia to find them a staunch audience.

Gary Bertini was a trained composer (he had studied with Arthur Honegger) whose restless energy was not satisfied with building up a reputation, both with the IPO and internationally, as an orchestral conductor. In 1955 he founded the Rinat Chamber Choir, which started in the kibbutzim and revolutionized vocal and choral music in Israel. It built up a huge following for madrigals and other choral works, and encouraged the composition of modern vocal music, including liturgical works. Bertini was not, however, content to stop there. Ten years later he founded the Israel Chamber Ensemble. This was divided into two sections, the Israel Chamber Orchestra and the Israel Chamber Opera.

The radio orchestra had done much to foster Israeli music. But, lacking continuous contact with a live audience, it had been unable to build up a following for that music. Bertini and his musicians decided to bring the music to the people. They wanted to give themselves a respite from the monotony of playing the standard repertoire over and over again, and they sensed a need among middle-aged and younger adults to have a change from that repertoire too. They wanted to provide young Israeli musicians with a permanent showcase, and to encourage and even commission them to compose. They wanted to look for new ways of encouraging musical enjoyment among young people and children. And they wanted to get out into the country. A measure of their eventual success was that in a typical season four out of five of their concerts were outside Tel Aviv, and they travelled ten thousand miles to play before eight thousand people.

The Chamber Opera arose from another need. Since before independence, it was true, Israel had had an opera company, devotedly given life by an American singer from Brooklyn, Edis de Philippe. But the National Opera was a depressing spectacle. It had a vast repertoire, of fifty-five operas and thirty-five ballets, which were ritually—and far from adequately—performed in the shabby old former cinema in Tel Aviv where the Knesset had initially met. The stage was too narrow, and the orchestra too small. The forlorn audience consisted mainly of pensioners, kibbutzniks, soldiers and children. Israel was simply too poor to support a Covent Garden or a Metropolitan, and these pathetic attempts to stage grand opera were almost worse than none at all. The Chamber Opera, with high musical standards, was a realistic answer to the country's requirements and possibilities.

Bertini had a finger in yet another pie. He was musical director of the Batsheva Dance Company. Israel had no tradition of classical ballet, and had wisely not attempted to mimic one. It could, however, draw on its folk dancing, which provided pleasurable entertainment at any informal celebration. One of the most individual dance traditions was that of the Yemeni Jews, and to preserve this Sara Levi-Tanai, a young kibbutznik of Yemeni origin, in 1949 founded the Inbal Dance Theatre. This continued as a haphazard unit until in 1952 it was discovered by Jerome Robbins. It then acquired a trainer and musical director and began making major public appearances. Inbal's exotic colour and charm gave it huge popularity; it made successful foreign tours and even appeared in a Hollywood biblical epic. But commercialization robbed it of its fresh spontaneity, and its popularity with its own Israeli public evaporated.

The Batsheva company was founded, averred Baroness Batsheva de Rothschild, because "there were two or three modern dancers around here with nothing to do, and that made a problem." But is was professional from the start. It was a modern dance company, founded in 1964 by the Baroness with the American balletic guru

Martha Graham as its adviser. It was perhaps being over-praised when Fernau Hall of the London *Daily Telegraph* described it as "one of the most exciting, enterprising and accomplished dance companies in the world." But it had achieved an undoubted professionalism and a distinctive style, and was even judged superior at dancing Martha Graham's works to that lady's own company. Encouraged, the Baroness in 1968 founded another group, Bat-Dor, with a very slight tendency towards classical ballet, and in 1971 provided the company with its own 380-seat theatre and teaching studios.

Both Baroness Batsheva and Bertini could agree that the comment of Noel Goodwin, music critic of the London *Daily Express*—"Israeli concert music is a confrontation between an abundance of talent and a lack of tradition"—was equally true of Israeli ballet. But it was hardly true at all of the Israeli cinema. Tradition was certainly lacking; but talent was far from obtrusive. And this was, in a way, perplexing. Jews were dominant figures in the film industries of every major country in the world. Their artistic contribution, as directors and writers, was as great as their commercial involvement. Yet, in a country where six out of every seven inhabitants were Jews, only the tiniest proportion of the film industry's output was worthy of notice, let alone serious criticism.

The audience was there. Because it was multilingual, it was readily receptive to foreign films. But it was still hungry for films in Hebrew, and responded eagerly to those of the slightest merit. A physical capability for movie-making in Israel had been built up steadily. The first studio was established in 1949, and by the early 1950s there were two studios together with black-and-white laboratories. Minor foreign films began to be produced in the country, and in 1958 a Law for the Encouragement of the Israeli Film was passed. The first local feature film, *They Were Ten*, was made in 1960, and the following year *I Like Mike*, a comedy about an American tourist, became the first full-length Israeli film to show a profit from its home screenings alone.

The first major film production in the country was, fittingly, Otto Preminger's American adaptation of *Exo-*

dus, the Leon Uris novel about Israel's birth. This, and two other foreign movies which followed fairly rapidly (*Judith,* with Sophia Loren, and *Cast a Giant Shadow,* with Kirk Douglas), helped to attract Israelis to film-making and to train them in how to do it for themselves. Still, however, they had to decide what kind of films they wanted to produce. There were three principal categories: Zionist films, dealing with the first years of the State; war films, starting with the independence war and going on to include any further wars as they broke out and were successfully concluded; and comedies about life in the new, ramshackle country that the Zionists had created and the wars had protected.

A comedy made in 1964 captured the national imagination so totally that it was seen by half the population of the country and established a permanent box-office record. This was *Sallah Shabati,* an episodic account of the integration of an Iraqi immigrant family. The lovably roguish main character—the film left no cliché unturned—was played with grizzled chin by Topol, providing his initial widely noticed demonstration of how a young man could effectively masquerade as an ageing patriarch. The scriptwriter-director was Ephraim Kishon, whose first film this was. For months after they saw the film, Israelis would go around maddening each other by humming the film's theme song, notable for expressive oriental gruntings.

If *Sallah Shabati* brought in money, *Three Days and a Child* won international recognition. This adaptation of an A. B. Yehoshua short story covered a three-day period during which a Jerusalem teacher found himself required to look after the small son of a girl he was once in love with, and who had come with her kibbutznik husband to sit for an examination in the capital. It was directed by Uri Zohar, a former comedy partner of Topol's. With this one movie he proved himself a natural film-maker. *Three Days and a Child* was not only a faithful adaptation of the original. It was also a near perfect piece of cinema in its own right. The mood of hot, heavy days in Jerusalem was accompanied by an air of sultry menace when the teacher, hating the boy because he was not his, yet loving him because he was his

mother's son, deliberately teased and frightened him until the situation got so out of hand that he scared himself.

It was a small film, and tried to be nothing more; but
on its own terms it was faultless. Zohar provided the first
truly erotic scenes in the Israeli cinema. He drew a performance of utter charm from the child. An Oded Kotler, as the teacher, gained for himself the Golden Palm
award at the 1967 Cannes Festival. This was the first
time that Israel had won an international cinema prize.

With the ending of the Six-Day War, film-making in
Israel really went ahead. With the bait provided by tariff
and tax concessions, the almost year-round good weath-
er, and increasingly available technical facilities, foreign
companies began to move in either to make films by
themselves or for productions with local companies.
Two modern colour laboratories were opened in 1970,
one at Herzlia, the other at Givatayim. This foreign in-
cursion delighted the Ministry of Commerce and Industry, which was eager to get its hands on the hard currency being imported. It was not, however, so satisfactory
for those who wanted to see genuine films about life in
Israel. The audience was huge. Even though the advent
of television had pushed cinema attendances well down
from the 1968 peak of fifty million, they still stood at
over thirty-five million in 1970. Yet of the fifteen feature films made in Israel in that year, only eight were
truly Israeli, the others being either foreign movies or
co-productions.

Even eight Israeli films could be reckoned an appreci-
able total, since there were in the country no more than
three directors regularly making movies. The most pro-
lific of these was Menachem Golan. Golan could make
anything: comedy, melodrama, war adventure. His work
had a certain minimal slickness but was entirely lacking
in taste or style. Yet he had studied both film and television production in the United States, where he had been
head of the films and TV department at the Israeli Embassy, and had returned to start making films in 1963. In
1969 he was invited to England to direct a Norman Wis-
dom comedy, *What's Good for the Goose,* which the British Film Institute's monthly film bulletin sympathetically

described as "the worst British comedy for some considerable time."

Back in Israel, Golan unconcernedly went on to make his biggest popular success, *Lupo*, a blatant imitation of *Sallah Shabati* (on which Golan had been the producer), complete with hummable theme tune and versatile young actor—Yehuda Barkan this time—as the elderly bumpkin father. *Lupo* was seen by 850,000 Israelis in its first six months on release, and encouraged Golan to go on and direct *The Highway Queen,* the trite but nauseating story of a gullible prostitute's downfall. This film was notable for its casting of a mongol child in the role of a mongol child. The jolly idea for this character came from the film's star, the exceptionally attractive Gila Almagor, who had a talent not only for thinking up film plots but also for playing film prostitutes, which she did repeatedly.

The real begetter of *Sallah Shabati*, Ephraim Kishon, continued to concentrate on quirky comedy. Kishon was a versatile writer, whose experiences in German and Russian camps had turned him into a humorist with a bitter after-taste. He wrote books, plays, and a regular satirical column in the evening newspaper *Maariv*. His films included *The Big Dig*, about an eccentric with a penchant for excavation which accidentally turned Tel Aviv into a Levantine Venice, and *Azulai the Policeman*, concerning a constable who won the affection of the criminal world by his constant inability to catch any of them.

If Kishon's film history was consistent, Uri Zohar's was entirely haphazard. He made his films to please himself, and had no clear idea of exactly how many they numbered. They might turn out to be poetic or vulgar, carefully shaped or messy. *Every Bastard a King* he described as a Western about the Six-Day War. *The Rooster,* of which he was slightly ashamed, was a really bawdy comedy about a soldier hopping from bed to bed along the route from the Suez Canal, where he was stationed, to Haifa, where his wife wanted him home for a divorce. Zohar was surprised that *Three Days and a Child* should be so much admired and thought it could have been much improved.

As well as being personally a charmer and politically a naïve idealist, Zohar appealed to other film enthusiasts by his unabashed affection for the medium, which had begun when as a boy he used to sneak into a broken-down old cinema on Ben Yehuda Street in Tel Aviv. He lamented the films which could be produced but were not, because of the conformism in Israel which made it difficult for original talent to emerge. But shortage of money played a part too. A film needed to win an audience of half a million people to break even; that meant that one-sixth of all Israel's men, women and children had to go to see it. In a small country with few rich men there was just not the cash available to risk on new talent, when even films by Kishon and Zohar were liable to lose money.

In almost all of the arts, her size and lack of resources held Israel back. Yet if she was unsuccessful it was not so much because of her lack of achievements, but because those achievements fell so short of ambitions more suited to a rich power with a population running to tens of millions. No one in New Zealand, which had a comparable population, became neurotic because his country had not produced a major playwright, or a great symphony, or a film comparable to *The Battleship Potemkin*. No one outside New Zealand could ever remember seeing a New Zealand film, let alone celebrate its winning a film festival prize. No New Zealand theatre company, however inadequate, had ever participated at a world theatre festival in London. New Zealand musicians did not at times give an impression of monopolizing the concert platforms in major Western capitals, nor had a New Zealand novelist won the Nobel Prize. The New Zealanders got along quite happily all the same.

But the Israelis, who had achieved all of these things, plus recognition of their art at the Venice Biennale, castigated themselves perpetually. They could not accept that being new and young was sufficient excuse; that a land so recently settled that three-quarters of its painters, writers and composers were not even born in the country must allow itself a little time. Israelis handicapped themselves by insisting on being judged by the standards of the big league; and often they fell far short of those standards. It was a pity that they tested themselves so unrelentingly. For by the standards of anyone other than an Israeli martinet, they were a runaway success.

10

A Free Country?

"WASP: *White, Anglo-Saxon Protestant"—definition of United States elite group, in Gale's* Dictionary of Acronyms and Initialisms

In a villa in the Shikun Hacottagim quarter of Jerusalem, a crowd had assembled for after-dinner drinks. Some of them were actually drinking alcohol, which made it a pretty specialized gathering in a country where "having a drink" generally entailed the imbibing of lemon tea, or fruit essence diluted with soda water. It was indeed a specialized gathering. There were present an ex-ambassador, an adviser to the Prime Minister, and senior civil servants from the Foreign Office and other government departments.

Someone came in late, bringing with him the latest *mot* which was making the rounds. "What is a WASP in Israel?" he asked. And to general approbation and merriment he provided the answer: "White Ashkenazi Socialist with *Protektzia.*" Everyone in the room agreed on the aptness of this felicitous invention. Everyone could afford to do so. For every one of these senior members of the state's administrative apparatus—all of them miserably paid, all of the highest integrity and the best intentions—was, by this new definition, a Wasp.

The question was posed: what was the aspect of Israeli life which most diminished its citizens' liberties? One guest suggested censorship. Another bugbear, it was felt, was religious domination of daily life and family decisions. There was a buzz of agreement when one of the most eminent bureaucrats present denounced the perva-

sive bureaucracy. Nobody mentioned the absence from
the room of a single person whose origin was Iraqi, Moroccan or Yemeni.

Censorship was undeniably a straitjacket on the nation's life. In a state which had been continually at war
from the day it came into being, the need for censorship
on security matters went unquestioned, even if the clum-
sy implementation of that censorship was intermittently
criticized. In any case, in a constricted country where almost every family had someone in the army, most military secrets were widely known even if, for decency's
sake, it was pretended that they were not. Long before a
corner of the veil on the Lavon Affair was lifted, a man
parked a large foreign car outside the Misadag Atlas in
Bat Galim, on the Haifa sea front, and limped inside
this gourmet restaurant. Pausing over a mouthful of the
Atlas's justly renowned hors-d'oeuvre, an Israeli pointed
after Benjamin Gibli and said, not too quietly, to his foreign guest: "See that man? He was one of the main figures in the Lavon Affair."

But if military censorship had to be accepted, even if
only for the sake of form, censorship of taste and oppressive guardianship of morals were more controversial. Israel remained a starchily puritan country. Long
after Sweden and the United States had decided that almost anything went, the appearance on the Tel Aviv
new-stands of girlie magazines, whose pictures went little farther than those available in any London tabloid
newspaper, aroused shocked distaste. Israel, defenders
of its standards insisted, was out of the mainstream of
the permissive world.

To ensure that this desirable state of affairs continued, the Films and Stage Plays Censorship Council
stood by to act as protector of the public. Inevitably this
body was a hang-over from the Mandate. The Minister
of the Interior—generally a Minister from the NRP—
had inherited the functions of the High Commissioner.
The eighteen-member Council consisted of representatives of the Ministries of the Interior, Education and Culture, Religious Affairs, Social Welfare and Police, as
well as writers and artists, all chosen in their personal
capacity and approved by the Government. Every mo-

tion picture required a licence from the Council, which had the right to refuse such a licence or grant one on special conditions, such as excision or classification. The Council operated by majority vote, and was provided with no set criteria on which to operate.

The criteria it set itself were arbitrary. Levi Geri, Chairman of the Council, in 1970 elegantly explained his attitude. "If the distributors feel that cutting scenes takes away from the artistic value of the film, they do not have to show the film. The general public is not concerned with art." Nor, it seemed, was the Council. In 1953, for example, it refused licences to three films; of these, an American product was banned "because it emphasized violence," and a French movie was rejected "for moral reasons." Nine other films were cut because, among other reasons, they "contained scenes of excessive brutality, nudity, offence to Jewish religion." One short play was refused a licence "because of its cynicism." In 1960, strip-tease acts were staged in Tel Aviv night-clubs without the Council's approval. "The shows were cancelled," it reported with some satisfaction, "and those responsible for the performances were arrested." In 1962, extending its intellectual range, the Council took "vigorous measures . . . to prevent the display of vulgar film posters."

It was difficult to discern any pattern in its activities. In 1964 it had cut three passages from Ingmar Bergman's widely praised film *The Silence,* and years later Levi Geri confirmed that those cuts must still stand. There was a strong feeling in the country against pornography, he insisted. Yet at the same time the Council gave a licence to Menachem Golan's shoddily vulgar *The Highway Queen,* which, quite apart from such irrelevant issues as taste, contained scenes far more pornographic than anything snipped out of *The Silence.* Similarly, the Council got itself into a great state over nude sequences in a silly American film called *What Do You Say to a Naked Lady?,* yet gave permission for nude scenes in both the Israeli stage version of the American rock musical *Hair,* and in *Jump,* a native attempt to leap on to the *Hair* bandwagon. On one matter, however, the Council was universally adamant. Sex education films must not be allowed. "Even the Labour Party think it's too much," explained Geri, playing his trump card.

More ominous was the Council's political censorship. Of the batch of films cut in 1953, some suffered because they gave "offence to Russia and offence to the Western powers." There was a rule that foreign powers must not be vilified. On the other hand, films from Germany were not even allowed into the country until diplomatic relations between the two countries were established. And a close watch was kept on films about Germany. A Hollywood version of Erich Maria Remarque's anti-war tract *A Time to Love and a Time to Die* was banned because its interpretation of the German standpoint was too favourable. Another Hollywood movie, *The Desert Fox,* whose subject was Erwin Rommel, was likewise rejected, because it was alleged to glorify the German general. "For me—no harm; for *sabras*—they don't know what happened," reasoned Geri. This attempt to obfuscate history was accompanied by the continuing national ban on the insidiously anti-Semitic music of Richard Strauss and Richard Wagner. Yet, as further bafflement for the innocent observer, in one typical year fifty-seven Egyptian and four Lebanese films were shown in Israel without any eyebrows being raised at the dangers of corruption at the hands of the nation's chronic enemies.

No wonder that Yeshaya Weinberg, director of the Cameri theatre, complained that censorship was carried out by "a handful of people who have no clear criteria other than their personal tastes," and that it was "marked by misjudgments and severe mistakes." He was supported by Judge Binyamin Cohen who, after fining a man and two women for showing pornographic films, said, on 1 April 1971: "Given today's reality, it makes no sense to ban pornography. Obscenity laws should be taken off the books."

As in many other Parliaments, however, support in the Knesset was strong for legislation restricting personal freedom. When, on 2 June 1971, Uri Avneri of Haolam Hazeh put forward a bill to legalize homosexual relations between consenting adults in private, it was not only the members of the religious parties who opposed him. A Labour representative, Mordechai Surkiss, declaimed that to repeal the existing law, which carried a maximum ten-year prison sentence for homosexual offences, would endanger Israel's very security and existence. On a free vote, the bill was defeated by thirty-eight to fifteen.

Parliament was at any rate a sovereign body which could, whenever it wished, change legislation which invaded individual freedom. It also had power to bring easement to those who felt that legalization of theocratic or rabbinical edicts was injuring their personal happiness. It was not simply a matter of the lack of public transport on the Sabbath, nor the closing of most places of public entertainment on that day; although, when innocent German entrepreneurs attempted to stage Grand Prix motor racing on a Saturday, they found that the power of the rabbis was an impassable road-block. They were not the first to learn that, in the words of the commentary accompanying a French documentary film, "compared with the Israeli Sabbath, the English Sunday is like carnival time in Rio."

Nor were the most serious complaints levelled against religious insistence that food on Israeli ships and aircraft must be kosher, or the threats by the Chief Rabbi of Tel Aviv to luxury hotels that their kosher licences would be withdrawn if they held New Year's Eve balls on the actual eve of 1972, which coincidentally happened to be the eve of the Sabbath as well. It was the most basic rights of the individual—the right to marry, the right even to citizenship—which were subject to religious obduracy. There was national commotion, and the Prime Minister herself was asked to intercede, when the rabbinate refused young people the right to Jewish marriage —the only marriage available in a land where civic weddings were not permitted—on the highly complicated technical ground that they were *mamzerim:* bastards. Periodically the whole question of the definition of a Jew would be raised, with its fundamental implications for citizenship under the Law of Return, as well as its effects on the right to marry. Groups claiming to be Jews would demand recognition and be denied it. Individuals might go to law and win their case, only to be thwarted by retrospective legislation rushed through on the insistence of the National Religious Party.

These were exceptionally serious questions, and all except the bigots recognized that solutions to them must be found. Yet at the same time it was seen that progress had to be made slowly. It was not only that parliamentary arithmetic gave the religious parties a stranglehold over the Government. When the Government made its mind up, as it eventually did on the need for some form of national service for girls from religious families, it was ready to face the political consequences.

Relatively unimportant issues could be faced or dodged according to convenience. But the major subjects for controversy involved the very future of the Jews as a people. As Ben Gurion put it, the Israeli state was not yet complete; while only a small proportion of Jews was living there it would be wrong to make basic and incontrovertible decisions in the name of the whole people. This was not racialism. A tiny group which had consistently been persecuted for thousands of years had no vested interest in purity or exclusivity of blood. Its blood had too often been shed because its adherents could be so easily distinguished.

Yet the Jews had survived all those thousands of years, to the point where they again had their own state in their own land, because they had taken the utmost care to maintain their identity. It was not out of fanaticism that young couples in the more prosperous suburbs of Manchester denied their middle-class dinner guests cream in their coffee after serving a meat meal. It was not because they felt revulsion at the prospect of scampi or paella that prospective tourists perused the *Jewish Travel Guide* to find kosher hotels in Riccione or Palma. This was how the Jews had survived to win Israel back, and how they would go on surviving if they ever lost Israel again. The rabbis were undoubtedly too stiffnecked. But even at the price of genuine individual misery, it was an error to suppose that all problems could be solved by placing those necks on the block of thoughtless or headlong reform.

Laws could gradually remedy this situation, in which unoffending individuals were made to suffer tragically.

The difficulty of dealing with the bureaucracy, however, was that its behaviour was not capable of improvement by the simple passage of a bill through the Knesset. Everyone raged about the bureaucrats. Immigrants were baffled and frustrated by the forms they had to fill in, and the offices at which they were required to attend. Foreign visitors were reduced to speechlessness by currency regulations which sometimes seemed to amount to good-humoured robbery. A driver accused of a traffic offence was immediately enmeshed in an administrative cobweb. Industrialists, too, complained of the tangled skein in which applications for government assistance involved them, requiring at least the services of a good lawyer and, if humanly possible, patience to wait through the months before a decision was handed down. A visitor to a government department could go wild with frustrated rage while the information clerk completed a personal telephone call at leisure before turning to deal with his intrusive query.

All this was routine. Yet the State Comptroller could put the situation in perspective by his injunction: "Look from here eastwards or southwards, and you'll have to have very good eyes to find something better." For Israel's civil service had a remarkably high standard of honesty, and was uninfected by corruption on any serious scale. Its shortcomings were the result of its beginnings. The new State of Israel had inherited no tradition of civil servants as servants of the public either from the Middle East, where it was situated, or from the Mandate administration, which it had succeeded, or from Eastern Europe or Germany, from which most of its leading figures had come. It possessed no standards of public administration on the European level. Orderly administration was not among its top priorities.

In the early years of independence the Ministries were staffed by members of the party of which the Minister himself was a member, who knew that party supporters expected favours from them. This was the classic *protektzia* situation, and the Ministries headed by NRP and Achdut nominees were its most devoted practitioners. A Cabinet decision of 22 November 1949 had changed the basis of civil service recruitment, with passage of an examination required for the higher grades. A Civil Service Commission was set up on 1 January 1951. But low pay made it difficult to attract suitably qualified personnel, and the bureaucrats had become entrenched during the transitional period when the urgent need had been to create administrative services fast, with the hope that incompetence could later be weeded out at leisure. A thrifty eye on keeping down expenditure was not felt to be so very essential. Centralist tendencies were increased by the small size of the country.

So Israel had become festooned in forms in triplicate, and infested with hordes of petty officials. This engendered much frustration, but there was remarkably little derogation of the rights of the citizen, or flouting of the laws which governed the bureaucracy. And when examples did occur, the State Comptroller was there to expose scandal. His revelations regularly plunged perfectionists into despair. The *Jerusalem Post,* in a leading article following the publication of his 1971 report, delivered itself of a jeremiad. "If the present trend remains unchecked and unreversed, then the road to becoming a real Levantine country is short." No greater doom could have been called down upon the people, following upon what the newspaper listed as "tales of how the Ministry of Finance bailed out failing companies and bankrupt banks; covered up for absurd transactions and the folly of officials; of how senior officials sign long-term contracts with firms and, soon after that, they emerge as their owners or directors."

Certainly over the years the State Comptroller revealed some remarkable goings-on. There was the case of the Boarding School for Gifted Children. This was a project of the Ministry of Education, given momentum by a substantial dollar donation from overseas. The building costs, however, went far beyond the estimate. The Ministry had entrusted the management and supervision of the work to a private company when, in accordance with standing orders, this should have gone to the Public Works Department. The earthworks jobs did not go to the lowest bidder. Unsatisfactory contract arrangements were made with a firm which had bid to construct the dormitory, and which got the job of building the school itself as a continuation of the dormitory contract, without it putting in any tender or any further specific contract being agreed. No competitive bids were called for. Although this firm—on to a very good thing—undertook to build the school at the prices fixed for the dormitory, it nevertheless demanded, and received, payment for higher costs. Changes were introduced. The original estimate had been 1,800,000–2,000,000 Israeli pounds; but the school's intake was cut from 200 to 120 boarders and from 24 to 16 classes; that should have cut costs. Yet the Ministry could happily report to the Budgets Department in 1962 and again in 1963 that construction would not cost more than three million pounds (the limit of the gift), as though this was some notable achievement. It knew however, and at latest by August 1962, that 4,500,000 pounds would be entailed. Scarcely surprisingly, a censorious State Comptroller's report found "grave deviations" from mandatory procedures and principles, mainly due to the Ministry's inexperience in building matters.

There was the affair of the empty government premises. In mid-1963 the Ministry of Agriculture had vacated eleven rooms it was occupying in the northern part of the country. These were taken over by the Ministry of Social Welfare—in April 1967. For four years the Treasury had been paying 400 pounds a month for the right to occupy empty offices.

There were the derelictions of the Licensing Department of the Ministry of Transport. In 1969 it had been laid down that an applicant should have his instructor with him when he took his driving test, in order to ward off complaints of unfairness if he failed, and to give the instructor the chance to note weak points in his pupil's driving, which he could then remedy in the course of further instruction. All excellent; except that, in Tel Aviv and Jerusalem, it was rarely happening. Testers refrained from telling the applicant why he had failed, or even from listing the reasons on the appropriate form. To restore the balance somewhat, drivers whose licences had been withdrawn by the courts or the police were still being allocated new licences during the period of their ban. Youths under eighteen were illegally passing tests

and obtaining licences by omitting to write their month
of birth on the application form.

There were, as well, the nepotistic practices hilarious-
ly current on the local council of the small town of Rosh
Haayin. In 1967 the council chairman's son was appointed as head of the education department, with his
father taking an enthusiastic part in the decision. This
rather blatantly violated a law which said that no local
authority could take on an employee whose superior
might be a relative. Between 1967 and 1970 the town
employed a religious-cultural organizer, even though no
tender was published for the job, which attracted a rabbi's salary, though not meriting it. It happened, too, that
the son of the gentleman who was appointed to this in-
flated position was a councillor, who lobbied for him
and even took part in the vote confirming his appointment. It was also revealed that the council, rather care-
lessly, failed to keep records of rate or water bills, which
prevented demands for the payment of such debts. This
was an undoubted convenience to nine of the town's
eleven councillors, who were discovered to be among
the tax-dodgers.

Corruption and incompetence, whether petty or on a
more ambitious scale, were certainly a serious matter,
and the shortcomings revealed by the State Comptroller's reports were sometimes grave. But at least the reports were compiled and published. Every official, in every one of the numerous and variegated bodies subject to
the Comptroller's inspection, was aware that any nefar-
ious activities in which he was involved were liable to be
distressingly exposed to the public view. No local authority in England was subject to the same public scrutiny as the sound family men of Rosh Haayin. And the
propagation of the reports themselves was a vindication
of Israel as an open society.

The exceptionally high standards of the State Comptroller's office had been laid down by one German immigrant—Dr. Siegfried Moses, a former auditor, who held
the post from 1949 to 1961—and maintained by another, Dr. Yitzchak Nebenzahl, an ex-factotum of the Bank
of Israel. Their *Yeke* stiffness and tidiness made them
singularly suited to the office and won them public re-

spect, even though a mischievous television programme did once catch Dr. Nebenzahl's official car exceeding the speed limit. Indeed, the role of the State Comptroller had been so successful that the Government decided that it should be expanded.

On 26 January 1970, the State Comptroller (Amendment No. 5) Bill was presented to the Knesset. The following year saw the enactment of this law, which awarded the Comptroller the additional function of Public Complaints Commissioner, or Ombudsman. In fact, even before this, the State Comptroller had been laying himself open to a report by the State Comptroller for exceeding his functions by investigating many complaints which had come to him, even without any legal authority. He had interpreted his authority, which gave him the right to criticize the efficiency of bodies open to his inspection, as permitting him to measure this efficiency by the quality of the service given.

Accordingly, he had looked into road safety and the development of the telephone network. He had got involved in the vexed question (religion again) of autopsies. He had explored the treatment of Israel's minorities: their roads, services and education, and the electrification of their villages. Although he was not allowed to deal with the complaints of soldiers on national service, he was able to accept those from men called up for reserve duty, and had become involved in the case of a barber who had been unconstitutionally called upon to cut his fellow reservists' hair; the law made it plain that a military man on call-up could be required to use only his military skills.

Now the Public Complaints Commissioner was given the specific duty to investigate any complaint, sent in either by a citizen or by a member of the Knesset on the citizen's behalf, against any act or omission of any body subject to the State Comptroller's inspection; labour relations and military discipline being excluded. The grounds of a complaint could be that an act or omission was contrary to law or to the principles of sound administration, unduly harsh, or manifestly unjust. The Commissioner was obliged to accept every complaint addressed to him, unless it was clearly only of nuisance value. Even anonymous complaints were to be accepted, since, as Nebenzahl understandingly put it, "the most suppressed sometimes have no other way of making complaints other than by anonymous letters." If the complaint turned out to be justified, the Commissioner was required to point out what corrective measures were called for, and a report was to be made to him about the steps to be taken. He was ultimately responsible to the Knesset. And he had a final shot in his locker. If a complaint did not stand up under his Public Complaints Commissioner terms of reference, he could always go back to it as State Comptroller.

Israel was unique in combining these two functions. Apart from other merits, this state of affairs should have won the Comptroller's approval because it was very economical with manpower. To the State Comptroller's staff of five hundred, which had remained almost stationary for ten years, only another twenty or so needed to be added. The Commissioner started work in September 1971. Regional offices, where complaints could be registered personally, were opened in Israel's three main cities. In the first two months, 1,600 were received. Of these, twenty per cent were justified. Both figures, claimed Dr. Nebenzahl proudly, constituted proportionately a world record.

It was not stated how many of these complaints had come from Israelis of oriental origin. But, as the 1970s progressed, it was this section of the population which continued to have the most justified grounds for grievance. By the end of 1970 they had become a dominant proportion of Israel's citizens. Out of a total of 2,561,500 Jews in the country at that date, 203,400 were *sabras* whose fathers had been *sabras;* 1,127,900 had either come from Europe or America themselves, or were children of immigrants from those areas; 1,230,200 were, on a similar basis, of Afro-Asian origin.

Yet the country's life remained in the benevolent but rigid grip of the Ashkenazim—the Wasps. They were in control of the Cabinet, Parliament, the political parties, the army, and the bureaucracy whose representatives had gathered for drinks in the Shikun Hacottagim. In

1971 Mordechai Ben-Porat, the Deputy Secretary-General of the Labour Party—himself of Iraqi origin—echoed the B'nai B'rith Anti-Defamation League in the United States by pointing out that, of 569 board members in Israel's big government corporation, only eighteen were of oriental origin. Avner Shaki, Deputy Minister of Education, alleged that only a small percentage of the employees in his Ministry were oriental, and that few men from this ethnic group were sent abroad by the Foreign Office. Almost every artist, writer, composer and film-maker originated from the West.

Even worse, this imbalance extended to the ordinary working population. The oriental's pay was low. In 1969 the average annual income for an Israeli-born Jew was 11,900 pounds, for a Jew born in Europe or America 12,000 pounds, for one born in Asia or Africa 8,300 pounds. In 1971 an inquiry commission headed by David Horowitz, then Governor of the Bank of Israel, found that oriental family incomes were only 69 per cent of the national average. It was true that this was an increase over the 63 per cent of ten years before, and that between 1963–4 and 1970 the Afro-Asian real family income had risen by 46 per cent, compared with 36 per cent for European-Americans and 27 per cent for native-born Israelis. But this narrowing of the family differential disguised an actual increase in the disparity per head of the population, brought about by larger families among the orientals.

The inequality extended to living conditions. The proportion of oriental families which had immigrated since 1948 and lived more than three to a room was 17 per cent, compared with 8 per cent nationally and 2 per cent among Westerners. To these over-crowded households it was little consolation that their 17 per cent was a reduction from 49 per cent in 1960. And there were insufficient amenities in these crammed residences. Ownership among them of refrigerators was 92 per cent, compared with 97 per cent for Europeans and Americans. For television sets it was 48 per cent, against 55 per cent among their Western neighbours. They had less opportunity of getting away from home; a mere 8 per cent possessed motor cars, effortlessly overtaken by the 19

per cent of Europeans and Americans. Only in ownership of washing machines did they have a slight edge:
46 per cent to 42 per cent.

Nor did it seem that this underprivileged group was in
the immediate future going to be able to narrow the gap
by profiting from the increased status and earning power
provided by higher education. Only one student in twenty from the oriental communities was in the early 1970s
achieving success in the *Bagrut* examination, compared
with one-third of the students of Western origin. In the
academic year 1969–70, 1,827 university students were
the children of *sabras,* 25,391 of European-American
origin, and just 4,347 Afro-Asian. While, in 1971, two-
thirds of the children in kindergartens were orientals,
only one-eighth of university students were. At Bar-Ilan,
it was true, the proportion had reached fifteen per cent.
Clearly, however, orientals were a long way from
achieving educational equality.

The orientals, in fact, were becoming a dominant
group in the population numerically while failing to
achieve parallel social and material advances. Like the
Arabs, if appreciably less so, they were an out-group
without satisfactory links with the élite or even the middle class. The political system did not help. If election
had been on the constituency basis, then some consti-
tuencies would have been oriental safe seats. Like the
NRP in the coalition, these members of the Knesset
could have used their bargaining power inside the Labour
Party to extract concessions. But under the list system
parliamentary membership was decided by the party's
bureaucracy, dominated by Wasp veterans. Of course,
orientals were not kept out; they were even admitted, if
minimally, into the Cabinet. But they were without any
substantial leverage.

This led to outbursts of frustration. In 1959 there
were riots by North Africans in Haifa and Beersheba in
protest against their own conditions and alleged police
brutality. A decade later, there grew up a movement of
young oriental Jews which took its name from the
American Black Panther Negro rights group. Among
many of Israel's leaders these Black Panthers aroused
either hostility or incomprehension. Ben Gurion had

never met any of them. Golda Meir could not understand them. Pinchas Sapir irritably discounted their importance. Yet there were others who supported them.
Yitzchak Ben-Aharon, General Secretary of the Histadrut, was foremost among those who demanded a campaign against poverty. There were suggestions that he
should begin in his own back yard since, as alleged by
Mordechai Ben-Porat, "when Asher Yadlin [head of
the Histadrut's Hevrat Ovdim] looks for executives or
business prospects he looks among his own social cir-
cles." Uzi Narkiss, conqueror of Jerusalem in the Six-
Day War, and later director of the Jewish Agency's immigration department, welcomed the Black Panther
demonstrations. They were right to shout about their demands, he said, because Israelis had been unduly preoc-
cupied with external problems and had neglected the
difficulties of the domestic situation.

One of those great debates, to which the Israelis were
irresistibly addicted, had begun. And Pinchas Sapir,
while hotly defending his record, at the same time put
measures in train to improve it. With characteristic sar-
casm he instructed an August 1971 meeting of the Labour Party's Central Committee: "I think it's high time
you all travelled around the country—we'll provide you
with air-conditioned buses—and see what has been
achieved in this land." But he also slipped into his
speech the information that the government had decided
to earmark funds to double the proportion of students
from oriental families to twenty-five per cent by 1980.

In her first decades, Israel's achievements had been
disappointing only to her own perfectionists. Under the
political system which had been evolved, with surprisingly little need for adaptation, the new nation had established itself as the only stable democracy in the entire
Middle East. Her safeguards for individual freedom,
though flawed, were strong and secure from the interference of the executive. With the burden of hundreds of
thousands of immigrants to carry, the education provided for Israeli children was comparable with that of
the most prosperous countries of the West. Against the
handicap of minimal raw material resources, an industrial economy was being steadily constructed; and the

opening up of desert lands was leading to increasing exploitation of such resources as there were. Access to the
arts was available on a scale unknown in much larger
countries, and to a massive section of the population;
not even in Sweden or the United States were one-third
of the population collectors of original paintings. A minority still themselves in a hundred and more countries,
the Jews of Israel were now staking their self-respect on
their ability to ensure for their Arab minority the equality and opportunities for advancement which Jews in the
Diaspora had often so cruelly been denied.

Now, assailed from within by accusations of discrimination, in their own State of Israel they were faced with
the supreme task of achieving what all Jewish communities everywhere had always regarded as their first duty:
the need to ensure that no Jew should be regarded as
less than his neighbour in the eyes of man, just as all were
equal in the sight of God; the need to ensure that no Jew
suffered want while others enjoyed plenty. In the savage
duel of war, as in the amenities of civilized peace, Israel
had demonstrated that she could beat other nations at
their own game. She was surely not going to fail on her
historic home ground.

Sources

It is possible to go on reading endlessly about Israel. No sooner has one work of reference been dutifully scanned than another, freshly completed, presents itself for perusal. Periodicals and newspapers add to the material available: I have found the *Jerusalem Post,* the *Jewish Chronicle,* and *Jewish Vanguard* indispensable. I have also consulted some scores of books briefly or at length. Of these, the following have been especially valuable:

Allon, Yigal. *Shield of David.* London, 1970

Barer, Shlomo. *The Magic Carpet.* London, 1952

Bar-On, Mordechai. *Education Processes in the Israel Defence Forces.* Tel Aviv, 1966

Bar-Zohar, Michael. *The Armed Prophet.* London, 1967

Ben Gurion, David. *Israel: Years of Challenge.* London, 1964

" " " *Rebirth and Destiny of Israel.* London, 1959

Ben-Porath, Yoram. *The Arab Labour Force in Israel,* Jerusalem, 1966

Bentwich, Joseph S. *Education in Israel.* London, 1965

Bentwich, Norman. *The Hebrew University of Jerusalem 1918–1960.* London, 1961

" " *Israel and Her Neighbours.* London, 1955

" " *Israel Resurgent.* London, 1960

"   "   *Israel: Two Fateful Years 1967–69.* London, 1970

Ben-Yosef, Avraham C. *The Purest Democracy in the World.* New York, 1963

Bermant, Chaim. *Israel.* London, 1967
"   "   *Troubled Eden.* London, 1969

Birman, Abraham (ed.). *An Anthology of Hebrew Poetry.* London, 1968

Blocker, Joel (ed.) *Israeli Stories.* New York, 1965

Branston, Thomas R. (ed.) *Recollections—David Ben Gurion.* London, 1970

Brod, Max. *Israel's Music.* Tel Aviv, 1951

Cohen, Abner. *Arab Border Villages in Israel.* Manchester, 1965

Cohen, Israel (ed.) *The Rebirth of Israel.* London, 1952

Comay, Joan. *Introducing Israel.* London, 1969

Crossman, Richard. *A Nation Reborn.* London, 1960

Darin-Drabkin, H. *The Other Society.* London, 1962

de Gaury, Gerald. *The New State of Israel.* London, 1952

Deshen, Shlomo A. *Immigrant Voters in Israel.* Manchester, 1970

Edelman, Maurice. *Ben Gurion.* London, 1964

Eisenstadt, S. N. *The Absorption of Immigrants.* London, 1954
"   "   *Israeli Society.* London, 1967

Elon, Amos. *The Israelis: Founders and Sons.* London, 1971

Emanuel, Muriel (ed.) *Israel.* London, 1971

Facts About Israel. Ministry for Foreign Affairs, Jerusalem.

Fein, Leonard J. *Politics in Israel.* Boston, 1967

Gamzu, Chaim. *Painting and Sculpture in Israel.* Tel Aviv, 1951

Golden, Harry. *The Israelis.* New York, 1971

Government Year Books. Jerusalem

Greenberg, David. *The Cinema.* Tel Aviv, 1967

"Green Flag." *The Jewish Travel Guide.* London

Halevi, Nadov and Klinov-Malul, Ruth. *The Economic Development of Israel.* New York, 1968

Halliday, Ruth. *The Skills to Make the Desert Bloom*. London, 1964

"Herodotus." *British Settlers in Israel*. London, 1971

Horowitz, David. *The Economics of Israel*. Oxford, 1967

Institute of Jewish Affairs and World Jewish Congress. *The Jewish Communities of the World*. London, 1971

Israel Economic Development. Prime Minister's Office, Jerusalem, 1968

Israel Today series. Jerusalem

Katz, Karl, Kahane, P. P., and Broshi, Magen. *From the Beginning*. London, 1968

King, Preston and Parekh, B. C. (ed.) *Politics and Experience*. Cambridge, 1968

Kleinberger, Aharon F. *Society, Schools and Progress in Israel*. Oxford, 1969

Kochan, Lionel (ed.) *The Jews in Soviet Russia since 1917*. London, 1970

Kohansky, Mendel. *The Hebrew Theatre—Its First Fifty Years*. Jerusalem, 1969

Kurzman, Dan. *Genesis 1948*. New York, 1970

Landau, Jacob M. *The Arabs in Israel*. London, 1969

Lau-Lavie, Naphtali. *Moshe Dayan*. London, 1968

Leon, Dan. *The Kibbutz—A New Way of Life*. Oxford, 1969

Litvinoff, Barnet. *Ben Gurion of Israel*. London, 1954
    "   "   *A Peculiar People*. London, 1969

Louvish, Misha. *The Challenge of Israel*. Jerusalem, 1968

Loveluck, Graham. *Secondary Education in Israel*. London, 1966

McDonald, James G. *My Mission in Israel 1948–51*. London, 1951

McIntyre, Ian. *The Proud Doers*. London, 1968

Marx, Emanuel. *Bedouin of the Negev*. Manchester, 1967

Meinertzhagen, R. *Middle East Diary*. London, 1959

Mintz, Ruth Finer. *Modern Hebrew Poetry*. Berkeley and Los Angeles, 1966

Pearlman, Moshe (ed.) *Ben Gurion Looks Back.* London, 1965

Penueli, S. Y. and Ukhmani, A. (ed.) *Anthology of Modern Hebrew Poetry.* Jerusalem, 1966

Prittie, Terence. *Eshkol of Israel: The Man and the Nation.* London, 1969

”   ”   *Israel: Miracle in the Desert.* New York, 1968

St. John, Robert. *Ben Gurion.* London, 1959

Samuel, Edwin. *The Structure of Society in Israel.* New York, 1969

Samuel, Rinna. *Israel.* London, 1971

Schmelz, U. O. and Glikson, P. (ed.) *Jewish Population Studies.* Jerusalem, 1970

Schwarz, Walter. *The Arabs in Israel.* London, 1959

Segre, V. D. *Israel: A Society in Transition.* London, 1971

Seitz, William C. *Art Israel.* New York, 1964

The Seventh Day: Soldiers' Talk About the Six-Day War. London, 1970

Statistical Abstract of Israel. Central Bureau of Statistics, Jerusalem

Statistical Year Books. Tel Aviv-Jaffa Municipality

Survey of Industry in Israel—1968. Ministry of Commerce and Industry, Jerusalem, 1969

Syrkin, Marie. *Golda Meir: Woman with a Cause.* London, 1964

Tammuz, Benjamin and Wykes-Joyce, Max (ed.) *Art in Israel.* London, 1966

Weingrod, Alex. *Israel: Group Relations in a New Society.* London, 1965

Weisgal, Meyer W. and Carmichael, Joel (ed.) *Chaim Weizmann: A biography by several hands.* London, 1962

Weizmann, Chaim. *Trial and Error.* London, 1949

Weizmann, Vera. *The Impossible Takes Longer.* London, 1967

Williams, L. F. Rushbrook. *The State of Israel.* London, 1957

Zweig, Ferdynand. *Israel: The Sword and the Harp.* London, 1969

I am grateful to Shlomo A. Deshen and to Manchester University Press for permission to reproduce from *Immigrant Voters in Israel* the anecdote quoted on page 24.

Index

289

ABOUT THE AUTHOR

GERALD KAUFMAN was born in Leeds, England, in 1930, the seventh child of Polish immigrant parents. Educated at Leeds Grammar School and Oxford University, he has followed twin political and journalistic paths. Starting as assistant general secretary of the Fabian Society, he joined the political staff of the DAILY MIRROR in London and was then appointed political correspondent of the NEW STATESMAN—until one day, while interviewing Harold Wilson at 10 Downing Street, he was invited to become the British Prime Minister's political press adviser.

After five years in this post he was elected MP for Ardwick, Manchester. In his spare time Gerald Kaufman has been film critic, television scriptwriter, and weekly columnist for the JEWISH CHRONICLE.

LISTEN!!

We represent world-famous authors (many published by Bantam), newsmakers, personalities and entertainers who know how to grab and hold an audience's attention and at the same time, make them enjoy listening. And their fees fit many budgets.

So if you, or someone you know, sets up discussions, debates, forums, symposiums or lectures you should get in touch with us.

We're the BANTAM LECTURE BUREAU and we'll send you a free copy of our catalog which will tell you exactly who we represent and what they talk about.

Bring out the books that bring in the issues.